Nothing Less than Literal

Mark Linder

Nothing Less than Literal

Architecture after Minimalism

THE MIT PRESS   CAMBRIDGE, MASSACHUSETTS   LONDON, ENGLAND

MIT Press books may be purchased at special quantity discounts for business or sales
promotional use. For information, please email special_sales@mitpress.mit.edu or write to
Special Sales Department, The MIT Press, 5 Cambridge Center, Cambridge, MA 02142.

This book was set in Berthold Akzidenz Grotesk by Graphic Composition, Inc. and was
printed and bound in the United States of America.

Library of Congress Cataloging-in-Publication Data
Linder, Mark, 1960–
    Nothing less than literal : architecture after minimalism / Mark Linder.
        p. cm.
    Includes bibliographical references and index.
    ISBN 0-262-12266-9 (hc : alk. paper)
    1. Minimal architecture. 2. Formalism (Art) 3. Architectural criticism — History — 20th
century. I. Title.
NA682.M55L55 2005
729′.09′045 — dc22

                                                            2004052423

to Julia
for Azriel

Stanley, see this? This is this. This ain't somethin' else. This is this.

The Deer Hunter (1978), screenplay by Michael Cimino, Louis Garfinkle, Quinn K. Redeker, and Deric Washburn

Contents

Acknowledgments

This book would have been inconceivable and forever unfinished without the help and encouragement of many people. Versions of its chapters were produced or refined as a result of invitations from Michael Hays at *Assemblage*, Marco Frascari at the University of Pennsylvania, Cynthia Davidson at *ANY*, John Hendrix at Cornell University, Catherine Ingraham at Pratt Institute, Sylvia Lavin at UCLA, Robert Levit at the University of Michigan, Linda Pollari at Woodbury University, and, of course, Roger Conover at MIT Press.

The Graham Foundation for Advanced Studies in the Fine Arts assisted with the procurement of image rights and reproductions. The Syracuse University School of Architecture provided support for much of the research and travel. Bruce Abbey and Art McDonald were generous—and critical—readers whose familiarity with and insight into Colin Rowe's influence were invaluable. My colleagues Ted Brown, Jonathan Massey, Anne Munly, and Francisco Sanin were constant sources of inspiration and information, as were my students, of whom McLain Clutter, Amador Pons, and Mark Rhoads deserve special mention.

Finding and gathering the diverse images in this book was a challenge made much easier by many people, but especially by Mel Bochner, Gene Gaddis, Bill Goldston, Steven Hillyer, Lynn Kearcher, Ellie Oliver, Barbara Opar, Howard Shubert, Michael Slade, and Laura Stella. At the MIT Press, Matthew Abbate, Paula Woolley, and Derek George made significant contributions to the text and design.

In ways unique to each of them, and in ways I may not even yet know, I am deeply grateful to Bob Somol, Charles Long, Sarah Whiting, Ron Witte, Tony Vidler, Catherine Ingraham, Mark Wigley, Homi Bhabha, Stan Allen, Joan Ockman, Robert Slutzky, Ellen Grimes, Miwon Kwon, Rodolphe el-Khoury, Detlef Mertins, Michael Meredith, Doug Garofalo, Tom Brockelman, and Brian Lonsway. Their work and friendship set the high standards to which I aspire.

Above all, Julia Czerniak made this book possible. She understood what and why I needed to do it, and offered every form of guidance, inspiration, dedication, tolerance, insight, and, perhaps most important, fun. Without her, this work would hardly matter.

Nothing Less than Literal

Introduction

This book attempts to come to terms with a theoretical question that is at once innocuous and insidious: How does architecture make its appearance? One kind of response to this question— by far the dominant and more legitimate kind of theoretical response—would research architecture's appearance in institutionalized modes of production and reproduction. This book offers another sort of response: it traces architecture's appearance outside—or seemingly outside, or at the very limits—of its own discipline by tracing a transdisciplinary "history of formalism" in the art and architectural criticism of the 1960s in America, and by documenting the role of architecture—its influence and effects—in the criticism that emerged to both attack and defend the art movement known as minimalism. It proposes that the events of the year 1967 comprise a "knot" or "navel" in that history, and that architecture played a key role in those events.[1] At once a distinct historical convergence as well as a time of confusion and hidden potential, the moment's very density—the complex of trends, exchanges, events, and individuals—establishes both an opening up and a closing down of practical possibilities. Such a knot might be conceived as an unconscious time in which "something [is] always missed" because it "closes up again as soon as it has opened."[2]

The history presented here does not attempt to unravel this knot but instead focuses on the particular ways that architecture appears to be tangled up in it. The primary subject, or site, of this research is not the architecture or art of the 1960s (buildings, projects, sculptures, paintings) but architecture's "undisciplined" appearances in the writings that emerged to explain, defend, and attack minimalist art and artists. Although those appearances have not gone unnoticed in the various histories of minimalism, they have not been treated seriously. An account of the attitudes toward (and uses of) architecture in the discourse around minimalism is crucial to understanding the reconfiguration of the space between the disciplines of architecture, painting, and sculpture that occurred in the 1960s. Each discipline was entangled in the events of 1967, and each emerged from those events with significant reconfigurations of its techniques and concepts. How we now understand the differences between those disciplines is a result of the reconfigurations, missed opportunities, and technical innovations of that dense discursive moment.

"Transdisciplinary" practices and research view the exchange of concepts and techniques between established disciplines in terms of translation and transference. Such an approach is distinct from more pervasive notions of *inter*disciplinarity, which endorse the crossing of disciplines as a means to establish shared methods or concepts. Rather, transdisciplinary work, as Homi Bhabha suggests, "happens at the edge or limit" of our own discipline where we become acutely aware of, and in need of, disciplinary knowledges.[3] Thus transdisciplinary work continues to use properly disciplinary techniques, concepts, and vocabularies but is open to the alterations that emerge when they appear in or are applied to other disciplines.

This research aims to continue—or recuperate, perhaps—the ongoing reconfigurations of formalism that at one moment in the 1960s produced entirely new modes of art and relationships between the arts. In this transdisciplinary scenario, formalism is a contested field of techniques, concepts, and terms deployed in altered modes in various mediums and materials. Form *appears* through the specific techniques of particular disciplines, be they descriptive, representational, interpretive, or productive. Those techniques are constantly reconfigured as they are shared by or shift between the various arts or disciplines. The transdisciplinary exchanges that were crucial to the emergence of minimalism, and their effects on formalist discourse in the following decades, can be characterized as a process of identity formation, and the dynamics of exchange can be likened to transference: the striving of one discipline—or "subject"—to assuage a perceived lack of identity by assuming that of another through dialogue. Thus, to scrutinize the *appearance* and seek the *significance* of architecture in the forms of other disciplines is an attempt to identify altered instances of architecture, even the alter ego of the architect, in a virtual mirror. Such an examination of art criticism operates on two presumptions. First, architecture will make its appearance in a significantly altered form. That is, because architecture is appropriated to suit the motivation of the borrowing discipline, something is lost or gained in the translation which not only reconfigures that discipline, but potentially can be returned to architecture. Second, the specific alterations in architecture's appearance will help to locate disciplinary limits. In other words, the precise *form* of the impropriety will reveal the differences between the identities of the disciplines at a particular historical moment. The point is not to enforce or clarify differences, identities, or limits, but to demonstrate the flexibility of disciplinary identities and to explain how negotiations between disciplines produce reconfigured modes of practice. The exchanges between art and architecture in the 1960s are unusually vivid and productive historical examples of fundamental disciplinary alterations, which serve as counterexamples to the more prevalent tendency to emphasize the conservative, institutionalizing character of discipline(s).

BETWEEN THREE FORMALISMS

The categorizing of art into painting, architecture and sculpture seems to be one of the most unfortunate things that took place. Now all these categories are splintering … and it's like an interminable avalanche of categories. You have about forty different kinds of formalism and about a hundred different kinds of expressionism.

Robert Smithson, "What Is a Museum?" (1967)

The various attempts to define the role of formalist criticism in the 1960s took shape as a conflict between "modernists" and "literalists."[4] Both terms are largely polemical and have seen their share of abuse in the last half-century of art discourse. Yet the persistent attempts by a few individuals to define and claim authority over these words make them particularly useful in understanding historical events. Over three decades, Clement Greenberg and then Michael Fried refined a critical vocabulary that established the "modernist" position. "Literal" is a crucial term in that vocabulary. It appeared at crucial, transdisciplinary moments in Greenberg's writings of the 1940s and 1950s, but it was Fried, in 1966 and 1967, who ultimately proclaimed literalism the antithesis of modernism and identified it as the most salient and objectionable characteristic of the minimalist artwork he hoped to "defeat." His term will be adopted here, not because this research ratifies his evaluations or conclusions, but because Fried's emphasis upon that artwork's literal qualities, as opposed to its minimal (or reductive) means, implies relationships to architecture that he was unwilling to acknowledge, and implicitly denied. Architecture plays a surreptitious role in Fried's argument (disguised as the derogatory terms "literalism," "theatricality," and "objecthood").

That is, by insisting that "art" must "defeat" literalism, theatricality, and objecthood, Fried rejects the aesthetic significance of numerous qualities, traits, and conventions that are identified with the architectural discipline: for example, "spatial recession," "scale," and "duration." Fried attacks these effects of objecthood and literalism for promoting an awareness of the physical "presence" of an artwork and an awareness of one's own body when "beholding" a work of art. Such awarenesses are distractions, he argues, from the state of absorption—or "grace"—that modernist art requires. The same might be said for any implication of (or tendency toward) an awareness of (or engagement with) architecture. This book extends the implications of Fried's position beyond his apparent *suspicion* of architecture, and details the ways in which his attack on literalism can be construed as a *denial* of the potential productive complicity of art and architecture. Fried's polemic, if understood as a proscription on the possibility of an architectural art, leads then to an examination of the architectural aspects of minimalism and, in turn, to the implications of a *literalist architecture.*

Contrary to their ambitions, the efforts of art critics such as Greenberg and Fried to establish disciplinary norms—especially their dismissal of any relationship between art and architecture—ultimately both provoked and enabled the reconfiguration of disciplinary limits, identities, and differences. However, the potential alterations far exceed the actual changes. The primary aim of this research is to reconsider the received histories of minimalist art and, in turn, to recuperate at least part of the architectural potential—the architecture of literalism—that is as yet still latent in the formalist reconfigurations of the 1960s. The presumed affinities between recent "minimal" architecture and the artwork of the 1960s are more a matter of visual resemblances than a development of the specific motivations and circumstances that inspired and provoked the artists of the 1960s. Most important, there has been no thorough examination of the specific ways that architectural concepts, representation, and practices played a role in the emergence of minimalism and its formal strategies.[5]

Just as architecture's role in the emergence of minimalism remains underexamined, recent important work on art *after* minimalism by theorists and critics such as David Batchelor, Maurice Berger, Hal Foster, and Robert Pincus-Witten also neglects the significance of architecture. However, three important essays initiate innovative, though quite distinct, approaches to understanding the significance of architecture for artists of the 1960s. Rosalind Krauss's 1979 essay "Sculpture in the Expanded Field" employs a structuralist Klein diagram to reconceptualize "sculpture" not as a medium, but as a term that operates semiotically in opposition to both "architecture" and "landscape." For Krauss, it is only by logically opposing sculpture to architecture and landscape that the seeming "infinite malleability" of recent sculpture can be reframed as a "historically bounded category."[6] Yve-Alain Bois suggests another relationship between architecture and sculpture in his 1984 essay "A Picturesque Stroll around *Clara-Clara*." Bois argues that Richard Serra's sculpture is an implicit but powerful critique of architecture and of architects, but in a wholly negative sense. For Bois, architects today have much to learn from Serra about space, perception, and form because of the way his work enacts a return to philosophical concepts of the sublime and to techniques of the picturesque without invoking or utilizing architectural conventions of representation.[7] A much less well known essay by Christian Bonnefoi, first published in French in 1979, explains the connection between architecture and minimalism in explicit terms that foreground architectural thinking. Bonnefoi argues in "Louis Kahn and Minimalism" that, for the artists of the 1960s, "sculpture's vitality resides in establishing a relation to architectural functions … enabling us to conceive of them as starting from the same basic dimension: *the wall* (one should recall that the origin of Minimalism is linked up with a denial of the wall as a place of exhibition for the plastic artwork.… [M]inimalism's first gesture was to lay the object upon the ground, to take it down, to affirm its volume in real space)."[8] Although Bonnefoi's argument is less historical than philosophical, it insists on the primacy of architecture for minimalist art, and for formalist thinking in general. For Bonnefoi, the work of Louis Kahn and minimalism are related to one another "in the sense that [for each] the formal solution is equivalent to the structural solution."[9] These few sources suggest the deep theoretical interdependencies of minimalism and architecture, even if much historical work remains to be done. This research examines one aspect of that historical project: the alterations in formalist discourse provoked by minimalism and the significance of architecture in the emergence of new understandings of form in art.

In the first four chapters of this book, the differing formulations of modernist and literalist criticism are presented through two pairings of critics. The first pairing (in chapters 1 and 2) examines the "postcubist" writings of Colin Rowe and Clement Greenberg, epitomized in essays each published in 1961. Despite the two critics' differing backgrounds, their approaches show remarkable affinities, including a shared analogy between cubist collage and architectural space. The second pairing (in chapters 3 and 4) contrasts the writings of Michael Fried and Robert Smithson. Their criticism developed simultaneously, and their conflict reached its greatest intensity in June 1967 when each published what is perhaps his most speculative and polemical essay in *Artforum*'s special issue on American sculpture. Most important, Fried and Smithson display attitudes toward architecture and space that are as opposed as their attitudes toward the new sculpture. Fried's invocation of "a continuous and perpetual present" as the epitome of aesthetic experience is an implicit denial of architecture's relevance to art, just as Smithson's proposal for "an esthetic method" that he calls "site-selection-study" takes an explicit interest in "buildings."[10] Whereas Fried sublimated space in his concept of the "radically abstract" and denied any architectural aspects in modernist sculpture, Smithson enthusiastically and explicitly embraced architectural concerns and devised a complex notion of space that would be displayed in its most refined form in his "non-sites," beginning in 1968.

While the appearance of architecture in Fried's and Smithson's debate is particularly intriguing, it is not an isolated instance in the history of formalist criticism. Both critics acknowledge that they worked in the shadow of Greenberg, whose writings of the prior two decades included a series of attempts to consider the relationship between architecture and art in modernism. The terms and issues that would be central to the arguments between Fried and Smithson had already emerged in Greenberg's criticism, particularly at those moments when he ventured to include architecture in his discussion.

This presentation of the work of four critics reveals an unappreciated exchange between the formalist discourses of architecture, painting, and sculpture in the 1960s, and identifies three related but competing modes of formalist criticism. The first—here called *pictorial formalism*—is codified in the medium-specific modernism of Greenberg and Fried that dominated postwar art and art criticism in America. For both, art is basically optical, and painting epitomizes the achievements of modernism. Whereas Greenberg ventured, and later abandoned, an effort to relate architecture to modernist painting and sculpture, Fried strenuously excluded architectural issues from his revised notion of modernist art. The second mode—here called *pictorial impropriety*—is exemplified by Colin Rowe's architectural criticism and design pedagogy, which operated as translations of abstract (especially cubist) painting and collage. Rowe's impropriety lies in his adoption of pictorial techniques and his simultaneous transgression of medium-specificity, as is evident, for example, in his suggestion that techniques of pictorial formalism can be transferred to the appreciation of *conceptual* devices such as architectural plans. The third mode—here called *literalism*—is advanced in the artwork and writings of artist-critics such as Robert Smithson, who engaged aspects of architecture to inspire, inform, and initiate a three-dimensional alternative to pictorial formalism. His non-sites, as well as the graphic design of his essays, build on the techniques, procedures, and language that he first encountered in his role as an "artist-consultant" to an architectural firm in 1966 and 1967. As in the work of numerous other artists such as Mel Bochner, Dan Flavin, Dan Graham, Don Judd, and Sol LeWitt, the architectural aspects of Smithson's work are overt. Yet Smithson's significance is distinct because of the way his work extended and consolidated an understanding of literalism in terms of architecture.

The literalist position initially took form as a rejection of modernist *painting*, as it had been defined by a continuous tradition of pictorial formalist criticism in the English language that began over a half century earlier with Roger Fry's essays on "post-impressionism," continued in Greenberg's essays of the 1940s and 1950s, and culminated in Fried's revision of Greenberg in the

1960s. Initially, the most innovative arguments of the 1960s emerged from, and in response to, new developments in what Donald Judd wryly called "the new three-dimensional work."[11] In their production of both criticism and artwork, the literalists not only engendered a sustained, prolific, and explicit reconfiguration of modernist criticism; they also identified a role for architecture that differs from the dominant modes of architectural criticism in the 1960s. That is, one of the lingering legacies of architectural formalism is a rejection of sculptural tendencies and a persistent assimilation and application of techniques that regard architectural representations and the buildings they produce as though they were a kind of painting, or at least a picture. At the same moment that architects intensified their interest in pictorialist practices, the literalist artist-critics advanced a "confused" relationship between architecture and sculpture to escape the dominance of pictorial formalism. In this way, the literalists initiated critical practices that can be understood as selective usurpations of the architectural discipline.

However, the crucial point here is that, despite working at cross purposes, both architecture's assimilation of pictorialism (via Rowe and others) and literalism's engagement with architecture constitute what I call *productive improprieties.* Both involve translations across disciplines that not only revise the borrower's own disciplinary conventions, but also potentially provide new material for the discipline from which each has borrowed. In the case presented here, over a period of just a few years in the mid-1960s, literalist sculpture and its criticism engaged architectural concerns and conventions — such as spatial perception and representation, inhabitation, scale, fabrication, the room as container, site documentation, and installation — and in the years that followed, a myriad of literalist practices emerged in the art world, each with peculiar and canny uses of architecture. The proliferation of installation, site-specific, and performance art in the 1970s and 1980s represents a first wave of productive engagement of architecture by artists. Today, nearly forty years after the advent of minimalism, artists such as Vito Acconci, Andrea Zittel, Jorge Pardo, and Glen Seator have been increasingly — and overtly — producing literally (though perhaps not literal*ist*) architectural work.

CRITICISM AND IDENTITY

What could be more ordinary than to identify? It even seems like the essential operation of thought.

Jacques Lacan, "From Interpretation to the Transference" (1964)

The concept of identity is fundamental in various ways to the modes of criticism discussed here. Modernist criticism established (some might say imposed) a certain identity for postwar art and artists. In his 1940 essay "Towards a Newer Laocoon," Greenberg described the modernist impulse as "an anxiousness as to the fate of art, a concern for its identity.... There has been, is and will be, such a thing as a confusion of the arts."[12] In 1966 Fried claimed that the task of the modernist critic is to avoid and correct cases of "mistaken identity."[13] For Fried, as for Greenberg, the viability of modern art depends on the ability to identify what is and what is not worthy of critical and aesthetic attention. In "Art and Objecthood," Fried writes: "the task of the modernist painter is to discover those conventions which, at a given moment, *alone* are capable of establishing his work's identity as painting."[14] Most important, modernist criteria of evaluation are medium-specific: modernist art *is* "art" only to the degree that it can be identified in the precise formal terms of a specific discipline—painting, sculpture, music, and so forth. According to Fried, not only are "the concepts of quality and value ... meaningful ... only *within* the individual arts,"[15] but what is "at issue ... is nothing less than the nature of painting and sculpture in our time, as well as the identities of the men and women whose enterprises they are."[16]

Yet within modernist criticism there have been evident difficulties in making such identifications. As Fried's opposition "Art and Objecthood" so neatly asserts, the foremost modernist problem involves the formalist understanding of *objects* and their literalist implications. Greenberg's writings reveal a struggle with questions of literalism and objecthood, and move from an endorsement of literalness to its wholesale rejection. Near the end of "Towards a Newer Laocoon," he states his well-known modernist position, but in literalist terms that he would later reject: "To restore the identity of an art the opacity of its medium must be emphasized. For the visual arts the medium is discovered to be physical; hence pure painting and pure sculpture seek above all to affect the spectator physically."[17]

In 1954 Greenberg reiterated that position in his claim that the modernist painting "has now become an object of literally the same spatial order as our bodies and no longer the vehicle of an imagined equivalent of that order."[18] But just two years later he would make a crucial shift and retreat from this emphasis on the "palpability" of modern art: "Modernist painting ... does call attention to the physical properties of the medium, but only in order for these to transcend themselves. Like any other kind of picture, a modernist one succeeds when its identity as a picture, and as a pictorial experience, shuts out awareness of it as a physical object."[19] Finally, in 1958, he introduced the concept of a "modernist 'reduction,'" which he claimed had become pervasive in *all* the arts, and which requires "[r]endering substance entirely optical, and form, whether pictorial, sculptural or architectural, as an integral part of ambient space."[20]

Thus Fried was following Greenberg when he identified objecthood as the antithesis of modernism: "It is as though objecthood alone can, in the present circumstances, secure something's identity, if not as non-art, at least as neither painting nor sculpture; or as though a work of art—

more accurately, a work of modernist painting or sculpture—were in some essential respect *not an object.*"[21]

Not only does Fried's oppositional logic brilliantly encapsulate the pictorial formalist position, but his declaration of a "war" between art and objecthood (non-art) and his identification of literalism as the chief enemy of modernist art also implicate architecture in the fate of modernism. Fried seems to have recognized, at least implicitly, that the literalist reconfiguration of formalism, with its refusal of the pictorial, embraces formal strategies, devices, and qualities that are literally architectural. With that transdisciplinary move, literalism swerved from what Yve-Alain Bois has characterized as "the vast corpus of American criticism of the late '60s and early '70s [which] was dominated by a reaction against Greenberg."[22] Striving to avoid "the closure of a whole universe of discourse whose divisions represented strategic positions on the same field," the literalists shifted that field by engaging architecture. Literalist artists and critics saw the prescriptions and exclusions of modernist formalism not as confusions to be eliminated, but as opportunities or openings for alternative practices and identities for the modern artist. They assumed an attitude toward Greenberg's and Fried's formalism that is similar to that of the literary critic Geoffrey Hartman who, in his 1966 essay "Beyond Formalism," maintained that his departure from the New Critics was "not due to their formalism as such but rather to their not being formalistic enough; and that, conversely, those who have tried to ignore or transcend formalism tend often to arrive at results more abstract and categorical than what they object to."[23]

ARCHITECTURE AND LITERALISM

Minimal works are readable as art, as almost anything is today—including a door, a table, or a blank sheet of paper. (That almost any nonfigurative object can approach the condition of architecture or of an architectural member is, on the other hand, beside the point. . . .)
Clement Greenberg, "Recentness of Sculpture" (1967)

As Donald Judd wrote in "Specific Objects," the essay that first formulated a literalist position, "Half or more of the best new work in the past few years has been neither painting nor sculpture. Usually it has been related, closely or distantly, to one or the other."[24] At one point in the essay, Judd turned to architecture and the window to illustrate his point: "In the new work the shape, image, color and surface are single and not partial or scattered. There aren't any neutral or moderate areas or parts, any connections or transitional areas. The difference between the new work and earlier painting and present sculpture is like that between one of Brunelleschi's windows in the Badia di Fiesole and the facade of the Palazzo Rucellai, which is only an undeveloped rectangle as a whole and is mainly a collection of highly ordered parts."[25]

Soon after, Robert Smithson would raise the formalist stakes, arguing that "[a]ll 'formal' criticism and art is based on representational space and its reduction."[26] Smithson's writings evaded such reductive formalism in large part by turning to architecture and, for example, explaining literalist sculpture as "a new kind of monumentality" inspired by "the slurbs, urban sprawl, and the infinite number of housing developments," "the discount centers and cut-rate stores with their sterile facades," "the 'moderne' interior architecture of the new 'art-houses' like Cinema I and II," and "the much denigrated architecture of Park Avenue known as 'cold glass boxes.'"[27] Then, in 1967, through an identification with the architectural details of the 1930s buildings on Central Park West, he imagined he could "transform the 'window' into an art form."[28] Smithson would achieve that aspiration in 1968 with his invention of the "non-site."

The final chapters of this book present the work of architects who have engaged the legacy of literalism: John Hejduk and Frank Gehry. Importantly, these architects' collaborations with artists have played a formative role in their practices. Hejduk, with the painter Robert Slutzky, curated the 1967 exhibition "The Diamond in Painting and Architecture." His essay for the exhibition catalog is consistent with his previous work of the 1950s and 1960s, which instituted many of the formal devices and processes that define postwar architectural formalism as a translation of the devices of modernist painting. Hejduk's Texas Houses (1954–63) and especially the Diamond Projects (1963–67) typify pictorial formalism in architecture. However, around 1968, as evidenced in the Wall House and Cube Houses, Hejduk's work began to acknowledge emerging literalist formal approaches that derive from minimalism and initiated a shift from systems of composition and projection to what he called his "new discovery" of the wall as "a Neutral Condition."[29]

Frank Gehry's architecture offers other evidence of the influence of 1960s art on architecture. Beginning with his project for the home and studio of the painter Ronald Davis (1969–72), Gehry conducted a series of experiments with design process that led to an explicit engagement with literalist strategies. Although Davis's manipulation of perspective in his work was decidedly pictorial, Gehry translated the latent literalism of the painter's devices into a design process that exceeded the painter's understanding of his own techniques, using architectural models to construct perspectival space as a three-dimensional object. Several years later, in three residential projects—including his own house—those experiments yielded a new language of construction and space. Gehry's literalism became fully explicit in his 1981 collaboration with Richard Serra when he first exposed his interest in the fish, a figure that would occupy him for nearly a decade. Neither sculpture nor architecture, Gehry's fish is what I call a "dumby building" that provokes a redescription of the architect's and architecture's identity.

DEFINING LITERALISM

The concept of a room is, most clandestinely, important to literalist art and theory.

Michael Fried, "Art and Objecthood" (1967)

One concise definition of literalism is *representation without idealization.* "This is this" is the axiom of literalism. Literalism locates the turning point (in this case, the "is") when language or representation *seems* entirely adequate and direct, but also utterly inflexible and maddeningly indeterminate. Literalisms lose their specific meaning as soon as they are removed from the circumstances of their utterance. Also, as the philosopher Stanley Cavell explains, literal usages can be *re*phrased but not *para*phrased.[30] Literalism is against interpretation and for application. Tony Smith's *Die* exemplifies this strategy (fig. 0.1). It is a black blank block that fabricates and deploys (empty) form to disrupt social conventions of space, to defer representation, to corrupt purity, to invite engagement in the slippages of the visual, actual, and textual fields. That slippage is why *literal translations* are more puzzling than they are obvious. By emphasizing direct correspondences between things—words, shapes, textures, etc.—one can suspend questions of intentionality and emphasize issues of conventionality or similitude (fig. 0.2). Apparent likenesses—"this is this"—quickly become critical when their presumed obviousness is open to interrogation.[31] That is one way to understand Frank Stella's claim that he tried "to keep the paint as good as it was in the can," or Eva Hesse's use of simple repetition (fig. 0.3), or Donald Judd's deployment of specific objects as "one thing after another."

Cavell offers a similar understanding of literalism when he advises a philosophical method that takes figural speech literally. He calls this *literalizing convention.* Cavell suggests that there is likely something to be learned by scrutinizing and playing out the conventional uses of seemingly plain words which despite their conventionality "strew obscurities across our path and seem willfully to thwart comprehension; and then time after time we discover that their meaning has been missed only because it was so utterly bare—totally, therefore, unnoticeably, in view."[32] This process is something like the reverse of the language used by the character Chance the Gardener in Kosinski's *Being There,* whose banal literal statements are misinterpreted as profound figures of speech. The reverse method is a matter of figures of speech being taken entirely literally. A didactic example of this in art occurs in the work of Robert Ryman, whose seemingly endless permutations of painting as a blank canvas literalize the conventions of his discipline, such as shape, whiteness, support, mounting, and frontality (fig. 0.4). With Ryman, as with Hesse and others, literalist techniques tentatively engage architecture. Walls, floors, space, and so on become an extension of, and even sustain, the artwork.

TRIAL PROOF II/X WITH PENCIL + INK ADDITIONS

0.1 *Representation without idealization:* Tony Smith, *Die*, 1962 (fabricated 1968). Steel with oil finish, 72 × 72 × 72 in.

0.2 *Literal translation:* Jasper Johns, *Words (Buttocks Knee Sock …),* trial proof ii/x, 1975–76. Lift ground aquatint with pencil and ink additions, 10.5 × 17.5 in.

0.3 *This is this:* Eva Hesse, *Repetition 19,* 1967. Aluminum screen, papier-mâché, glue, polyester resin, paint, each unit c. 10 × 8 × 8 in.

0.4 *Literalizing convention:* Robert Ryman, *Pace,* 1984. Acrylic on fiberglass, wood, aluminum, 59.5 × 26 × 29 in.

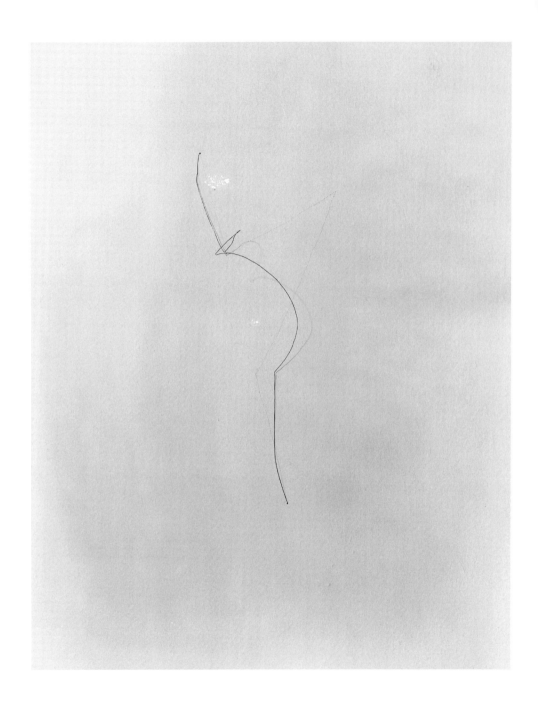

0.5 *Literal figures:* Richard Tuttle, *33rd Wire Piece,* 1972. Pencil, wire, nails, 35 × 18 in.

Literal figures transgress the assumed gap between virtual and actual, seeming and seaming, as in Richard Tuttle's *Wire Piece* series (fig. 0.5). To make those works Tuttle first draws a faint, idiosyncratic, shaky line on the wall in pencil. A wire is attached to the wall at the upper end of the line, then is bent to follow the shape of the (much craggier) line. When it is released, the wire springs up and away from the wall and casts a shadow. The interplay of the three linear figures (wire, pencil, shadow), each with subtle yet noticeable distinctions, constitutes the work. This is this is this. Each is a literal figure and the differences between them heighten that literalness. The work cannot be reduced to any single medium. Most important, if we think of these works in a radically literal way—if we read the figural features literally (and vice versa)—the question of whether the work engages architecture or "is" architecture becomes crucial. Where does the artwork start and architecture end? What about the gallery and its constraints on our perception of the piece? What about the floor upon which we walk? Where does this elaborate diagram end? A literalist reading suggests that the answers to these questions are not definitive but require an examination of techniques and their contexts. These works are quite literally architectural, but only if we insist on taking them literally. They insinuate that the appearances of architecture, contrary to the all too common criticism, can never be "too literal."

Chapter 1

Blankly Visual: Colin Rowe's Pictorial Impropriety

Formalism and Colin Rowe circulate in architectural discourse as a dedicated couple, but their relationship, while intimate, is more intriguing, unconventional, and agonized than is usually assumed. The tendency to equate Rowe with a constrained, discipline-specific version of formalism is the result of the brilliance and focus of his early essays, which have come to exemplify a distinct genre of historical criticism founded in formal analysis, as well as the techniques of design that emerged from his teaching in two deeply formalist architecture programs, briefly at the University of Texas and more lastingly at Cornell.[1] Yet Rowe's application of formalist methods to architectural problems—from his earlier efforts to ascertain the broader significance of modern architecture's formal devices in essays such as "The Mathematics of the Ideal Villa" (1947), "Mannerism and Modern Architecture" (1950), "Transparency: Literal and Phenomenal" (1956, coauthored with the painter Robert Slutzky), and "Dominican Monastery of La Tourette" (1961) to his later concern with urbanism in his 1978 book *Collage City*—is a product of a broader discourse.[2] To view Rowe's criticism as either a specifically architectural mode of close reading or the handmaiden of design practice neglects the intricacies and, most important, the continuity of his effort to intervene across disciplines in the development of Anglo-American formalism.

The conventional wisdom that separates the early "idealist" Rowe from the later "pluralist" Rowe—while perhaps an accurate representation of a shift in temperament and cultural outlook—is misleading when applied to his consistent fascination with the pictorial techniques of formalism. Rowe's shift in emphasis from the formalist devices of painting (in the 1950s) to those of collage (in the 1970s) has been characterized as at once a revision of the method of his early essays, an affirmation of the pluralist ethics of American postmodernism, and an apologia for a "neotraditional" urbanism. Yet his formalist sources and modes in *Collage City* are not different from those in his earlier essays; and while there are important changes in Rowe's thinking over those three decades, he displayed an incisive, suspicious, and nuanced attitude toward high modern architecture long before the general anxiety about the fate of modernism emerged in the late 1960s.

If there is a defining event in Rowe's engagement with formalism, it is not a decisive shift of attitude sometime in the late 1960s, but an earlier moment of originality and insight. Rowe's 1961 essay on Le Corbusier's monastery La Tourette marks the most intensive development of his formal methods and offers the reading of architecture that most explicitly transgresses disciplinary conventions. "Dominican Monastery of La Tourette" is as much the culmination of the pictorialism of his earlier essays as it is the initiation of the preoccupations with collage and context in his later work.

The chronology and development of Rowe's work is complicated, however, by the unusual delay in the broad dissemination of his early writings. Between 1947 and 1961, in Britain and in America, Rowe wrote ten innovative and now influential essays, but published only half in that same period. Two of the most famous, "Transparency: Literal and Phenomenal" and "Transparency: Literal and Phenomenal, Part II," were written with Slutzky in 1955–56 but were not published until 1963 and 1971, respectively. Nine of the ten essays—the exception is the second "Transparency" essay—would be collected in the book *The Mathematics of the Ideal Villa and Other Essays,* which was published in 1976—three years *after* Rowe "completed the text" of *Collage City.*[3] This untimely juxtaposition of the earlier and later work likely made the differences between them seem more obvious, and those differences tend to be emphasized over the inherent continuities in Rowe's methods and observations. When his essays appeared, or reappeared, as a book in 1976, they were seen less as consequential and strategic interventions in the development of formalist thinking than as brilliant but suspect work on what was already past. The intellectual sources and discursive context of the early work were considered less important than its contemporary significance for architectural criticism and design.

On the other hand, the equivocating erudition of *Collage City* has been credited with (or accused of) converting Rowe's earlier critical techniques into tools of amelioration and accommodation. *Collage City* has also been seen as shifting the concerns of formalism from "objecthood"—an intensive scrutiny of the formal configurations of individual buildings—to "contextualism"—an extensive elaboration of the incidental heterogeneity of American urbanism and the altered form of post–World War II European cities.[4] A realistic ambivalence (or a liberal pragmatism) seemed to replace the abstract precision of formal analysis, and Rowe has since been both assailed and admired for swerving from the close reading method that fueled his earlier criticism. Rowe's attack in *Collage City* upon "modern architecture's object fixation" is often cited as evidence of a significant change in his outlook, and certain other writings also seem to support the notion of a postmodern conversion.[5] In 1973, the same year he finished writing *Collage City,* Rowe wrote an addendum to "The Mathematics of the Ideal Villa," in which he admits the "limited value" of the "Wölfflinian style of critical exercise" of that essay and several others that followed.[6] Yet even while Rowe described his earliest methodology as antiquated—"painfully belonging to a period c. 1900"—he reserved the hope that the method of the early essays "might still possess the merit of appealing primarily to what is visible…. It might, in other words, possess the merits of accessibility" because it "mak[es] the minimum of pretenses to erudition and the least possible references outside itself." By comparison, in his introduction to *Collage City* (which was likely written in the same year as the addendum to "Mathematics") Rowe announces that his new approach is more inclusive and has neither obvious scholarly limitations nor a specific art historical origin.

Rowe's insistence, in the 1973 addendum to "Mathematics," on the accessibility of visual analysis and the vitality of cubism and its criticism suggests that he believed that his earlier essays establish a justifiable *beginning* of a project that not only remains based in formal analysis but continues to insist upon a translation of the aesthetic innovations of modern art into architectural terms. The ironic ambivalence of *Collage City* should not be seen as a disavowal of the abstract precision of formal analysis. Nor should his criticism simply be understood in the context of the architectural values and trends that made the implications of his approach so appealing to "postmodernists." The deeper alignments are transdisciplinary. Much attention has been given to Rowe's evolving interest in political theory and the philosophy of science and history—namely, the work of Karl Popper and Isaiah Berlin—but his concerns with the devices of cubism and the legacy of formalism are both more fundamental and more focused than his other interests.

Rowe's distinct and durable contribution to the architectural discipline is his persistent attempt to translate the pictorial rigor of cubism into architectural terms.

Yet the desire persists to identify an obvious split in Rowe's subject. The fact that his early essays and later book are separated by a seemingly absent decade of writing encourages the periodizing, as does the fact that in the 1960s the legacy of formalism in art discourse was intensely reconfigured. Curiously, though, neither *Collage City* nor the revisions to the essays in *The Mathematics of the Ideal Villa* offer any significant alterations to Rowe's understanding of cubism or formal analysis. Nor does his work ever acknowledge or account for the emergence of minimalist and pop art, the reassessment of artists such as Picasso, Duchamp, and Pollock, or the renewed interest in movements such as dada and surrealism. Cubism and formalism appear in Rowe's work as a basically stable set of principles, and *Collage City* is less a rejection of the formalist modes of the early essays than a revision of their purposes and applications.

All the same let us now recognize that, by 1976, rather than camouflage and cover-up, what might be called extensive manipulation was coming to be required.

Colin Rowe, "Ideas, Talent, Poetics: A Problem of Manifesto" (1989)

Rowe's early work usually is described as a reaction against the technological and functionalist pieties of postwar architecture as exemplified by Sigfried Giedion's 1941 book *Space, Time and Architecture* and the curriculum Walter Gropius instituted in the 1940s at Harvard's Graduate School of Design. On the other hand, the greatest positive influence on Rowe, it is assumed, was Rudolf Wittkower, with whom Rowe studied from 1945 to 1947 at the Courtauld Institute in London. At that time Wittkower was revising the several essays that would become *Architectural Principles in the Age of Humanism,* the 1949 book that is so often associated with the first "half" of Rowe's work.[7] While Rowe never abandoned his praise for Wittkower, citing his work as the "best example of criticism directed towards … the correlation of form and meaning in architecture," other influences are equally significant even if they are less distinct.[8] Rowe's formalism also should be seen in the context of a more perceptually based and generally applicable *pictorial formalism* that derives from art criticism—especially that of painting—and which pervaded Anglo-American culture for nearly the entire twentieth century. As Meyer Schapiro pointed out as early as 1936, architects, critics, and historians, generally "overlook the degree to which the designs of the architect are affected by pictorialism, by the modes of seeing and drawing developed in modern, and especially abstract, painting."[9]

Nowhere is Rowe's pictorialism more apparent than in the two "Transparency" essays he wrote with Robert Slutzky. Although Rowe would later tactfully distance himself from the "leading ideas" of those essays by crediting them to Slutzky, he also has suggested that they were present—as "juvenile enthusiasm"—as early as 1950 in his "Mannerism and Modern Architecture" and would return as "themes" in later lectures and essays.[10] If there is a shift, then, in Rowe's approach, it is a move not away from pictorial formalism but away from its explicit application. If anything, the *subtext* of Rowe's (and all) pictorialism—a liberal humanism that places faith in subjective visual judgment to discern reality's true appearance and arrive at shared cultural values—becomes the *pretext* of his later writing, while his formalist methods move into the background.[11]

The roots of pictorial formalism lie in German aesthetics and art history of the nineteenth century.[12] They were famously (and reductively) reformulated by the British critics Roger Fry and Clive Bell in the second decade of the twentieth century as the theory of "significant form."[13] By 1950, that reformulation had become pervasive in America, as is evident in books such as Alfred Barr's *Picasso: Fifty Years of His Art* (1946), Henry-Russell Hitchcock's *Painting toward Architecture* (1948), Gyorgy Kepes's *Language of Vision* (1944; fig. 1.1), and László Moholy-Nagy's *Vision in Motion* (1947).[14] Rowe and Slutzky were certainly aware of and interested in these books. The "Transparency" essays refer to Barr, Kepes, and Moholy-Nagy, and Rowe reports that a statement of "principles and policies" that he wrote in 1954 to introduce a new curriculum at the University of Texas "was based on Hitchcock's *Painting toward Architecture*."[15] In fact, Rowe first traveled to America in 1951 to study with Hitchcock at Yale, and it seems that that experience, as much as his work with Wittkower, inspired Rowe's historical and critical approach. Most important, the position Hitchcock outlined in *Painting toward Architecture*—the critique of functionalism, the reiteration of Alfred Barr's discussion of cubism, and the characterization of modern architecture as a rejection of stylistic imitation in favor of the formal "architectonic" of later cubism and a reinterpretation of purism and De Stijl—is similar to Rowe's own thinking at the time and in the next several decades.

Rowe's approach also has significant affinities with Hitchcock's first book, *Modern Architecture: Romanticism and Reintegration* (1929).[16] Although Rowe was more insistent than Hitchcock that architecture's appearance is strongly influenced by intellectual developments, the appeal of Hitchcock's "remarkably penetrating account of the new architecture which had appeared in the twenties" was likely its emphasis on a long period of gradual change that could be demonstrated through the visual analysis and description of carefully chosen examples.[17] Hitchcock's thesis is that modern architecture must be understood as a development spanning five centuries, beginning with "an increasing substitution of visual logic for organic logic" in the Flamboyant Gothic

Picasso. *Portrait of Kahnweiler*
Courtesy of Mrs. Charles B. Goodspeed

Amadee Ozenfant. *Purist Still Life*
Courtesy of Art of This Century

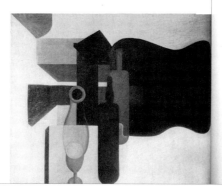

G. F. Keck. *Detail of a House*
Photograph by W. Keck

Contemporary architecture utilizes the transparent quality of synthetic materials, glass, plastics, etc., to create a design that will integrate the greatest possible number of spatial vistas. Inside and outside are in close relationship, and each viewpoint in the building offers the widest visible comprehension of space. Reflections and mirrorings, transparent and translucent building materials are carefully calculated and organized to focus divergent spatial vistas in one visual grasp.

L. Moholy Nagy.
Space Construction 1930

1.1 Page spread from Gyorgy Kepes, *Language of Vision*, 1944.

interiors of the fourteenth century, and he argued that "the phases [of] European architecture … since … the thirteenth century are not to be considered as constituting successive independent styles … but rather as subsidiary manners of one Modern style" that exhibits architects' "more or less conscious intellectual interests in abstract form."[18]

Rowe apparently was attracted also to Hitchcock's "superior judgment"[19] (relative to Giedion's) of the evolving "relation between technics and aesthetic expression."[20] Hitchcock did not believe that technology was the catalyst for what he calls the "New Tradition" which emerged in the second half of the nineteenth century or the "New Pioneers" that followed in the early twentieth century. Nor did he see a decisive break with the past: "however much there may be progress technically, aesthetically there is only more or less sequential change."[21] For Hitchcock, what truly distinguishes the New Tradition and New Pioneers from earlier phases of modern architecture is that their technical achievements were integrated with a more explicit, and distinctly architectural, formal experimentation. The work of the New Pioneers in particular was the result of an altered relationship between painting and architecture. Although influenced by abstract painting, the New Pioneers eventually departed from it, and promised to supersede it by attempting to "achiev[e] on another scale and in three real dimensions the effects then found in painting to be of aesthetic significance.… It is probable that the influence of abstract painting on architecture will prove also to have been temporary. Indeed it may appear that its point of view is better satisfied by architecture than by painting, and that it will be continued in architecture alone."[22] This concern with the relationship between the arts is crucial to Hitchcock's claim that, following a distinct decline during what he calls the "age of romanticism" (c. 1750–1850) which was due in part to architecture's dependence on "picturesque" modes of composition derived from landscape painting, the New Pioneers enacted what might be understood as a "return" to architecture that recovered its identity as an art.[23] This is nowhere clearer than in the final sentence of Hitchcock's book: "The great change has been that while Romanticism made of architecture the least of the visual arts, it is to-day nearer to being the most important."[24]

Certainly Rowe was fascinated by the pictorialism inherent in modernist architecture and the potential to advance a specifically architectural tradition of formal experimentation. His work can be understood as an extended effort both to investigate the "influence of abstract painting on architecture" and to undermine the assumptions of contemporary architects who treated modernism as a purely social or technological project. Rowe was persistent in his efforts to connect the emergence of visual modes of composition in architecture at the end of the nineteenth century to the work of architects who have denied any such connection. His critique of the pronouncements of architects such as Mies and Gropius was founded on an insistence that constructivist and especially De Stijl composition had a pronounced influence on virtually all

8

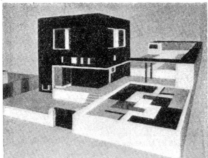

9

10

7, facing page, Gropius's building at the Deutsche Werkbund Exhibition of 1914, and 8, his Haus am Horn 1923, still exhibit, if only in composition, the elements of academic theory. The space-time factor has not emerged. How-

11
12

ever, in Ferenc Molnar's design for a house, 9, the Red Cube, 1922, and even more in Van Doesburg's project, 10, of 1923 the theory of composition based on a picturesque viewpoint has entered into a definite conflict with a system of personal abstraction deriving from Cubism. With the Bauhaus, 11 and 12, elements of the strictly functional programme are given unity in a Cubist composition. The elements exist in tension, and the total abstraction is intelligible only from the air.

1.2 Images from Colin Rowe, "Mannerism and Modern Architecture," *Architectural Review*, 1950.

1.3 Page from Colin Rowe and Fred Koetter, *Collage City*, 1978.

Theo Van Doesburg: Counter-
construction, maison particulière, 1923

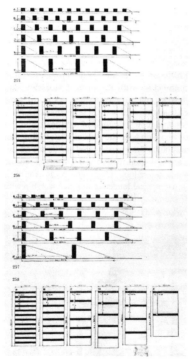

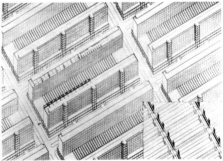

Ludwig Hilberseimer: project for
central Berlin, 1927

Walter Gropius: diagrams showing the
development of a rectangular site with
parallel rows of apartment blocks of
different heights, 1929

The villa by Le Corbusier at La Chaux-de-Fonds, built in 1916. It was omitted from the Oeuvre Complète presumably because 'the didactic emphasis of the collection might have been impaired' by its inclusion. The formal ambiguity it displays, with the remarkable focus on a blank, framed panel, provides an interesting comparison with some designs of the sixteenth century Mannerists in Italy.

clusive, rectilinear, self-sufficient form seems to deny the type of pyramidal composition, which reveals itself from the garden.

The flat vertical surface of the two upper floors is divided into three panels. The outer ones, narrow and vertical, are pierced by elliptical lunettes, while the central one, elaborately framed, comprises an unrelieved blank, white surface. It is towards this surface, accentuated by all the means within the architect's control, that the eye is immediately led. The low walls, screening service rooms and terrace, are curved inwards rising towards it; two entrance doors prepare the duality to be resolved; the projecting marquise with its supporting columns completes the isolation of the upper wall, where the composition is to be focused; the emphatic elliptical windows in the outer panels increase the demand for a dominant; and with the mind baffled by so elaborately conceived an ambiguity, the eye comes to rest on the immaculate rectangle and incisive detail of its brick frame.

Contemplating this façade for any length of time, one is both ravished and immensely irritated. Its mouldings are of extreme finesse, lucid and complex; the slightly curved window reveals are of considerable suavity: the contrast of wall above and below the canopy is permanently exciting; the sharp and dogmatic change of texture refreshes and soothes; but the blank surface is both a disturbance and a delight. The masses and the modelling impel the eye towards it, but it is the activity of emptiness, which the intellect is called upon to enjoy.

Since this motif was presumably intended to shock, its success is complete, for it imbues the façade with all the qualities of a manifesto. In this abrupt composition, if nowhere else in this villa, there appears a tension which seems to foreshadow the later development; and it is the panel with its intensifying frame which establish for other elements of the façade—columns and canopy—their apparent precocity. Distinct and deliberate, drawing attention to itself, and yet without apparent content, at once distributing attention over the rest of the house; by its conclusiveness the whole building gains significance; but by its emptiness it is, at the same time, the problem in terms of which the whole building is stated. Thus, as an

apparent outcome of its systematically opposite values, there issue a whole series of disturbances, of which it is both centre and periphery.

Behind the panel lies the staircase, the lighting of which can only be impaired, and one must assume that an architect as apt as Le Corbusier, could, had he wished, have chosen some alternative and functionally more satisfactory organization; while even if it were to be supposed (improbable as it appears) that the frame was intended to receive some fresco or inscription, it is still a motif sufficiently abnormal and recondite to stimulate curiosity and encourage a hunt for possible parallels. The most probable and certainly the most rewarding field of investigation seems to be Italian; not that with Le Corbusier any direct allusion could be expected, but that in general terms he so frequently appears to be descended from the architectural traditions of Renaissance humanism.

In early Renaissance loggia and palace façades, sequences of alternating windows and panels do not appear to be uncommon. In such more frequent sequences from the sixteenth century, panels and windows acquire almost equal significance. Panels may be expressed as blank surfaces, or become a range of inscribed tablets, or again they may form the frames for painting; but whatever their particular employment may be, the alternation of a developed system of panelling, with an equally developed system of fenestration, seems always to produce complexity and duality of emphasis in a façade. This quality must have given considerable pleasure to the generation of architects subsequent to Bramante; and in the pages of Serlio, for instance, panels occur in an almost embarrassing profusion.[2] Sometimes they are to be found in the typical alternation, or on other occasions absorbing entire wall surfaces; in elongated form they are used to intersect two whole ranges of windows, or they may appear as the crowning motif of a triumphal arch or Venetian palace. It was probably Serlio who first employed the panel as the focus of a façade. In some cases he has groups of windows arranged on either side of this reduced but evocative form of central emphasis; but it also seems likely that in only two instances does the panel make a central appearance within an eleva-

The use of the blank panel to provide central emphasis is illustrated in the first two of the façades above. 2, the so-called Casa di Palladio at Vicenza, 1572, a subtle exercise in the inversion of classical rules, bears an obvious relationship to the villa at La Chaux-de-Fonds. 3, Zuccheri's casino at Florence, 1578; the design of this house remained in the repertoire of academic archi-

[2] See Serlio: *Tutte l'Opera d'Architettura.* The panel alternating with windows occurs in Book IV, pages 15, 23, 25, 27, 29, 33, 43, 45, 49, 55, 151, 159, 187, 221, 229. The example in Book VII, p. 187, suggests itself as a possible source for Palladio's scheme. It was perhaps through the influence of Serlio that this motif penetrated France, where for instance, alternating with a range of attic windows, it is to be seen in such a scheme as Lescot's Louvre.

1.4 Page from Colin Rowe, "Mannerism and Modern Architecture," *Architectural Review*, 1950.

modern architects. In 1952 Rowe claimed that "no theory of contemporary vision is possible" without taking into account "the compositional schemes which derive from cubist painting by way of Constructivism and the Dutch De Stijl group.… The influence of this formal experiment upon Modern architecture has often been denied, but it cannot be overlooked that every historically important architect of the 1920s was affected by it" (figs. 1.2, 1.3).[25] By 1994 Rowe was equally adamant about the influence of this "pictorial rebellion" even if he had changed his mind about its ultimate value. In *The Architecture of Good Intentions,* Rowe suggests that the assimilation in architecture of "mostly Viennese theories of pure visibility" (Fiedler, Hildebrand, Riegl, and Wölfflin) and the derivative English notion of significant form (Berenson, Scott, Fry, and Bell) were as debilitating to the production of meaning in architecture as the "functional and technological bias of most of modern architecture's apologists."[26]

Rowe's revised evaluation of formalism reveals that his work and its influence are caught in a double bind. On the one hand, he acknowledged and engaged the pervasiveness of pictorialism. On the other hand, he realized that that very pervasiveness weakens pictorialism's critical potential and makes it all too easy to assimilate his formal readings stripped of their historical and architectural specificity. The consequential issue is whether pictorialism in architecture is habitual or critical, derivative or productive, and whether those who gravitate to either of the two presumed periods of Rowe's thinking have avoided the more difficult and original aspects of his work that emerged in the overlap between his early and later writings, as well as in the transactions between architecture and art criticism. A careful reading of Rowe's early writings, which culminate in the intensely vivid pictorialism of "La Tourette," reveals unappreciated critical innovations as well as specific affinities with the concurrent thinking of the art critic Clement Greenberg. Although there is no direct relationship between Rowe and Greenberg, and despite many differences between them, their essays "La Tourette" and "Collage," both published in 1961, mark an intriguing convergence in the modernist discourses on formalism in art and architecture.[27] Both critics' arguments grow from a consideration of relationships between cubism and architectural space, and each advanced formal strategies in these essays with affinities to those of the literalist artists and critics who would emerge later in the 1960s. Most important, the problematic of the blank canvas is central to the thinking of both critics, although Rowe's consideration of the pictorial implications of blank surfaces began in 1950, while Greenberg's first mention of the empty canvas occurred in 1962 (fig. 1.4). The fact that these two critics converge on similar issues, but from different disciplines and with vastly different concerns, is a fascinating event in the history of formalism. Considered together, the two 1961 essays demonstrate the limits of pictorial formalism as well as suggest the potential of what might be called pictorial impropriety.

> By violating a unity at conception, by jamming two discrete elements within the same block, Le Corbusier … has guaranteed a stimulus so acute that the visitor is not aware of the abnormality of his experience.
> *Colin Rowe, "La Tourette" (1961)*

It is surprising that Rowe never made a single reference to Greenberg, who, from the publication of his first essay in 1939, "Avant-Garde and Kitsch," to his 1961 book, *Art and Culture,* had emerged as the most persuasive American advocate of modernist art.[28] The publication of *Art and Culture,* a selection of previously published but significantly revised essays, marked the height of Greenberg's influence; that same year he also published what would become his most infamous essay, "Modernist Painting," which even more than his book has come to be identified with his version of formalism.[29] Whereas *Art and Culture* was a collection of mostly topical essays on the major figures and events of modernism, "Modernist Painting" distilled a general theory. For the first time since he had published "Towards a Newer Laocoon" in 1940 (a self-described "historical apology for abstract art," which was not included in *Art and Culture*), Greenberg condensed his thinking into something approaching a definitive statement.[30]

The relationship between Rowe's and Greenberg's formalism and their understanding of modernism is addressed in Rosalind Krauss's 1980 essay "Death of a Hermeneutic Phantom."[31] Formalism, for Krauss, is a generally applicable historical term—the "central analytical model" of "the modernist tradition"—which allows her (even though she admits "no particular competence in architectural criticism") to confidently and directly apply her understanding of art to a discussion of architecture. Krauss describes formalism as a method that calls attention to the numerous *devices* ("the actual procedures") behind or within the appearance of an artifact which make its forms' appearance legible. In other words, formalism turns "opaque" the otherwise "transparent" techniques of art, and it is this "baring of the device," rather than the sheer appearance of artifacts, that gives them significance in aesthetic terms.[32] Most important, these devices are "medium-specific": "it is the first law of this type of analysis that the device to be bared, the use of art to reveal art, must be distinct for the separate arts."[33]

Krauss bases her summary of Greenberg's position on a reading of "Modernist Painting" where, in a well-known passage near the beginning of the essay, he proposes that modernism is synonymous with "self-criticism"—the tendency of modernist art "to turn around and question its own foundations."

> I identify modernism with the intensification, almost the exacerbation, of this self-critical tendency that began with the philosopher Kant. Because he was the first to criticize the

means itself of criticism, I conceive of Kant as the first Modernist. The essence of Modernism lies, as I see it, in the use of the characteristic methods of a discipline to criticize the discipline itself, not in order to subvert it, but to entrench it more firmly in its area of competence.[34]

This brief passage is Greenberg's baldest explanation of the importance of the concept of medium, which by 1960 had become the single dominating issue in his criticism. While the definition of medium in his earlier writings remained relatively open, or at least implicit, "Modernist Painting" is specific and programmatic: "The limitations that constitute the medium of painting [are] the flat surface, the shape of the support, [and] the properties of pigment."[35] But Greenberg was not satisfied with three equally important criteria; he insisted that "the ineluctable flatness of the surface," unlike shape or color, is "unique and exclusive to pictorial art.... Because flatness was the only condition painting shared with no other art, Modernist painting oriented itself to flatness as it did to nothing else."[36] The following year, in "After Abstract Expressionism," Greenberg reformulated his definition of modernist painting into what is perhaps the exemplary statement of pictorial formalism:

> the irreducible essence of pictorial art consists in but two constitutive conventions or norms: flatness and the delimitation of flatness; and the observance of merely these two norms is enough to create an object which can be experienced as a picture: thus a stretched or tacked-up canvas already exists as a picture—though not necessarily as a successful one. (The paradoxical outcome of this reduction has been not to contract, but actually to expand the possibilities of the pictorial: much more than before lends itself now to being experienced pictorially or in meaningful relation to the pictorial....)[37]

Appropriately, modernist painting reaches its epitome in an ironic example of *pure opacity*—a featureless "picture."[38] The very fact that the empty canvas can be *seen* as a picture confirms the success of the formalist effort to, in Krauss's words, "force the viewer to encounter the picture as *first of all* a flat object" and thus treat the modernist painting as "internally coherent, inwardly referential to its own laws or norms, and logically distinct from everything that is not painting."[39] Yet, for Greenberg, all art participates in the expanded possibility of the pictorial that is instigated by painting, although different visual devices (which he never defines) would be required in each of the other arts.

Krauss seizes upon this important point, and suggests that something is awry in Rowe's application of the pictorial model to architecture: "Rowe, in analogizing the reading of buildings to the reading of paintings, transforms what is physically true of buildings—that they exist in three-dimensional space and are therefore experienced through time—and makes them instead a series of *pictures,* framing temporal experience as a set of static images."[40] According to Krauss, Rowe's pictorialism required the invention of "a hermeneutic phantom." As a result of his conceiving of the building-as-picture(s), Rowe postulates the existence of a conceptual building: spatial form, as opposed to pictorial form, appears as what Krauss calls a "transcendental object" that cannot properly be considered a device of the medium of architecture because it is not "an actual procedure" but a mental operation (figs. 1.5, 1.6). But it is precisely this duality of conceptual and pictorial form that is crucial to Rowe and Slutzky's advocacy of "phenomenal," versus "literal," transparency. Krauss explains:

> The split between literal and phenomenal transparency can be likened, then, to the difference between what can be called an actual and a virtual object. The real or actual object—inert, fossilized in time and space—is one thing, while the virtual object—a function of the viewer/reader's capacity to organize and reflect—is another. Insofar as the architectural critic wishes to make discriminations along this virtual/actual axis, he works in tandem with the other formalists in their efforts to distinguish literary from ordinary language or art objects from objects of common use. But to the extent that in order to make this distinction he must construct a hermeneutic phantom, his activity shears away from theirs.... Rowe ... is suppressing the facade itself in favor of another edifice: the facade as pretext or stimulus for a set of mental configurations; the creation of a transcendental object.[41]

Krauss suggests that because Rowe systematically applied pictorial formalism to architecture without isolating a properly architectural device to be bared, his work is fraught with "ambivalence … half in and half out of formalism." But that ambivalence, or (one might say) that task of translation, should be considered not as evidence of formalism's limitations in architecture, as Krauss suggests, but as a distinct and durable contribution to architectural criticism. Rowe and Slutzky were promoting what can be called a pictorial impropriety, and something of critical value is at work in such transactions. The authors' failure to identify a properly architectural device not only confuses the mediums of architecture and painting, it is also an evasion of architectural propriety, one that both disturbed and attempted to counter what Rowe at that time believed to be the pervasive, but logically obscure, modernist definition of the architectural medium: "In any final analysis of its theory, modern architecture seems to rest upon a conviction that authentic architectural form can only be engendered by recognizing the disciplines which *function and structure* impose."[42]

Thus Rowe not only transgresses the notion of medium-specificity but seems to situate himself outside of the "central analytical model" of modernist architectural theory. By his own account, Rowe was far from properly modernist in Greenberg's sense. Greenberg emphasized vision and the "strictly optical" devices that produce aesthetic effect,[43] while Rowe's formalism operated as a dialectic of vision and concept, with concept being privileged.[44] For example, in 1950, Rowe wrote: "[Cubism's] influence, and that of abstract painting in general upon the modern movement in architecture has been consistently emphasized, and its effects are obvious.... But it is clear too, that though working with a visual medium, the abstract art of today is working with a not wholly visual purpose, for abstraction presupposes a mental order of which it is the representative."[45] This "continuous dialectic between fact and implication" (or between "perceived object" and "conceiving subject") would become a staple of Rowe's criticism.[46] Greenberg, on the other hand, would explicitly reject such a distinction in his later writings. Increasingly his formalism would rely upon a technical description of the devices and appearance of abstract art.

Clearly, the two critics' "formalisms" are in no way identical. Neither are their understandings of cubism. Rowe's sources on cubism are not individuals with whom Greenberg concurred, and the two critics are particularly at odds in their reading of cubist collage. From the beginning, the writings of Alfred Barr are the touchstone for Rowe's presentation of cubist principles. This affiliation with the most central of cubism's American critics is the most telling continuity in Rowe's writings, and in aligning himself with Barr, Rowe takes up cubist collage precisely where Greenberg departs from it. Greenberg's "Collage" opens with a dismissal of critics like Barr who see cubist collage as achieving "a renewed contact with 'reality' in face of the growing abstraction of Analytical Cubism."[47] This realist argument was most famously proposed and successfully promoted by Barr a quarter of a century earlier, and Greenberg's essay attacks the notion that cubism is an advanced, conceptual form of representation that displaced perspective and thereby severed the traditional link between representation and similitude. Greenberg instead insists upon the autonomy of modern art, and argues that collage is entirely consistent and continuous with "the inner, formal logic of cubism."[48] In "Collage," he presents an intricate, dialectical explanation of the formalist concerns that led Picasso and Braque from analytical cubism into collage and, finally, to Picasso's construction sculptures, epitomized by *Guitar* (1912), which was first seen in the United States in 1967 at the Museum of Modern Art's major exhibition "The Sculptures of Picasso" (fig. 1.7). That presentation of Picasso's work both revised Barr's earlier interpretation and initiated a contentious debate about the role of collage in the evolution of cubism and abstract art.[49]

Rowe, however, continued to embrace Barr's realism and even used the key artifact in Barr's history of cubism, Picasso's collage *Still Life with Chair Caning* (1914), as *Collage City*'s emblematic image (fig. 1.8).[50] Cubist construction sculptures and any acknowledgment of the contemporary discourse on collage are absent from that book. Rowe was particularly taken with Barr's

Plate 64 Fernand Léger, *Three Faces*, 1926.

Plate 65 Bauhaus, Dessau. Walter Gropius, 1925-26.

Plate 66 Picasso, *L'Arlésienne*, 1911-12.

Die Anwendung des Begriffs der Transparenz im übertragenen Sinne auf Bauten des ersten Schaffensjahrzehntes von Le Corbusier erschließt wesentliche Einsichten in die Prinzipien seiner Raumorganisation und vermag eine kennzeichnende Eigenart der Le Corbusierschen Raumwirkung aufzudecken und zu erfassen. Noch nie ist die Dialektik von praller Körperlichkeit und untief wirkendem Raum, die Mehrfachdeutbarkeit der Formbeziehungen, die Zuordnungsart von Nutzung und Form in Le Corbusiers Bauten deutlicher gemacht worden. Und zwar von der Sache her, ohne ‹außerarchitektonische› Assoziation. Der von Rowe und Slutzky definierte Transparenzbegriff wird zum Werkzeug der Betrachtung; er ermöglicht Verstehen und Werten. Er wird zugleich aber auch sofort zum operativ einsetzbaren Mittel, mit dessen Hilfe während der Entwurfsarbeit Formordnung gedanklich ermöglicht und zeichnerisch erstellt werden kann.

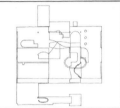

allgemein:
Transparenz entsteht immer dort, wo es im Raume Stellen gibt, die zwei oder mehreren Bezugssystemen zugeordnet werden können – wobei die Zuordnung unbestimmt und die Wahl einer jeweiligen Zuordnungsmöglichkeit frei bleibt.

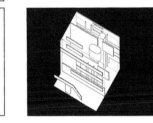

Das puristische Bild von Le Corbusier ist der kubistischen Tradition entsprechend in Schichten aufgebaut. Der Versuch, die Bildordnung **eindeutig** in tatsächliche Ebenen aufzulösen, zeigt, daß es unmöglich ist, alle Formen eindeutig im Raume zu fixieren. Es ist typisch für Transparenz im übertragenen Sinne, daß die **Lage einzelner Formen** im Raum **mehrdeutig** ist.

«Die Fassade wird aufgeschnitten und Tiefe im entstehenden Schlitz eingefügt» (S. 26).
«Die Wirklichkeit des tiefen Raumes wird fortwährend in Gegensatz zu Andeutungen eines untiefen Raumes (die wirklichen und impliziten Raumschichten) gebracht» (S. 29). **Das wird an jeder Stelle im Raum spürbar;** der Betrachter kann sich in bezug auf die eine oder andere Ordnung sehen, «und durch die resultierende Spannung wird Lesart um Lesart erzwungen».

1.5 Page from Colin Rowe and Robert Slutzky, "Transparency: Literal and Phenomenal," in *The Mathematics of the Ideal Villa,* 1976.

1.6 Page spread from Bernhard Hoesli, *Transparenz,* 1968.

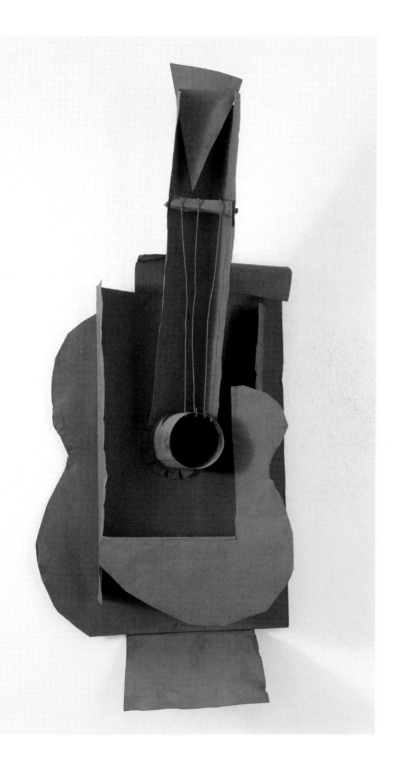

1.7 Pablo Picasso, *Guitar,* 1912. Construction of sheet metal and wire, 30.5 × 13.75 × 7.5 in.

1.8 Pablo Picasso, *Still Life with Chair Caning,* 1912. Oil on oil-cloth on canvas edged with rope, 29 × 37 in.

claim in 1946 that collage subverts any manner of illusionism, and the idea that the *Still Life* is doubly "realistic": first, because it introduces a new representational device—it embeds actual pieces of reality in its pictures; second, because it harbors no illusions—it frankly admits that "what seems most real is most false."[51]

… the anticipated frontal views never do, in fact, materialize.
Colin Rowe, "La Tourette" (1961)

Over a period of thirty years, the versions of Rowe's pictorial impropriety shift subtly, from the conceptual approach of "Mathematics," "Mannerism," and "Transparency" that Krauss describes, through an increasingly focused pictorialism that is epitomized in "La Tourette," to the realism that drives *Collage City*. Rowe's work first takes a decidedly pictorial turn in 1950 in "Mannerism and Modern Architecture," an essay that attempts to demonstrate how cubist methods have the potential for modern architecture to build upon the pictorial tendencies that emerged in the facades of sixteenth-century mannerists such as Federico Zuccheri. Rowe analyzes cases in which both mannerist and modernist architects begin with a pictorial basis—the facade as frontal, flat, and framed condition—and employ a different version of the dialectic between vision and concept to produce complex effects. The blank panel in the facade of Le Corbusier's Villa Schwob at La Chaux-de-Fonds compels Rowe's careful and creative analysis of the mannerist works, and his preoccupation with that facade continued at least until 1961, when he returns to it and compares it to the blank wall of the chapel at La Tourette (fig. 1.9).[52] Thus a central figure in Rowe's thinking for at least a decade is remarkably similar to Greenberg's empty canvas. But a change will occur in "La Tourette." Seemingly, as a result of his increasing application of cubist principles, the conceptual/pictorial dialectic that appears in Rowe's earlier essays becomes intensely pictorial. Thus the sequence of essays from 1950 to 1961 is developmental: each explicitly notes the correspondence between cubist painting and architectural design, and each is increasingly pictorial in its approach.

This is not to suggest there is not a more general continuity that begins with the earlier essay "The Mathematics of the Ideal Villa," in which Rowe's interest in geometry is also predominantly two-dimensional. But "Mathematics" makes no reference to cubism or painting. It is not until "Mannerism and Modern Architecture" that Rowe draws a direct parallel between abstraction in architecture and contemporary painting. Most important, in the earlier essay Rowe's pictorial impropriety is hardly acknowledged, and the analysis attains the kind of opacity that Krauss suggests is at the heart of formalism. That is, in "Mathematics" plan-making is the device that is bared: the geometries, or mathematics, are not visible in the architecture, but rather are devices

trails, the so-called *canons-à-lumière*, might seem to quiver like the relics of a highly excruciating martyrdom, while the general blankness of the spectacle might seem to be representative of religious anonymity and while a variety of phantasies infiltrate his consciousness, the

2, *the villa built by Le Corbusier at La Chaux-de-Fonds in 1916. Colin Rowe argues a similarity between this and the approach side of La Tourette (below), in that both have as visual focus an element without high intrinsic interest which absorbs the eye but does not retain attention.*

visitor, since he feels himself to be presented with a random disclosure of the building, is at this stage disinclined to attribute any very great importance to his experience.

The north side of the church this wall is instinctively known to be. It is doubtful if any other element could be so opaque. So much is evident. But, therefore, while the visitor interprets it frontally, he also attributes to this inscrutable visual barrier the typical behaviour patterns of an end elevation. This wall may indeed be a great dam holding back a reservoir of spiritual energy. Such *may* be its symbolical reality. But the visitor also knows it to be the part of a building; and he believes himself to be approaching, not this building's front, but its flank. The information which he is being offered, he therefore feels, must be less crucial than simply interesting. The architect is displaying a profile rather than a full face. And, accordingly, since he assumes that the expressive countenance of the building must be around the corner, rather as though the church were the subject of a portrait *en profil perdu*, the visitor now sets out to cross an imaginary picture plane in order to grasp the object in its true frontality.

A certain animation of contour—the oblique cut of the parapet and its intersection with the diagonal of the belfry—will focus his eye and lead him on. But if, for these reasons, the building first insists on a rapid approach, as he climbs the hill or moves along the alley within the trees, the visitor is likely to discover that, somehow, this gesture of invitation has vanished and that the closer he approaches it the more unsympathetic the building seems to become towards his possible arrival.

This is one aspect of a disconcerting situation; but another should be noticed:

that at a certain stage in the approach route the building suddenly comes to seem utterly drained of importance. For, as one leaves behind the courtyard of the old chateau, which is the socket of the enclosure in which one believed oneself to be, one is obliged to exchange a reliable womb for an unpeopled arena. The whole deserted sweep of the upper valley of the Turbide has progressively come into view; the field of experience is transformed, and the nature of the stimuli to which one is subjected becomes systematically more concentrated and ruthless.

Thus, the eye which was previously directed towards the left of the church façade, towards the point of entrance, is now violently dragged away towards the right. The movement of the site has changed. The visual magnet is no longer a wall. Now it has become an horizon. And the wall which previously had acted as the backdrop to one field of vision, as a perspective transversal, now operates as a side screen to another, as a major orthogonal, which directs attention into the emptiness of the far distance but which, by foiling the foreground incident—the three entrails—also serves to instigate an insupportable tension between the local and the remote. In other words, as the church is approached, the site which had initially seemed so innocent in its behaviour becomes a space rifted and ploughed up into almost unbridgeable chasms.

This is conceivably to provide too lurid an analysis; but, though it may exaggerate the intensity, it does not too seriously distort the quality of an experience which

is unexpected as it is painful. It would be possible, and maybe even justified, to interpret this preliminary *promenade architecturale* as the deliberate implication of a presumable tragic insufficiency in the visitor's status. The wall is exclusive. The visitor may enter, but not on his own terms. The wall is the summation of an institutional programme. But the visitor is so placed that he is without the means of making coherent his own experience. He is made the subject of diametric excitations; his consciousness is divided; and, being both deprived of and also offered an architectural support, in order to resolve his predicament he is anxious, indeed obliged—and without choice—to enter the building.

It is possible, but it is not probable, that all this is uncontrived. However, if one happens to be sceptical of the degree of contrivance and if one is temperamentally predisposed to consider the game of hunt-the-symbol as an over-indulgence in literature, then it will be desirable to continue an inspection of the building's exterior. It is not an easy decision to make. For the vertical surface of the church wall slices both the higher and lower approach roads like a knife and, when this psychological obstacle is penetrated, though something of the interior of the convent is at last presented, a further discovery is made. The visitor now finds that the anticipated frontal views never do, in fact, materialize. He becomes aware that the only surface of the building which actively encourages a frontal inspection is indeed exactly that north wall of the church which it had been

[*continued on page 407*]

5, *air-view showing the blank north wall of the monastery (that of the church), which is all that is seen as the visitor first approaches it. At the foot of the wall is a side chapel lit by three canons-à-lumière. It is of some interest that Le Corbusier, who does not normally publish air-photographs of his buildings, has included this in his recent autobiographical anthology*—My Work.

that sustain the spatial and structural organization that produces perceptible (pictorial) architectural effects.

As Rowe's subsequent essays become increasingly pictorial, he is increasingly attentive to the impropriety inherent in his approach. Even in "Mannerism and Modern Architecture," he recognizes the need for violating the "purity" of "the pictorial approach" in architecture: "It is a defect of the pictorial approach, taking account chiefly of masses and relationships in their effect upon the eye, that frequently the object itself and its detail suffer a devaluation. Subjected exclusively to the laws of human sensation, it is seen in an impressionistic manner, and its inner substance, whether material or formal, remains undeveloped."[53] In his effort to explain and analyze the introduction of cubist form into architecture, Rowe dutifully acknowledges the pictorial impropriety of his analogies. Through a series of qualifications and remarks, he reminds the reader that his pictorial treatment of architecture is a deceiving, but nonetheless fundamental, explanation of modernist architectural principles.

It is through Rowe's collaboration with Slutzky in "Transparency: Literal and Phenomenal" that the impropriety becomes truly productive. That is also the essay in which Rowe first references Alfred Barr. Perhaps more important, the primary references in that essay—Kepes and Moholy-Nagy—are purely visual or pictorial and not specifically cubist, or even particularly concerned with the propriety of medium.[54] From those sources, Rowe and Slutzky established the meanings of transparency that initiate the essay, meanings which, they suggest, apply equally to painting or literature, and presumably to architecture. Nonetheless they emphasize that transparency in architecture has its own peculiar problems: "at the very beginning of any enquiry into transparency, a basic distinction must be established. Transparency may be an inherent quality of substance, as in a wire mesh or glass curtain wall; or it may be an inherent quality of organization. One can, for this reason, distinguish between a literal and a phenomenal transparency."[55] This proposition is followed by a further distinction: "Our feeling for literal transparency seems to derive from cubist painting and from … the machine aesthetic. Our feeling for phenomenal transparency probably derives from cubist painting alone" (46 [162]). Thus Rowe and Slutzky set architecture against itself. The machine aesthetic is, as Rowe suggested in "Character and Composition," a visual affect of the presumed proper medium of modern architecture. The formal devices of cubism, on the other hand, are external to architecture and can be deployed in architecture to produce phenomenal—that is, conceptual—transparency. As Rowe does in "Mannerism and Modern Architecture," Rowe and Slutzky propose in "Transparency" that a formalist understanding of modern architecture is enhanced by both a conceptual emphasis and a knowledge of cubism. Their subsequent comparisons of cubist paintings bear this out, for in each case the painting described as more properly cubist is the one that manages to maintain a phenomenal reading. This amounts to a higher value placed on "flat" rather than "deep" space, limited rather than indeterminate backgrounds, and frontal versus oblique views. After establishing these exemplary readings of transparency in works by Braque, Gris, and Léger, and before launching their famous comparison of Le Corbusier's villa at Garches (Villa Stein) and Gropius's Bauhaus, Rowe and Slutzky again warn the reader of a too hasty application to architecture:

> In considering architectural rather than pictorial transparencies, inevitable confusions arise; for, while painting can only imply the third dimension, architecture cannot suppress it. Provided with the reality rather than the counterfeit of three dimensions, in architecture literal transparency can become a physical fact. However, phenomenal transparency will, for this reason, be more difficult to achieve; and it is indeed so difficult to discuss that generally critics have been willing to associate transparency in architecture exclusively with a transparency of materials. (49 [166])

That warning proves more than necessary, for no less than three paragraphs later, the reader is invited to accept a scandalous impropriety. After first explaining that "Le Corbusier is primarily occupied with the planar qualities of glass and Gropius with its translucent attributes," Rowe and Slutzky ask the reader to imagine that at "Garches the ground is conceived of as a vertical surface" (49 [167]). In other words, the conceptualism inherent in "Mathematics" here becomes a specifically cubist pictorialism. Rowe and Slutzky discuss not only the facade, as Krauss notes, but also the plans as though they were one of the paintings analyzed earlier in the essay. They purposely suppress the possibility that either the facade or the plans represent the actual spaces in the villa, and criticize Kepes for implying that the "architectural analogue" of pictorial transparency "must be found in the material qualities of glass and plastics" (49 [166]). They also attack Sigfried Giedion for the literalness of his reading of the "all glass wall at the Bauhaus," as well as for daring "to reinforce this suggestion with a quotation from Alfred Barr." Instead, Rowe and Slutzky show how at Garches "Le Corbusier is primarily occupied with the planar qualities of glass and … we can enjoy the sensation that *possibly* the framing of the windows passes behind the wall surface" (49 [167]) (fig. 1.10):

> This system of spatial stratification brings Le Corbusier's facade into the closest relationship with the Léger…. At Garches, Le Corbusier replaces Léger's concern for the picture plane with a most highly developed regard for the frontal viewpoint … ; Léger's canvas becomes Le Corbusier's second plane; other planes are either imposed upon, or subtracted from, this basic datum. Deep space is contrived in a similar coulisse fashion with the facade cut open and depth inserted into the ensuing slot. (50 [168])

1.10 Le Corbusier, Villa Stein, 1927.

1.11 Pablo Picasso, *Accordionist,* 1911. Oil on canvas, 51.25 × 35.25 in.

But then, as is characteristic of Rowe's writing, the essay proceeds to "qualify" this impropriety: one should not "infer that, at Garches, Corbusier had indeed succeeded in alienating architecture from its necessary three-dimensional existence." This is demonstrated through "some discussion of the building's internal space," and is followed by a repetition of both the caveat and the invitation that introduced the discussion of the facade: "Thus, after recognizing that a floor is not a wall and that plans are not paintings, we might still examine these horizontal planes in very much the same manner as we have examined the facade" (51 [169]). Through this alternation of proposition and qualification, Rowe and Slutzky demonstrate the "continuous dialectic between fact and implication" in Le Corbusier's architecture, a dialectic that characterizes phenomenal transparency and provides a connection back to Greenberg (51 [170]). The opposition of fact and implication resembles Greenberg's analysis in "Collage" of the dialectic between "depicted flatness" and "literal flatness" inherent in cubist painting, the dialectic that led, he argues, to the invention of cubist collage.

This parallel between formalist criticism in art and architecture reaches an uncanny convergence in Rowe's and Greenberg's 1961 essays, "La Tourette" and "Collage," where both critics are fascinated by what they describe as a confusion of structure, material, and space. Despite their differing interpretations of collage — Rowe's realism and Greenberg's illusionism — and their differing uses of formalism, key aspects of the two critics' thinking converge in 1961. Rowe's critical conclusions regarding Le Corbusier's monastery resonate not with Greenberg's polemic in "Modernist Painting," but rather with his explanation in "Collage" of the relationship between cubist collage and Picasso's construction sculpture. According to Greenberg, construction sculpture was an outgrowth of pictorialism, or a productive pictorial impropriety that confuses structure, material, and space. In "Collage" Greenberg returns to the cross-disciplinary, conceptual thinking that had surfaced in his earlier essays on Mondrian, and explains that cubist collage converts cubist pictorialism into sculptural and even "architectural" modes. This began, Greenberg argues, in 1911 when analytical cubism had grown decorative, homogeneous, and flat (fig. 1.11):

> flatness had not only invaded but was threatening to swamp the Cubist picture. The little facet-planes in which Picasso and Braque were dissecting everything visible now all lay parallel to the picture plane. They were no longer controlled, either in drawing or in placing, by linear or even scalar perspective.... The main problem at this juncture became to keep the "inside" of the picture — its content — from fusing with the "outside" — its literal surface. *Depicted* flatness — that is, the facet-planes — had to be kept separate enough from the *literal* flatness to permit a minimal illusion of three-dimensional space to survive between the two.[56]

At first Picasso and Braque merely played with this problem by adding "a conventional, *trompe-l'-oeil* suggestion of deep space *on top* of Cubist flatness," as in Braque's "very un-Cubist graphic tack-with-a-cast-shadow." Other devices include the artists' use of painted "block lettering" and mixing sand with their paint (72–74) (fig. 1.12). But then, Greenberg writes, the innovations of cubist collage shattered the picture plane, and liberated Picasso and Braque from the overwhelming relentlessness of their painting techniques: "Instead of isolating the literal flatness by specifying and circumscribing it, the pasted paper or cloth releases and spreads it." At its most radical, cubist collage jettisons representation entirely and initiates a new, three-dimensional illusionism "in *front* of, *upon,* the surface" of the picture (fig. 1.13). The collages "seem to thrust out into real, bas-relief space" (75).

At this point, Greenberg proposes, "Picasso and Braque were confronted with a unique dilemma: they had to choose *between* illusion and representation.... In the end, Picasso and Braque plumped for the representational, and it would seem they did so deliberately" (77). This is the path represented by *Still Life with Chair Caning* and all of synthetic cubism. Illusion provided a second path, leading to the traditions of abstract painting, from Pollock to Olitski, that Greenberg consistently praised. But in "Collage," Greenberg suggests a third path for cubism that leads to modernist sculpture, and which is able to refuse the choice between illusion and representation: *Guitar,* Picasso's first construction sculpture, initiates an entirely new kind of art that possesses an unprecedented *literal* autonomy. Assembled from found objects and materials—cardboard, wire, wood, fabric, metal—construction sculpture renders easel painting, murals, and monolithic statuary obsolete. The new sculpture no longer needs to represent "reality" because it is real itself. Illusionism becomes emphatically *literal* and *spatial:* "Picasso had glimpsed and entered, for a moment, a certain revolutionary path in which no one had preceded him. It was as though, in that instant, he ... had suddenly tried to escape all the way back—or forward, to literal three-dimensionality. This he did by using utterly literal means to carry the forward push of the collage (and of Cubism in general) *literally* into the literal space in front of the picture plane" (79). Greenberg claims that "here, at last, the decorative is transcended and transfigured ... in a monumental unity" (82), and in the final sentence of "Collage," he explains how painting, sculpture, and architecture are combined in a new art form: "The monumentality of Cubism in the hands of its masters is more a question of a vision and attitude—an attitude toward the immediate physical means of pictorial art—thanks to which easel paintings and even 'sketches' acquire the self-evident self-sufficiency of architecture. This is as true of the Cubist collage as of anything else in Cubism, and perhaps it is even truer of the collage than of anything else in Cubism" (83).[57]

In "La Tourette" Rowe begins to articulate a literalist reading of architectural form with clear affinities to Greenberg's notion of an architectural and monumental cubism. Rowe's analysis

1.12 Pablo Picasso, *Violin, Glass, Pipe, and Inkwell,* 1912. Oil
on canvas, 32 × 21.25 in.

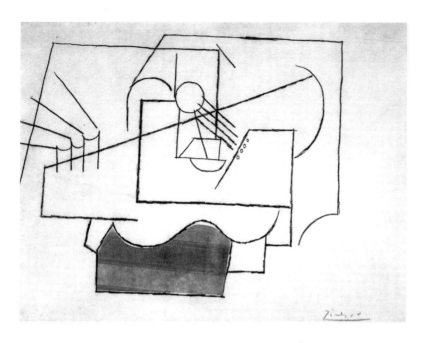

1.13 Pablo Picasso, *Table with Guitar*, 1912. Charcoal and pasted paper on cardboard, 18 × 24 in.

1.14 Le Corbusier, La Tourette, 1960. (Figure 8 in Colin Rowe, "La Tourette," 1961.)

obsessively describes the pictorial effects of the monastery, beginning with the blank north wall. He compares its surface, with its sloping parapet, to the blank panel in the facade of Villa Schwob which he had analyzed in detail in "Mannerism and Modern Architecture." At both buildings, the "first experience" is of a blank wall, "an element without high intrinsic interest which, while it absorbs the eye, is unable to retain its attention."[58] However momentary, that experience parallels the structure of pictorialism presented in Greenberg's ironic parable of the empty canvas that optimizes and isolates the optical ambivalence between literal flatness and phenomenal image at its degree zero.

In "Mannerism and Modern Architecture," Rowe explains that he was attracted to the entrance facade of Villa Schwob because it "presents quite distinct problems of appreciation" if its forms are understood simply as a pictorial composition.[59] He then offers a precise and evocative description that emphasizes the visual effects and the inherent complexities of the facade's organization, as well as the affinities and contrasts between the spatial organization of the building and the visual organization of the facade.

> The flat vertical surface of the two upper floors is divided into three panels. The outer ones, narrow and vertical, are pierced by elliptical lunettes, while the central one, elaborately framed, comprises an unrelieved blank, white surface. It is towards this surface, accentuated by all the means within the architect's control, that the eye is immediately led. The low walls, screening service rooms and terrace, are curved inwards rising towards it; two entrance doors prepare the duality to be resolved; the projecting marquise, with its supporting columns, completes the isolation of the upper wall, where the composition is to be focused; the emphatic elliptical windows in the outer panels increase the demand for a dominant; and with the mind baffled by so elaborately conceived an ambiguity, the eye comes to rest on the immaculate rectangle and the incisive detail of its brick frame.

> Contemplating this facade for any length of time, one is both ravished and immensely irritated. Its moldings are of extreme finesse, lucid and complex; the slightly curved window reveals are of considerable suavity: the contrast of wall above and below the canopy is permanently exciting; the sharp and dogmatic change of texture refreshes and soothes; but the blank surface is both a disturbance and a delight. The masses and the modeling impel the eye towards it, but it is the activity of emptiness, which the intellect is called upon to enjoy.

> Since this motif was presumably intended to shock, its success is complete, for it imbues the facade with all the qualities of a manifesto. In this abrupt composition, if nowhere else in this villa, there appears a tension which seems to foreshadow the later develop-

ment; and it is the panel with its intensifying frame which establish for other elements of the facade—columns and canopy—their apparent precocity. Distinct and deliberate, drawing attention to itself, and yet without apparent content, at once distributing attention over the rest of the house; by its conclusiveness the whole building gains significance; but by its emptiness it is, at the same time, the problem in terms of which the whole building is stated.[60]

In his attempt to explain the significance of the blank panel, Rowe then returns to "the architectural traditions of Renaissance Humanism." Particularly in the sixteenth century, he writes, "panels may be expressed as blank surfaces, or become a range of inscribed tablets, or again they may form the frames for painting." But "in only two instances does the panel make a central appearance within an elevation so restricted as that at La Chaux-de-Fonds; ... the so-called Casa di Palladio at Vicenza and Federico Zuccheri's casino in Florence."[61] Rowe's description of Zuccheri's facade applies the conceptual dialectic: "it is a dilemma of dual significance, a distinction between the thing as it *is* and as it *appears*, which seems to haunt all these three facades." In writing about the work of Zuccheri, who was a "painter, sculptor and architect," Rowe is most successful at demonstrating the functional and structural irrelevance of the design, and showing that a visual reading of the facade, as a formal "organization," begins to alleviate the seemingly "violent" approach to detailing and surface.[62]

A decade later, in "La Tourette," Rowe's criticism again begins with a pictorial premise, then proceeds to make distinctions that engage the literalness of the wall, and in doing so he comes very close to Greenberg's analysis of construction sculpture in "Collage": "while at La Chaux-de-Fonds the fundamental structure of the ambiguity ... is confined to a plane and causes largely an oscillation in the evaluation of surface, at La Tourette we are presented with a far more evasive condition.... The wall of the church, which is constantly invested with a high figurative content and then deprived of it, acts both to call attention to itself and simultaneously to shift attention outwards onto the visual field of which it is the principal component."[63] While at Villa Schwob the blank panel epitomizes and initiates the formal problematic of the building, depth is produced at La Tourette because the experience of the wall is not truly "frontal"; it is an "end elevation" (fig. 1.14). When Rowe "sets out to cross an imaginary picture plane in order to grasp the object in its true frontality," he is confronted by a pictorial impropriety that does not occur in mannerism, at Villa Schwob, or at Garches: "the anticipated frontal views never do, in fact, materialize.... [There is] an elaborate divorce of physical reality and optical impression."[64] In other words, at La Tourette Rowe is unable to conceptualize what Lacan calls the "phantom." This incapacity is exemplified in an uncannily Lacanian passage (reminiscent of "The Mirror Stage" as well as Lacan's discussion of pictures in *The Four Fundamental Concepts of Psycho-Analysis*)[65] in which Rowe describes the visitor's initial encounter with the building as

> an experience which is [as] unexpected as it is painful. It would be possible, and maybe even justified, to interpret this preliminary *promenade architecturale* as the deliberate implication of a presumable tragic insufficiency in the visitor's status … [who] is so placed that he is without means of making coherent his own experience. He is made the subject of diametric excitations; his consciousness is divided; and, being both deprived of and also offered an architectural support, in order to resolve his predicament he is anxious, indeed obliged — and without choice — to enter the building.[66]

La Tourette cannot be treated as a painting; it is a collage, or more specifically, an architectural construction sculpture that has expanded pictorialism beyond flatness, has abandoned frontality, and has engaged what Greenberg calls real, literal space.[67] That is, Rowe sees La Tourette as enacting aspects not only of Barr's realism but also of Greenberg's illusionism. On the one hand, Rowe's realism leads him to imagine that, just as Picasso places cloth in his 1914 *Still Life* (see fig. 1.8), so Le Corbusier situates a simple block (or "*megaron volume,* one of those open-ended tunnel spaces compressed between vertical planes"), analogous to the literal form of projects such as Villa Stein, within a cloister that acts as a framing device and a mounting surface.[68] Simultaneously, the wall of this block itself acts as a frame and surface for the side chapel, and so on through numerous scales and incidents, from the arrangement of the courtyard to the various concrete slabs and blocks that occupy window openings and, like tiny megarons, block one's view (figs. 1.15–1.18). Thus Rowe's realism leads him to imagine that Le Corbusier, as collagiste, "deliberately tore the fragment from one context in order to press meaning on it in another."[69] On the other hand, La Tourette enacts a version of the sculptural arising out of a literalization of the pictorial similar to the scenario that Greenberg proposes in "Collage." This is apparent in Rowe's description of two "spirals," one of which exhibits a "pictorial opportunism" (the foreshortening of the sloping north wall) and the other a "sculptural opportunism" ("those three, twisting, writhing and even agonized light sources") (figs. 1.19, 1.20): "There is a spiral in two dimensions. There is a contradictory spiral in three. A corkscrew is in competition with a restlessly defective plane. Their equivocal interplay makes the building."[70] This conflict between the optical illusions of the two spirals and their dependence on the literal support of the wall (of the megaron volume) to conjoin them epitomizes Rowe's hyperpictorial cubist analysis in "La Tourette." With these two figures, Rowe brilliantly illustrates how the conventions of cubist pictorialism are overwhelmed at La Tourette by the devices that Greenberg attributes to cubist collage and construction sculpture.

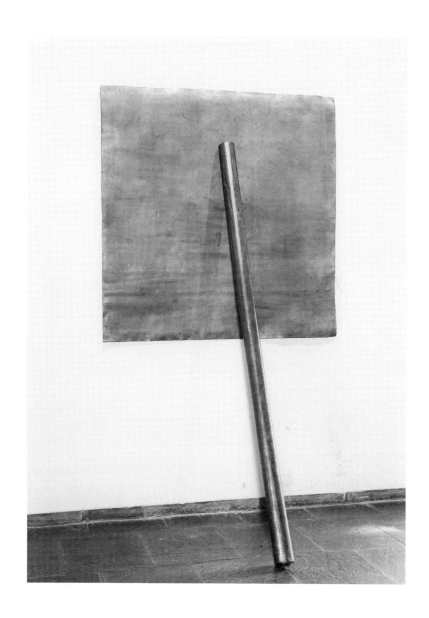

1.15 Le Corbusier, La Tourette, 1960.

1.16 Richard Serra, *Prop,* 1968. Lead antimony, 97.5 × 60 × 43 in.

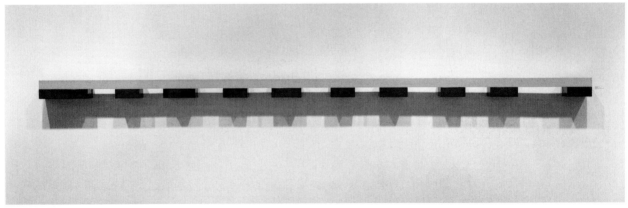

1.17 Le Corbusier, La Tourette, 1960.

1.18 Donald Judd, *Untitled,* 1965. Aluminum, 8.25 × 253 × 8.25 in.

1.19 *Two "spirals":* Le Corbusier, La Tourette, 1960.

1.20 Pablo Picasso, *Still Life,* 1914. Painted wood with upholstery fringe.

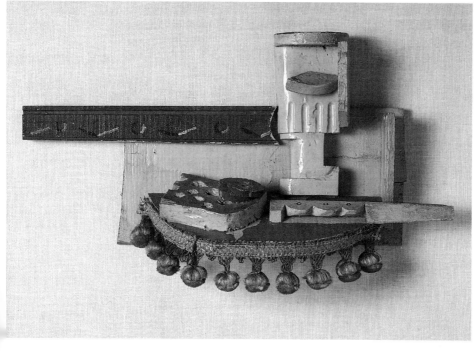

Apparently, Rowe did not recognize or fully accept the affiliation with construction sculpture, because ultimately this imagined convergence of two critics deflates. Near the end of the essay Rowe retreats to a description of effects proper to cubist painting, and equates them with Le Corbusier's "style," which at La Tourette is "very much along the lines that previous evidence of his style might lead one to predict": that is, the ability "to charge depth with surface, to condense spatial concavities into plane, to drag to its most eloquent pitch the dichotomy between the rotund and the flat."[71] Rowe's concluding remarks are entirely compatible with both his earlier essays and his later interpretation of the *Still Life* as a "realist" cubist picture. Although numerous historians and critics have suggested that the cubist collage is an altogether different "picture," Rowe does not exploit the full potential of this difference. When he shifted his model from painting to collage, he simply extended his earlier pictorial argument and missed, like Greenberg perhaps, the potential of pictorial impropriety in architecture that is so provocatively articulated in "La Tourette." So if there is a discontinuity in Rowe's criticism, it is not between his early and late writings; rather, it is a singular moment in 1961 when his pictorial impropriety is pushed to its limit and he ventures a fabulous translation of disciplines, leaving traces from which architects might derive a transdisciplinary formalism, one that avoids reductive applications of pictorial formalism. For example, in "La Tourette," Rowe describes the megaron volume as not only combining vertical and horizontal blank surfaces in a single block, but also combining the two versions of cubist collage: the ambivalent realism of the *Still Life* and the spatial architectonic of *Guitar*. Most important and surprising is how, in the final paragraph, Rowe's reading of the megaron approaches the understanding of space, vision, and objects that would be central to the literalist critique of pictorialism: "To a block one attributes a structural continuity, a textural consistency of space and a homogeneity of spatial grain or layering. While recognizing it to be hollow and to be empty, one still conceives its emptiness as, in some way, a metaphor for a block of stone or a block of wood."[72]

Although Rowe retreats from this reading, he does not abandon the intrigue of the literal. "La Tourette" can be read as a revision of his professed preference for phenomenal transparency. Whereas in the first "Transparency" essay Rowe discusses the plans of Garches as conceivably vertical surfaces and describes the "inevitable confusion" that arises if one ignores the fact that "a floor is not a wall and that plans are not paintings," he shifts in "La Tourette" to a literal conflation of walls and floors. In 1961, Rowe noted that La Tourette can be seen not only in terms of megaron volumes, but also in terms of "sandwich volumes where the pressure of the horizontal plane is more acute. A history of the cross fertilization of the megaron and sandwich concepts throughout Le Corbusier's career would be entirely relevant; but ... it is scarcely ... within the scope of a short critique."[73] The several paragraphs Rowe added in 1976 to what was the final page of the 1961 essay begin to sketch that history by pursuing a direct comparison of La Tourette and the "hybrid condition of Garches" (Villa Stein), which is "a megaron which is anxious to become a sandwich (or vice versa)" (that is, an ambivalent hybrid between Maison Citrohan and Maison Dom-ino) (figs. 1.21, 1.22).[74] In the 1976 passage, rather than pursuing a discussion of facades or vertical planes, Rowe adds an extensive discussion of "Le Corbusier's passion for walls," and includes a long quotation from *Vers une architecture* that ends by claiming that a "floor ... is really a horizontal wall." By implication, then, a megaron can be seen as a vertical sandwich. When Rowe recalls the language of *Vers une architecture* to explain that "the most audacious innovation which La Tourette presents" is that its "floors are horizontal walls" and "presumably, walls are vertical floors," he achieves a literalness that could not have appeared in "Transparency" and was only latent in 1961. Nevertheless, in 1976, Rowe maintains his preference for the less literal and more pictorial vertical surfaces at Garches: "these facades conceal rather than expose the reality of the structural components. They are articulated ... so as to comply with a structural argument; but in terms of an entirely literal induction from the physique of the building [as at La Tourette], they can only be considered a *non sequitur.* Like so many other Corbusian elements they are obedient to the exigencies of the eye rather than those of the work, to the needs of the conceiving subject rather than the perceived object.... Their predicament is optical."[75]

Still, Rowe's application of formalism in "La Tourette" demonstrates that the assumed distinctions between his early and later writings becomes difficult to maintain precisely when his pictorialism and its impropriety are most acute. In "La Tourette" collage emerges as a practice that might intensify pictorial methods to allow architecture to exploit its surfaces in ways that combine the real and the imaginary, writing and pictures, literal and phenomenal, seaming and seeming. Thus, it is possible to draw a shaky line between Rowe's conclusion that such transpositions of walls and floors make "the building a form of dice," and Tony Smith's literalist sculpture of the following year: a six-foot steel cube titled *Die.* In the years to come, literalists from Tony Smith to Robert Smithson would offer a myriad of translations of Greenberg's empty canvas into Rowe's blank wall (figs. 1.23–1.25).

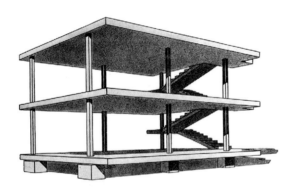

1.21 *Vertical sandwich:* Le Corbusier, drawing of Maison Citrohan, 1920.

1.22 *Horizontal sandwich:* Le Corbusier, drawing of Maison Dom-ino, 1914.

1.23 Tony Smith, *Die,* 1962. Installation in Paris for "Art of the Real," 1968.

1.24 Pablo Picasso, *Glass and Die,* 1914. Construction of painted wood, 9.25 × 8.5 in.

1.25 Robert Smithson, *The Shape and the Future of Memory,* 1966. Collage, 8.25 × 6.25 in.

2

Chapter 2

Flatly Confused: Clement Greenberg's Formalism across Disciplines

Clement Greenberg published two of his most important essays in 1961, each of which exemplifies a divergent formalist legacy in modernist criticism. "Modernist Painting" insists on the "purity" of medium as the criterion that establishes a "proper" modernist genealogy; "Collage" embraces and capitalizes upon an "impropriety" of medium—that is, a controlled and productive "confusion" of techniques applied across disciplines.[1] Thus, at the very moment Greenberg was codifying the terms of his criticism in "Modernist Painting"—the essay that is generally presumed to be his definitive theoretical statement on medium-specificity—he also published his final—and most compellingly intricate—attempt to devise a genealogy that could explain the complex and puzzling relationships between modernist painting and sculpture.[2] Most important, architecture plays a key role in Greenberg's transdisciplinary thinking. In fact, three related essays in his 1961 book *Art and Culture*—"Collage," "The New Sculpture," and "Modernist Sculpture, Its Pictorial Past"—each conclude with the claim that modernist sculpture, though derived from painting, aspires to a monumentality that relates to the "self-sufficiency" of architecture. All three essays are significantly revised versions of previously published magazine articles which in their original forms (and sequence) record Greenberg's fitful yet persistent attempts to discuss space, literalism, and the historical and technical affiliation of modernist painting and sculpture with architecture.[3] When he revised those essays for *Art and Culture,* the transdisciplinary relationships were made clearer, even if the precise connections between the three arts are configured somewhat differently in each essay.[4]

Greenberg's characterization of modernist sculpture as a "new, quasi-pictorial mode born of the Cubist collage and bas-relief construction"[5] is quite distinct from the categorical clarity of medium that he professes in "Modernist Painting," and to understand Greenberg only in terms of the orthodoxies of that infamous essay is to accept something of a caricature of a more complex critic. Of course, Greenberg's writings of the 1960s did little to discourage the caricature.[6] After the publication of *Art and Culture,* Greenberg mounted an increasingly stubborn and reactionary defense of his notion of "the avant-garde tradition."[7] His criticism seemed no longer able to account for developments in American art, not the least of which was the rise of sculpture as an expanding discipline not identifiable with any specific medium. Faced with numerous efforts to challenge his critical strategy and its legacy, Greenberg would constantly restate and defend his tastes and standards with greater force and in simpler terms.[8] He refused to turn his critical attention to anything other than (what he considered) "major" painting and sculpture. Where others saw vitality, variety, and new possibilities in the art of the 1960s, Greenberg saw a series of inconsequential reactions against the continuation of coherent disciplinary standards:

> Everything conspires, it would seem, in the interests of confusion. The different mediums are exploding: painting turns into sculpture, sculpture into architecture, engineering, theatre, environment, "participation." Not only the boundaries between the different arts, but the boundaries between art and everything that is not art, are being obliterated. At the same time scientific technology is invading the visual arts and transforming them even as they transform one another. And to add to the confusion, high art is on the way to becoming popular art and vice versa.[9]

Such apparent confusion, Greenberg argued, is a consequence of the refusal to recognize the stylistic continuity and legitimate genealogy of modernist art. To Greenberg, the 1960s were a period of absurd reactions and superficial revolts: he believed that, contrary to the artists' claims, there was an actual decrease in the innovation and originality of the art of the 1960s: "Approached strictly as a matter of style, new art in the 1960s surprises you—if it *does* surprise you—not by its variety, but by the unity and even uniformity it betrays *underneath* all the appearances of variety. There are Assemblage, Pop, and Op; there are Hard Edge, Color Field, and Shaped Canvas; there are Neo-Figurative, Funky, and Environmental; there are Minimal, Kinetic, and Luminous; there are Computer, Cybernetic, Systems, Participatory—and so on."[10] All of the new movements, Greenberg argued, adhere to the basic standards of what he termed "Post Painterly Abstraction,"[11] the most recent manifestation of modernist painting: "Design of layout is almost always clear and explicit, drawing sharp and clean, shape or area geometrically simplified or at least faired and trued, color flat and bright or at least undifferentiated in value and texture within a given hue."[12] Greenberg saw the 1960s as another phase of the historical tendencies he had previously identified in abstract art; the seeming confusion was less an aspect or effect of the art objects than of the explanations and conceptions of the artists and their criticism. Those who saw variety and change were overlooking the underlying formal continuity of modernism.

Discussion as to purity in art and, bound up with it, the attempt to establish differences between the various arts are not idle. There has been, is and will be, such a thing as a confusion of the arts.

Clement Greenberg, "Towards a Newer Laocoon" (1940)

In his earlier writings, despite his professed aversion to confusion, Greenberg was both more nuanced and more willing to examine the issues raised by transdisciplinary relationships that are analogous to those that emerged in the 1960s. Greenberg's speculations in the 1950s on the relationships between the arts—particularly his writings on sculpture—identified problems and made distinctions that would be revisited and reconfigured in the 1960s by critics and artists who both extended and contested his theory of medium-specificity. Although Greenberg had clearly emerged as the dominant critic and the most persuasive advocate of American painting in the 1950s, his writings on sculpture were less influential. In part, this is because two aspects of his criticism remained unresolved: his varying attitude toward the traditional art historical problem of the "confusion of the arts," and his increasing emphasis on "flatness" as a "limiting condition" of pictorial art. By the late 1950s, in "Sculpture in Our Time," Greenberg attempted to reconcile the two aspects in the guise of what he called the "modernist 'reduction'"—the proposition that all modes of modernist art have become pictorial by "rendering substance entirely optical, and form, whether pictorial, sculptural or architectural, as an integral part of ambient space":[13]

> Under the modernist "reduction" sculpture has turned out to be almost as exclusively visual in its essence as painting itself.... Modernist sensibility, though it rejects sculptural

painting of any kind, allows sculpture to be as pictorial as it pleases. Here the prohibition against one art's entering the domain of another is suspended, thanks to the unique concreteness and literalness of sculpture's medium. Sculpture can confine itself to virtually two dimensions … without being felt to violate the limitations of its medium, because the eye recognizes that what offers itself in two dimensions is actually (not palpably) fashioned in three.[14]

That special dispensation for sculpture, granted by virtue of the "literalness that was once its handicap [but] has now become its advantage," provides an opening for Greenberg to consider confusions between and within the individual arts. When he does, his thinking begins to address many of the same issues that would be central to the 1960s debates on the propriety of the new sculpture. So rather than understanding the debates between "modernists" and "literalists" as a battle for or against Greenbergian orthodoxy, we might recast those controversies as a contest between divergent claims on distinct aspects of Greenberg's work.

These claims were implicitly and explicitly articulated by critics, artists, and those who combined the two roles in several exhibitions, from 1964 to 1966, that introduced and promoted what would become known as minimalist or literalist sculpture (figs. 2.1–2.3).[15] But the exhibition "American Sculpture of the Sixties," staged in the spring of 1967 at the Los Angeles County Museum of Art, served as their culmination, not only because of its ambition to be a comprehensive survey of current work (the show included 166 works by 80 artists), but as a result of its prominence and the diverse assessments of its success or, for most, its failures. Maurice Tuchman, its curator, edited a catalog that was as ambitious as the exhibition, presenting samples of the artists' writings as well as original essays by ten prominent critics. Foremost among them was Greenberg, who presented a concise defense of his notion of modernism and his first direct attack upon the "Minimalist" trend.[16] Essays by Barbara Rose and Lucy Lippard supported and consolidated Greenberg's premises yet challenged his conclusions, while several other critics directly refuted Greenberg.

Wayne Andersen, in his essay for the catalog,[17] challenges Greenberg's 1965 claim that "American abstract sculpture ran more or less parallel, stylistically, with abstract painting" for the past two decades.[18] Instead, Andersen offers a brief survey of postwar American sculpture as an independent and coherent historical category. According to Andersen, sculpture appeared to parallel the style of painting only because there were no independent groupings of artists or convincing critical assessments of the development of modern sculpture. This situation began to change in the 1960s as sculptors formed their own alliances and, more important, fostered an allied criticism, just as abstract expressionism had grown prominent in the 1950s in tandem with the art criticism of Greenberg, Harold Rosenberg, and Thomas Hess.[19] An expanded version of Andersen's catalog essay appeared two months after the LACMA show in a special issue of *Artforum* titled "American Sculpture," which included essays by the sculptor-critics Robert Smithson, Robert Morris, and Sol LeWitt, as well as Michael Fried's "Art and Objecthood," the essay that is unquestionably the most powerful attempt to reconfigure and sustain Greenberg's legacy.[20]

Philip Leider, the magazine's editor, has described that issue of *Artforum* as "probably the best we ever had. It was like the *moment*."[21] In effect, though not by design, that special issue of *Artforum* served as a rebuttal, an extension, and an alternative to the Los Angeles catalog. The leading article, by Leider, was an at times sarcastic review of the Los Angeles show (figs. 2.4, 2.5). Although he was generally sympathetic to the sculpture, Leider admonished both the curator and the museum for the selection and installation of the work. But Leider's most scalding attacks were on the new museum building, designed by William Pereira, which was widely criticized and generally disliked (fig. 2.6):

> The major drama of the exhibition lies in the tension of hatred that is generated between the work and the building, most especially that considerable part of the exhibition that is installed outdoors on the "Norton Simon Sculpture Plaza." No work escapes the tearing involvement with the kitsch fountains, looney lamp-posts, plastic-domed walkways, concrete railings, the whole unstructured jumble of senseless frills that make up the design of the museum buildings. The sculpture is an insult to the building, but the building is an insult to the sculpture, too, and finally drags the latter down to its own miserable level, so that the entire installation becomes an offense.[22]

The prominence of architecture in Leider's essay is not entirely explained by the widespread enmity toward the new building. Rather, Leider's displacement of his criticism from the sculpture to its relationship with the architecture is symptomatic of a larger difficulty, a confusion about the identity and limits of the various disciplines, and of modern art in general, provoked in part by a lack of agreement on the proper critical and curatorial approach for the new sculpture. If nothing else, Leider's review calls attention to how the LACMA show revealed architecture's complicity in the critical and disciplinary confusion generated by the new sculpture.

Still, much remains obscure in this battle over the space between disciplines. By documenting and organizing the artifacts and texts, the catalog and the *Artforum* special issue reveal that the conflict was not only a confrontation of opposing theoretical positions, but also a much deeper and more tangled quarrel over the genealogy and identity of abstract art.[23] In that sense, LACMA's "American Sculpture of the Sixties" and *Artforum*'s special issue "American Sculpture" together constitute a significant *event:* they condense and collapse multiple

2.1 Installation, "Black White and Grey," Hartford Atheneum, 1964.

2.2 Installation, "10," Dwan Gallery, New York, October 1966.

2.3 Installation, "Primary Structures," Jewish Museum, 1966.

conflicts from various times and situations, resulting in a reconfigured relationship to the past and opening new possibilities for the future.[24] What is missing from most accounts of the new sculpture of the 1960s is a recognition of the degree to which those future possibilities can be understood as reconfigurations of Greenberg's past criticism. The intensity and oppositional character of the discourse has obscured that complex relationship, as has Greenberg's dogmatic writing of the 1960s.

For example, Greenberg's 1967 article for *Vogue* magazine, "Where Is the Avant-Garde?" frankly presents the pictorially based "taste" at the core of his defense of the "avant-garde tradition," a tradition in which "the avant-garde," "abstraction," and "modernist painting" are virtually one and the same.[25] Drawing upon the principles of painters such as Hoffman, Kandinsky, and Mondrian, as well as the aesthetic theory of Kant (and, at times, Hume),[26] Greenberg reviews his notion that the avant-garde maintains a self-critical attention to the concerns of "art itself." Since the impressionists, he claims, avant-garde art has been concerned with visual aesthetic experience. Painting has proven to be the art most adequate to its exploration for two reasons: first, a painting's flatness allows it to be experienced, and reexperienced, as a whole in a single instant of visual sensation, and second, such "pure" optical form appears to have a nonreferential, self-critical capacity.[27]

From the publication of his first essay "Avant-Garde and Kitsch" in 1939 to well into the 1960s, those basic aspects of what Greenberg calls the "rationale" of the avant-garde (or modernism, or abstract art) persist in his writings. But Greenberg faced a dilemma in the 1960s: key traits of the "confusion" that he saw in the art and art criticism of the 1960s were also evident in his early writings. In fact, he removed many of the more tentative speculations—"all the haste and waste involved in my self-education"—from the versions that are republished in *Art and Culture*.[28] These excised or edited passages often treat disciplinary and formal problems similar to those that preoccupied artists in the 1960s, which suggests that Greenberg should not have been entirely surprised by the experiments of that decade. Most important, just as architecture plays a key role in the development of 1960s sculpture, it also persistently emerges at key moments in Greenberg's early, albeit aborted, transdisciplinary efforts. For these reasons, retracing Greenberg's remarks on sculpture, with particular attention to his discussions of relationships between the arts, reveals the status of architecture in his narrative and his standards.

AMERICAN SCULPTURE AT THE LOS ANGELES COUNTY MUSEUM OF ART

PHILIP LEIDER

Dusty: How about Pereira?
Doris: What about Pereira?
*   I don't care.*
Dusty: You don't care!
*   Who pays the rent?*
Doris: Yes, he pays the rent
Dusty: Well some men don't and some men do
*   Some men don't and you know who*
Doris: You can have Pereira
*   — T. S. Eliot, Sweeney Agonistes*

Two years ago ARTFORUM based a special issue ("The New York School") on the first exhibition Maurice Tuchman prepared for the Los Angeles County Museum of Art. The show was impressively large, well-cataloged, nicely installed, slightly erratic both in the choices of artists and individual works. Since then, Tuchman has established himself as the most energetic curator in the country, and the exhibitions schedule of the Los Angeles County Museum of Art has gone unmatched. To be sure, certain characteristics of that very first exhibition have tended to become permanent features of most County Museum exhibitions: they tend to be gigantic, they are all well-cataloged, there is a consistent bias in favor of quantity over quality, and all the exhibitions seem to be presented in a wildly indecorous, carnival atmosphere (the current exhibition, *American Sculpture of the Sixties*, even has buttons) designed, it would appear, to overwhelm *Newsweek*. Many of these qualities are built into the museum plant forever: William Pereira's buildings are a circus in stone, a monument to quantity over quality, and every exhibition must first overcome the indignity of the setting, which is often, as in the case of *American Sculpture of the Sixties*, not possible.

Indeed, the major drama of the exhibition lies in the tension of hatred that is generated between the work and the building, most especially that considerable part of the exhibition that is installed outdoors on the "Norton Simon Sculpture Plaza." No work escapes the tearing involvement with the kitsch fountains, looney lampposts, plastic-domed walkways, concrete railings, the whole unstructured jumble of senseless frills that make up the design of the museum buildings. The sculpture is an insult to the building, but the building is an insult to the sculpture, too, and finally drags the latter down to its own miserable level, so that the entire installation becomes an offense.

Lyman Kipp sculpture about to be absorbed into the architecture.

6

Anthony Caro (two sculptures), lamp-post, rail, squares and plant.

2.4 Page from Philip Leider, "American Sculpture at the Los Angeles County Museum of Art," *Artforum*, 1967. (Photo caption reads: "Lyman Kipp sculpture about to be absorbed into the architecture.")

2.5 Photo with caption ("Anthony Caro (two sculptures), lamp-post, rail, squares and plant") from Philip Leider, "American Sculpture at the Los Angeles County Museum of Art," *Artforum*, 1967.

2.6 Edward Ruscha, *Los Angeles County Museum on Fire*, 1965–68. Oil on canvas, 53.5 × 133.5 in.

[Mondrian's] pictures … are no longer windows in the wall but islands radiating clarity, harmony, and grandeur.… Space outside them is transformed by their presence. Perhaps Mondrian will be reproached for the anonymity with which he strove for the ruled precision of the geometer and the machine in executing his paintings: their conceptions can be communicated by a set of specifications and dimensions, sight unseen, and realized by a draftsman. But so could the conception of the Parthenon.

Clement Greenberg, "Art" (1944)

Greenberg's 1967 essay for *American Sculpture of the Sixties* contains a definitive passage:

> Minimal works are readable as art, as almost anything is today—including a door, a table, or a blank sheet of paper. (That almost any non-figurative object can approach the condition of architecture or of an architectural member is, on the other hand, beside the point; so is the fact that some works of Minimal art are mounted on a wall in the attitude of bas-relief.)[29]

Greenberg doesn't explain why facts such as the mounting of art objects or their seeming architectural qualities are "beside the point," but his motives become clearer if his position is understood as a revision and recurrence of the claims put forth in his parable of the "empty canvas." Published five years earlier, that passage reveals not only why he believed—in 1967—that "almost anything is readable as art," but also why architecture, or a relationship to architecture, is irrelevant to that claim:

> The irreducible essence of pictorial art consists in but two constitutive conventions or norms: flatness and the delimitation of flatness; and the observance of merely these two norms is enough to create an object which can be experienced as a picture: thus a stretched or tacked-up canvas already exists as a picture—though not necessarily as a successful one. (The paradoxical outcome of this reduction has been not to contract, but actually to expand the possibilities of the pictorial: much more than before lends itself now to being experienced pictorially or in meaningful relation to the pictorial.…)[30]

The two passages have an almost identical rhetorical structure. Both begin with a bold assertion: within certain very broad norms, "almost anything" now can "exist as a picture" or "be readable as art." Setting aside for now the important difference between "a picture" and "art," or between "existing" or "being readable," each passage establishes—implicitly and explicitly—the premise that the possibility of art depends on certain limiting conditions—flatness and the delimitation of flatness—which Greenberg follows in each case with parenthetical qualifiers. One qualifier is positive: he is open to expanding the pictorial, as is clear in his later claim that flat objects such as doors and tables are readable as art. The other is negative: he is closed to expanding the architectural—it is "beside the point." There is a logic to this difference. Whereas Greenberg was able to accept the way painting depends on its condition of support—the stretcher, the flat surfaces of the canvas and even the wall—he wanted to detach sculpture from its "architectural condition," an aim that is largely reactionary. It derives from his wish to avoid *literal* ambiguities of medium—a wish that stems in large part from difficulties in his earlier criticism with concepts of space and their effect upon the nature of art.

Instead, Greenberg emphasizes medium-specificity, a concept that first appeared in his 1940 essay "Towards a Newer Laocoon," where he prescribed a classification of the various arts in terms of technique and medium relative to "pure" abstraction. Like Lessing, in his 1766 treatise *Laocoön: or, On the Limits of Painting and Poetry,* Greenberg insists on avoiding a confusion of the arts, but he devises new criteria and a new reciprocity. Rather than accepting one art in "the dominant role" as "the prototype of all art" (a condition that leads, Greenberg argues, to its own confusions),[31] Greenberg proposes that each art avoid confusion with the others through "purism," or "the acceptance, the willing acceptance, of the limitations of the medium of the specific art": "The avant-garde arts have in the last fifty years achieved a purity and a radical delimitation of their fields of activity for which there is no precedent in the history of culture. The arts lie safe now, each within its 'legitimate' boundaries, and free trade has been replaced by autarchy.... The arts, then, have been hunted back to their mediums, and there they have been isolated, concentrated and defined."[32]

Clearly, Greenberg's protest against the appearance of confusion in the New York scene of the late 1960s reiterates the most explicit tenets of his earliest criticism—purity and the legitimate limits of each medium—but with a crucial variation of emphasis. In 1940 he had hoped that each art would find its own "autonomy," but by 1960 he had abandoned his argument for an "autarchy" of the arts and recognized painting as the leading art. Greenberg's development might be reduced to this formula: his advocacy of the "flatly pure" in 1940 eventually led him in the 1960s to insist upon the "purely flat." For if abstraction guaranteed a reductive enforcement of disciplinary boundaries as well as autonomy for art (the "flatly pure"), flatness *as a condition of abstraction* served as the first principle of painting's elevation as the exemplary art (the "purely flat"). In other words, Greenberg's preoccupation with flatness in the 1960s not only derives from his initial emphasis on "purity" and the legitimate limits of each medium, but is also compelled by the past successes of painting, the only medium to unambiguously confirm his claims of 1940 and his subsequent critical judgments. Painting's success was being challenged in the 1960s by transdisciplinary experiments, and Greenberg responded by focusing upon the specific terms of a single medium at the cost of continuing to develop or question his initial premises.

Greenberg's turn from general principles to specific criteria was also a reaction to the explicit politicization of art in the 1960s. Greenberg always had advocated a separation of art and politics. When he wrote "Avant-Garde and Kitsch" in 1939, Greenberg and others affiliated with *Partisan Review* were in the process of breaking with the pro-Soviet stance of the American Communists, as well as with their support for social realism (which Greenberg considered to be kitsch).[33] Rather than advancing a positively socialist art, one allied with and participatory in a political program, the editors of *Partisan Review* began to establish a distinction between cultural values and political aims.[34] In the final paragraph of his essay, Greenberg encapsulated this policy in his statement that "we no longer look toward socialism for a new culture—as inevitably as one will appear, once we do have socialism. Today we look to socialism *simply* for the preservation of whatever living culture we have right now."[35] In effect, socialism was seen as the last best hope for high art, but not a proper subject for it. Greenberg "simply" wanted to clear a space for the continuation and preservation of "major" art.

The following year, in "Towards a Newer Laocoon," Greenberg theorized the principal attributes of a depoliticized art by reconfiguring the neoclassical debate between Winckelmann and Lessing. Whereas Lessing elevated the literary arts—poetry and theater—above the visual arts, Greenberg attempted to reverse the hierarchy, not by siding with Winckelmann but by accusing Lessing of underestimating the influence of the visual arts upon literature. More important, he considered Lessing's argument obsolete since the "purist" trend of the twentieth century "insists upon excluding 'literature' and subject matter from plastic art." The avant-garde strives to sustain artistic standards and project the high arts into the future by shielding them from "ideas": "The avant-garde saw the necessity of an escape from ideas, which were infecting the arts with the ideological struggles of society. Ideas came to mean subject matter in general. (Subject matter as distinguished from content: … subject matter is something the artist does or does not have in mind when he is actually at work.) This meant a new and greater emphasis upon form."[36]

By the end of "Towards a Newer Laocoon," Greenberg wryly admits that his argument "has turned out to be an historical apology for abstract art."[37] The premise and substance of his position—the definition and defense of the avant-garde tradition—would not vary over the next three decades. What would change was the status of modern art. Not only was modern art "secure" in the early 1960s, it was triumphant. But Greenberg identified a new threat, this time *internal* to the avant-garde: besides becoming corrupted by ideas and politics, the arts were also becoming confused with each other. By reasserting, in more extreme terms, the necessity for a separation of the various disciplines, Greenberg was able to diagnose the apparent confusion of the 1960s as a failure of artistic nerve.

Although it was clearly not an innocent, purely formal concern that led Greenberg to empha-size the achievement of painting, and as a consequence to weaken his critical basis for discussing modernist sculpture and architecture, his predicament was in part a result of formal problems, many of which involved his conception of space. Greenberg's efforts to come to terms with both corporeal space and the representation of space can be traced in his 1961 revisions to the essay "Abstract and Representational." Originally published in 1954, that essay was written in response to Leo Steinberg, who in the previous year had disparaged "the modern critic who belittles all rep-resentational concerns, because he sees them only as solved problems, [and] underrates their power to inflame the artist's mind and to intensify his vision and touch."[38] Assuming that Stein-berg was referring to him, Greenberg produced a vehement defense of abstraction, arguing that neither abstraction nor representation is inherently superior; rather, "actual experience" had con-vinced him that "the best art of our day tends, increasingly, to be abstract," and this "saddens our eyes" not because art no longer represents objects, but because it abandons the illusion of visual depth, "those spatial rights it used to enjoy back when the painter was obliged to create an illu-sion of the same kind of space as that in which our bodies move. It is this illusion and its space that we may miss even more than the things, as such, that filled it." Greenberg then makes a star-tling proposition: "The picture has now become an object of literally the same spatial order as our bodies and no longer the vehicle of an imagined equivalent of that order. It has lost its 'inside' and become all 'outside,' all plane surface [and] the abstract...picture...returns [the spectator] to that space in all its brute literalness."[39] In his 1961 revisions, however, Greenberg altered the essay to avoid the implications of corporeality and literalness. The painting is no longer characterized as an object but as an "entity": its role is not to return the spectator to literal space, but to refuse an "escape" into the *illusion* of literal space "from the space in which he himself stands."[40]

Thus Greenberg shifts from understanding abstraction as a positive force (that returns us to "space in all its brute literalness") to a defensive strategy (that prevents our "escape" into "an imaginary equivalent of" literal or corporeal space). This refusal of literalism and erasure of cor-poreal space allows him to apply his pictorialism to sculpture, and becomes entirely explicit in his notion of the "modernist 'reduction'"—a mode of abstraction that converts the brute literal-ness of actual space into a purely optical phenomenon: "The human body is no longer postu-lated as the agent of space in either pictorial or sculptural art; now it is eyesight alone, and eyesight has more freedom of movement and invention within three dimensions than within two."[41] The result of this optical reduction, despite the advantages of "freedom" and "invention" that it gives to sculpture, is to devalue sculpture in relation to painting. Sculpture may allow more visual complexity, and thus "sculpture—that long-eclipsed art—stands to gain by the modernist 'reduction' as painting does not," but only painting remains a "pure" medium.[42] Sculpture is caught between two modalities of vision: it is flatly confused—simultaneously optical (seemingly flat) and three-dimensional (literally spatial). Thus it should be no surprise that later in the same essay Greenberg would write that "the hopes I had placed in the new sculpture ten years ago, in the original version of this article, have not yet been borne out—indeed they seem to have been refuted. Painting continues as the leading and most adventurous as well as the most expressive of the visual arts."[43]

But what *is* surprising is the remark that follows: "In point of recent achievement architecture alone seems comparable with it."[44] Once again architecture appears at a key moment in Greenberg's writing on sculpture. What Greenberg means by "architecture" here is not clear, given how little he wrote about it, but in the 1940s he most likely was thinking of the International Style and perhaps in the late 1950s of the Miesian commercial architecture that was appearing in New York City, forms of architecture that, in his view, assert planarity as the counterpart to painting's "flatness."[45] Greenberg's high esteem for architecture was clear as early as 1940 in "Towards a Newer Laocoon" where he proposed that formalism in art might be understood to work something like functionalism in architecture: "Painting and sculpture can become more completely nothing but what they do; like functional architecture and the machine, they *look* what they *do*."[46] But while the aim in 1940 was to free each of the arts to "function" according to the visual potential of its medium (to "*look* what they *do*"), Greenberg eventually came to profess that how art "looks" simply *is* what it "does."

Greenberg's tendency toward the modernist reduction, which culminates in the late 1950s, had its beginnings in the late 1940s, a period when he made a point of reviewing exhibitions of modern sculpture. In 1948 he was drawn to the flat, bas-relief-like works in an exhibition of Naum Gabo's sculptures at the Museum of Modern Art. He mentions three pieces, each with affinities to both painting and architecture—*Construction in a Niche* (1930), *Construction with Alabaster Carving* (1938), and *Circular Relief* (1925) (fig. 2.7). Near the end of the review, Greenberg admits his interest in the way those objects take on the problems of painting (although he hedges about whether he gave in to the pictorial temptation): "It may be that I liked these pieces especially because of their frontality, their affinity with the easel picture, which makes them easy to see from a single point of view. But I doubt it."[47] Greenberg's doubt (or confusion) is granted some legitimacy the following year in a review of a show of Isamu Noguchi's at the Egan Gallery (fig. 2.8).[48] On the one hand, he expresses an interest in how Noguchi sometimes "works in bas-relief and manipulates his forms against the naked wall as a background," admitting a particular fondness for a piece called *Open Window* and another which he describes as "a flat slab of wood placed on the wall like a picture." On the other hand, he also praises Noguchi for being "fully in the midst of the adventure in genres that is modern advanced sculpture." Thus Greenberg could

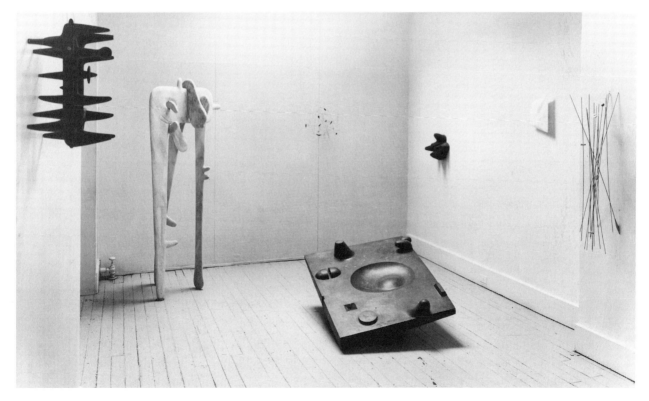

2.7 Naum Gabo, *Circular Relief,* 1925. Plastic on wood base,
9 × 19.75 in.

2.8 Isamu Noguchi, installation at Egan Gallery, 1949. *(Open
Window* is on the far left.)

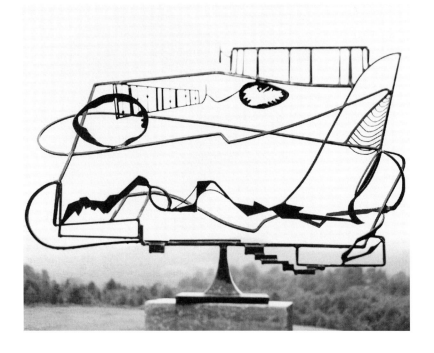

2.9 David Smith, *Hudson River Landscape,* 1951. Welded steel, 49.5 × 75 × 16.75 in.

simultaneously praise one sculpture that was "flat ... like a picture," and another that was morphologically and metaphorically allusive to architecture and space.

These anecdotes from the late 1940s exemplify two difficulties that recur in Greenberg's critical development. The first is his wavering assessment of the prospects of modern sculpture, which can be traced from the late 1940s to the mid-1960s. In the earlier essays, he was enthusiastic about the potential of what he called "the new sculpture" (which he defines as an outgrowth of cubist collage, not painting proper), but by the late 1950s he had become disappointed with the work that actually had been produced, ultimately retracting his earlier positive speculations and forwarding his idea of the "modernist 'reduction.'" Greenberg's retraction and reduction can be understood as a direct consequence of his own canny, early support for yet to be famous painters such as Pollock, Newman, and Rothko. By comparison, except for David Smith, the sculptors he supported did not attain nearly the equivalent level of success. Thus painting increasingly inspired the terms and criteria of his criticism, while he was unable to offer an equally coherent, consistent, or convincing critical assessment of the problems of sculpture.

Greenberg's retraction is also part and parcel of the second difficulty inherent in his critical development: his attitude toward the confusion of the arts. Beginning with his proclamation, in 1947, of David Smith as "already the greatest sculptor this country has produced," he continued to champion Smith's "pictorial" work over what he called "monolithic" work of other sculptors (fig. 2.9).[49] In the 1940s, his hopes for sculpture were allied with Smith and others—particularly David Hare and Theodore Roszak—who "point to the possible flowering of a new sculpture in America, a sculpture that exploits modern painting and draftsmanship, new industrial methods, and industrial materials. Certainly, of all arts, the new pictorial or constructivist sculpture relates best to American décor, understands it best, and would affect it most directly.... Last but not least, the new sculptor has the advantage of working in a virgin medium."[50] But less than ten years later, in 1956, Greenberg praised only Smith, and was entirely frank about the dominance of painting: "in the thirties and forties ... it looked as though sculpture might shortly become the dominant vehicle of figurative art.... These hopes have faded. Painting continues to hold the field.... And sculpture has become a place where, as hopes have turned into illusions, inflated reputations and inflated renaissances flourish."[51] Contrary to his "autarchic" hopes in 1940, by the late 1950s Greenberg recognized painting as the dominant art: only a few sculptors could achieve the "illusion" of flatness and be further nourished by that aim. Unlike painting, which he believed has been characterized since the Renaissance by a "resistance to the sculptural," sculpture he held to be not only *not* resistant to painting but wholly dependent upon it, both historically and formally. Greenberg never wavered from his claim that the new sculpture "is a product of cubism," in particular cubist collage.

Collage was a major turning point in the evolution of Cubism, and therefore a major turning point in the whole evolution of modernist art in this century.... The writers who have tried to explain their intentions for them speak, with a unanimity that is suspect in itself, of the need for a renewed contact with "reality" in face of the growing abstractness of Analytical Cubism.... But the term "reality" [is] always ambiguous when used in connection with art.

Clement Greenberg, "Collage" (1961)

According to Greenberg's account in "Collage," a radical break in the sculptural tradition occurred around 1911 or 1912. At the very moment Brancusi was producing his radically reduced, disembodied heads, and thus, Greenberg believed, announcing the endgame of the monolith, Picasso and Braque were undertaking the experiments that Greenberg saw as the origin of modernist sculpture. Contrary to his rival Herbert Read, Greenberg did not see a potential for monolithic sculpture in modernism, and so for him Brancusi's sculptures mark the end of sculpture "in the round" (fig. 2.10).[52]

But there is one significant convergence in Greenberg's narrative: both the monolithic and cubist trajectories brought sculpture close to architecture: "Brancusi, under the influence of Cézannian and Cubist painting as much as anything else, pursued the monolith to an ultimate extreme, to the point indeed where sculpture suddenly found itself back in the arms of architecture. This time, however, it was not sculpture as ornament, but as a kind of art that approached the condition of architecture itself—as pure architecture or as monument. And in this condition sculpture became accessible once more to flat and linear handling."[53] That "flat and linear handling" was achieved in cubist "construction-sculpture," where "at last, the decorative is transcended and transfigured ... in a monumental unity. This monumentality has little to do with size.... The monumentality of Cubism in the hands of its masters is more a question of vision and attitude—an attitude toward the immediate physical means of pictorial art—thanks to which easel paintings and even 'sketches' acquire the self-evident self-sufficiency of architecture."[54] Thus Brancusi was inspired by cubism to push premodern sculpture to one architectural extreme, while Picasso and Braque used cubism to invent modernist sculpture, which was also inherently architectural but in a different way. As Greenberg would later realize, particularly in "Sculpture in Our Time" and "Collage," modernist sculpture was caught between the reductive opticality of painting and the literal spatiality of architecture.

In many essays, beginning in the late 1940s, Greenberg argued that modernist sculpture derives, both historically and formally, from painting (a result of what he called "cross-breeding" or "its pictorial past"). At the same time, in his earliest writings, he believed modernist sculpture

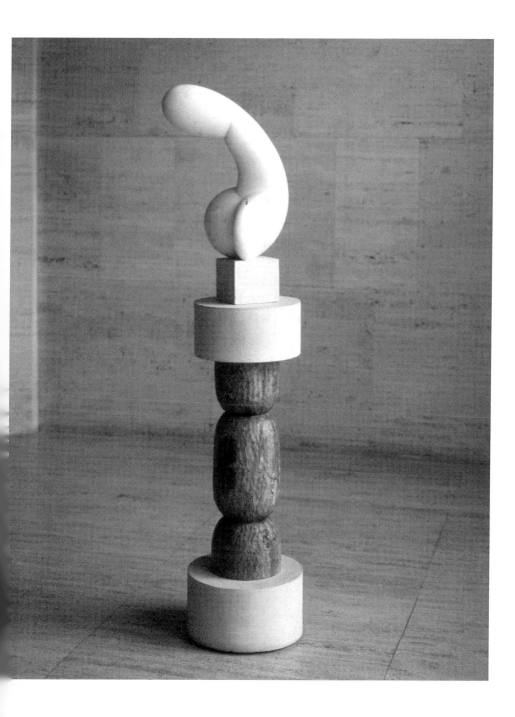

10 Constantin Brancusi, *Princess X*, 1916. Marble.

benefited from a strict separation of the arts. His hope for an independent sculpture peaked in 1949 in his first essay devoted exclusively to developments and possibilities in modern sculpture. In "The New Sculpture," he went so far as to speculate that "painting's place as the supreme visual art is now threatened, whether it is in decline or not…. [Sculpture] has lately undergone a transformation that seems to endow it with a greater range of expression for modern sensibility than painting now has. This transformation, or revolution, is a product of Cubism."[55]

Greenberg's enthusiasm is marked by confusion. There is a tension between origins and medium in this narrative: the heroic *origins* of sculpture are cubist ("springing up out of a mode of painting that thrusts forms outward from the picture plane instead of drawing them back into the recessions of illusionary space"), while its proper *medium* is "virgin" ("the new sculpture has almost no historical associations whatsoever—at least not with our own civilization's past—which endows it with a virginality that compels the artist's boldness and invites him to tell everything without fear of censorship by tradition").[56]

But the very title of Greenberg's next major essay on sculpture suggests an abandonment of this notion of a "virgin medium." In "Cross-Breeding of Modern Sculpture" (1952), Greenberg resists seeing sculpture as a successfully autonomous art, and he reconfirms that resistance when republishing the essay in 1961: all of the hopeful speculations have been excised or fundamentally rewritten.[57] Greenberg wrote in 1952 that "sculpture is on the point of turning the tables on painting," but that claim is removed from the 1961 version of the essay, which is transformed into an evaluative narrative highlighting the triumphs of cubism in sculpture. Greenberg's continuing insistence that sculpture is of cubist origins ultimately limits his assessment of the later directions of sculpture, and he continues to emphasize the origins of modernist sculpture in the shift from "the natural-hued monolith" to "an entirely new, open, linear, pictorial kind of [cubist] sculpture." Sculpture is revolutionized by this translation of cubism into a three-dimensional practice: modernist sculpture "was no longer a *statue,* but an *object.*"[58]

Even the art *object* is an ambivalent—if not confused—medium, as is clear in Greenberg's remarks on the Gabo and Noguchi sculptures and in his 1954 claim that abstract painting is "an object of literally the same spatial order as our bodies." For a short time Greenberg explored the potential of that ambivalence in both sculpture and painting, but by 1965 his narrative would itself assume a very reduced form, perhaps out of a concern to not legitimate literalist sculpture historically as a medium-specific reinvention of the monolith (analogous to modernist painting's reinvention of flatness).[59] In the 1960s, Greenberg deemphasized the origins of modernist sculpture; instead of a genealogical account of the discipline's own means or medium, Greenberg focused on the *formal* dependence of sculpture on painting after World War II.

Yet Greenberg's earlier writings suggest that it is also possible to take a more generous view, one that embraces "confusion" and the impure status of modern sculpture as a literal object, a status that allies it with the material, technical, spatial, and conceptual complexity of architecture. A detailed version of this revisionist view is presented by Yve-Alain Bois in *Painting as Model,* but whereas Bois revises Greenberg by contesting his chronology (through a revised and more precise dating of Picasso's collages), thus using "history" to undermine "criticism," it is also possible to fight "criticism" with "criticism"—that is, to reconstruct Greenberg's critical development by tracing those abandoned and eventually repressed ideas that return in the 1960s in the work of his opponents, the literalists. An examination of the internal and contextual development of his criticism helps to explain why Greenberg's attempt to trace the origins of modernist sculpture to painting ended in the late 1950s, even though it inspired his essay "Collage." Bois explains how, in that essay, Greenberg was the first American critic "to understand what was crucial in the evolution of cubism … [and] the first to comprehend that a rupture had occurred for Picasso … during the summer of 1910. Above all, he alone recognized … that the construction titled *Guitar* completed by Picasso in 1912, is at once the origin of 'synthetic' cubism and of a new era in Western sculpture."[60]

Although Greenberg's interpretation produces a contradiction that he is unable to resolve between an inexorable progress toward a purity of medium and lingering implications of transdisciplinarity, Bois wants at least to credit Greenberg for his astute understanding of cubist collage, even while dismantling his conclusions. Bois characterizes Greenberg's analysis as a direct, but veiled, adaptation of the Western tradition of bas-relief, as theorized by Adolf von Hildebrand (a connection that is apparent in Greenberg's reviews of Noguchi and Gabo).[61] Bois bases his argument in part on that of Greenberg's French contemporary, the critic Daniel-Henry Kahnweiler, and claims that a formalism like Greenberg's treats sculpture as a kind of "'painting' that dared not speak its name." Bois argues that the "frontality and pictorialism" emphasized by both Greenberg and Hildebrand "were aberrations resulting from *fear* of space, fear of seeing the sculptural *object* lose itself in the world of objects, fear of seeing the limits of art blur as real space invaded the imaginary of art."[62]

More precisely (and less polemically, perhaps), Greenberg and Hildebrand harbor not so much a fear of space, as an abhorrence of spatial *confusion.* On one hand, Greenberg held the view that Picasso's *Guitar* is a move from flatness into "literal three-dimensionality," that is, a painting "in real and sculptural space to which there clung only the vestige of a picture plane."[63] On the other hand, Greenberg's claim that Picasso's move into real space spawns a revolution in sculpture also produces morphological confusions between visual and literal form—and between pictorial ("flat") and literal ("round") space. Greenberg eventually escapes these contradictions by embracing the modernist reduction and identifying the contradictions as "illusionism."[64] In this case, modernist

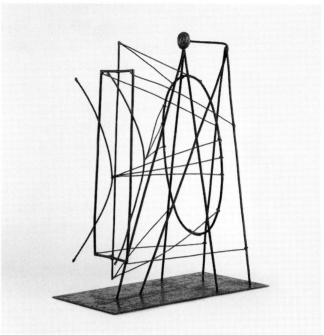

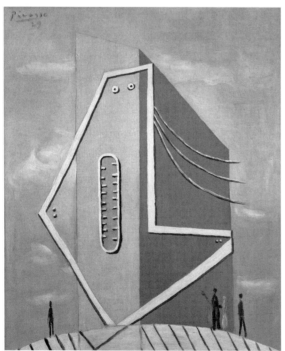

2.11 Pablo Picasso, *Woman in a Red Armchair*, 1929. Oil on canvas, 25.5 × 21.25 in.

2.12 Pablo Picasso, *Construction in Metal Wire (Proposed Monument to Guillaume Apollinaire)*, 1928–30. Iron and sheet metal, 19.5 × 10 × 6.75 in.

2.13 Pablo Picasso, *Study for a Monument (Woman's Head)*, 1929. Oil on canvas, 25.5 × 21.25 in.

sculpture has produced an illusion that is the reverse of perspective—pictorial space *in front of* the picture plane—and Greenberg's brilliant explanations of the pictorial and optical illusions induced by flatness are efforts to avoid such spatial contradictions. Bois considers Greenberg's reductions, however ingenious, an abuse of cubism: "This mixing of real space and the space of art … is at the heart of cubism, of the *objecthood* that it wishes to confer on the work of art and that Greenberg's reading tends to minimize if not efface."[65] But Greenberg's earlier writings do not logically exclude Bois's and Kahnweiler's interpretations. Rather, they begin to analyze the ways sculpture and architecture might be involved in the spatial problems of painting, without "looking like" painting at all. Thus it becomes possible to value the transdisciplinary experiments of painters who venture into sculpture (such as Matisse or Picasso) or architects who venture into painting (namely, Le Corbusier), rather than dismissing them as curious but failed detours, as Greenberg did.[66]

For example, in two essays published in 1956 and 1957, Greenberg offers an adamantly negative assessment of Picasso's sculpture of the late 1920s, work which is decidedly "impure." In the first essay, a 1956 review of Frank Elgar's *Picasso,* Greenberg writes that Picasso's painting entered a period of decline around 1926, a development related to the artist's interest in sculpture and architecture at that time.[67] In the second essay Greenberg notes that Picasso's painting was again "weak" from 1950 through 1953, and how, as in the twenties, Picasso "resorts to sculpture to work things out."[68] Greenberg calls that sculpture "lamentable," and seems to suggest that this must be the case if sculpture is to be translatable back into painting. As if trying to reinforce his emphasis on the year 1926 (Picasso's supposed point of decline in the first essay), he notes Kahnweiler's discussion of Picasso's interest in architecture and monuments in the late twenties (figs. 2.11, 2.12). Elgar also remarks on Picasso's "keen interest in architecture" in his book (in which he is obviously paraphrasing passages from Kahnweiler's 1948 *Les sculptures de Picasso*),[69] writing that by 1929,

> calm, majestic figures began to appear in the depths of [Picasso's] canvases, like massive monuments. With their volumes stressed by contrasts of light and shade, their simplified colouring and their isolation in an unrelieved space, they are almost like painted sculptures.… At the same time as this adventure into pure plastic form he began to take a keen interest in architecture, in which he was helped by Cubism.… He invented open wire sculpture … thus wresting from the architects a whole field which had hitherto been their private preserve, that is to say spatial creation.[70]

While the second part of this passage reinforces Greenberg's account of the birth of constructed sculpture, it also points to the spatial ambivalence that troubled Greenberg and which, after 1956, he would work against in his criticism. Of course, Greenberg also was probably dismayed by the fact that Picasso's sculptural designs of the late twenties were not constructed but modeled in bronze and clay, and were studied repeatedly in numerous media, including etchings, paintings, and drawings. Again in his 1957 essay, Greenberg casts this use of multiple media as a period of decline; he reiterates the implication that a painter's turning to architecture or sculpture is a weakness. Despite his respect for Kahnweiler, Greenberg disagrees with him about the value of working across mediums, and makes no mention of Kahnweiler's most interesting observation (which is quoted by Elgar). According to Kahnweiler, Picasso had some extremely odd, hybrid ideas which derived from a desire to deal not simply with space but with scale (fig. 2.13): "In 1929 he [Picasso] conceived of gigantic monuments, meant for erection on the Mediterranean shore as houses which at the same time would be enormous sculptures representing the female head. 'I have to paint them because nobody's ready to commission one from me' he said to me."[71] Kahnweiler sees Picasso's experiments not as mere trials that ultimately led him back to painting, but as decisive moments in which he engaged architecture in order to produce innovative sculptures. Such confusions (or productive improprieties) might therefore be seen as offering architectural precedents or, at the very least, unconventional insights into the terms and techniques of the architectural discipline.

Yet Greenberg was reluctant to grant sculpture or architecture an identity distinct from painting. When he did consider architecture as a collaborator with painting, he viewed the exchange as taking place on painting's terms: "'International style' architecture, cubist and post-cubist painting and sculpture, 'modern' furniture and decoration and design are the manifestations of a new style.... The new style arose independently in architecture and would, I feel sure, have come to fruition there without painting's aid. But painting—cubist painting—did serve to reveal the new style in architecture to itself."[72] Greenberg was even less generous toward sculpture: "as far as sculpture is concerned, the new style was created by painting, and by painting alone."

By the late 1950s these transdisciplinary speculations are no longer included in his writings; at the same time, Greenberg's concept of space is at the heart of the problems that began his turn away from sculpture and architecture. Greenberg's early writings address the spatial relationships between painting and architecture in two ways. The first involves a conflict between exterior surface and interior surface: that is, two kinds of flatness and two "visions" of space. By the 1960s, Greenberg will eliminate this problem by opting for a pure interiority: the autonomy of the shaped canvas. But, as noted earlier, in 1954 Greenberg asserted precisely the opposite concept:

the picture has now become an object of literally the same spatial order as our bodies, and no longer the vehicle of an imagined equivalent of that order. It has lost its "inside" and become all "outside," all plane surface.[73]

In 1952, he had yet another—more ambivalent—formulation; he contrasted the painting of Barnett Newman with that of Mondrian and proposed that each exemplified an inverse relationship to architectural space:

> [Newman's] paintings … constitute, moreover, the first kind of painting I have seen that accommodates itself stylistically to the demand of modern interior architecture for flat, clear surfaces and strictly parallel divisions. Mondrian aims more at external walls, and at the townscape that replaces the landscape wherever men collect together. Newman … aims at the room, at private rather than public life.[74]

Four years earlier, in 1948, Greenberg had offered a more general reflection on the spatial conflict between the landscape and the room. In fact, he believed that it had provoked a "crisis" in modernist painting which he saw as a consequence of "the contradiction between the architectural destination of abstract art and the very, very private atmosphere in which it is produced."[75] In other words, the crisis could be characterized as that between the (objective) exteriority of architectural space and the (subjective) interiority of pictorial space. Nonetheless, in the mid-1940s Greenberg had imagined that a shared concern for abstraction could overcome such dichotomies and lead to a new kind of unity of the arts, one that is pictorial, not spatial: "architecture, sculpture and painting" all share a "common tendency to treat all *matter,* as distinguished from *space,* as two-dimensional."[76] Contrary to the position he would adopt in the 1960s, he speculated that Mondrian's "exterior" formalism seemed to promise a system for aligning architecture, sculpture, and painting. In his 1944 obituary of Mondrian, Greenberg was explicit about the connection between architecture and Mondrian's painting: "Mondrian was the only artist to carry to their ultimate and inevitable conclusions those basic tendencies of recent Western painting which cubism defined and isolated. His art has influenced design and architecture more immediately than painting … I am not sure whether Mondrian himself recognized it, but the final intention of his work is to expand into the décor of the man-made world—what of it we see, move in, and handle."[77]

Unlike his writings of the 1950s and 1960s, Greenberg was intrigued in the early 1940s by the potential confusion of "real" and "pictorial" space, as is seen in the Gabo and Noguchi reviews, when his reductive tendencies do not quell his speculative thinking. The most instructive example is his 1943 review of Frederick Kiesler's Gallery of the Twentieth Century, designed to house Peggy Guggenheim's collection of painting and sculpture (figs. 2.14, 2.15).[78] Greenberg seems to have taken an interest in Kiesler, for even as late as 1952 he wrote that Kiesler "personifies the recent stylistic union of painting, sculpture and architecture in an exemplary way. He, in particular, has given us only a sample of all he has to say."[79] Nevertheless, in his generally positive review of the Guggenheim gallery, he could not resist criticizing Kiesler for his aggressive installation of the abstract paintings. On the one hand, Greenberg applauds Kiesler's effort to extend into architecture a "tendency dominant in painting since cubism … which, by means of abstraction, collage, [and] construction … tries almost literally to disembowel the painting. Its pictorial content no less than the physical fact of the canvas itself is to enter the actual presence of the spectator on the same terms and as completely as do the walls, the furniture, and people." On the other hand, "the same terms" are always the terms of painting and pictorial space; the architecture is judged by the degree to which it emulates and heightens the experience of the abstract paintings. Greenberg professes a varying tolerance for the efficacy of "actual presence," depending upon which kind of painting is being viewed. He distinguishes between the requirements of the "abstract and cubist" painting and the "fictive" work of Paul Klee and the surrealists—which Greenberg refers to with the diminutive term "easel painting." He explains that Kiesler hung the surrealist paintings in "indefinite space" (they were mounted from behind on single poles), an approach that was "exactly right because it emphasizes the traditional discontinuity between the spectator and the space within the picture." But he was dissatisfied with the installation of the abstract paintings, which were hung from "ropes [which] should have been covered with dark cloth." The ropes made the abstract rooms "a little crowded and scrappy," and Greenberg wanted to see "a more unified background.… As it is, the eye is unable to isolate them [the paintings] easily." Apparently the ropes accentuated the physical qualities of the abstract paintings, and did not "set off the high-keyed colors and pale tints." It is likely that Greenberg would have preferred that the illusion of flatness permeate the whole "abstract" room. Conversely, he insisted that the surrealist canvases require an exaggeration of their objecthood in order to reveal the devices of their illusions.

Clearly, Greenberg's notion of art entering "the actual presence of the spectator" requires a discriminating acknowledgment of the conflict between literal and pictorial space. In his 1949 review of Noguchi, Greenberg revealed this fear of spatial confusion, expressing his general desire to bracket the space of art and his specific preference for abstract paintings that are easily isolated from their surroundings: "The artist who deals with three dimensions is more easily hypnotized, it would seem, by his own facility than is the one confined to a flat surface.… The object … does not lose itself in the décor as readily in the picture—which, on the other hand, has the advantage of not being confused with the furniture."[80]

Greenberg's various attempts to negotiate the spatial conflict between architecture and painting provide the context and the material to begin to understand the role of architecture in the sculpture and criticism of the 1960s. Ultimately, by situating the criticism and practices of the 1960s historically and concentrating upon the spatial problems inherent in literalist art, we can see

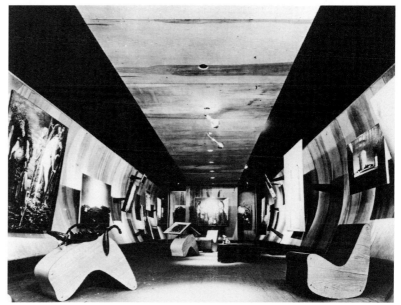

2.14 Frederick Kiesler, Art of This Century gallery, Cubist
Room, 1942.

2.15 Frederick Kiesler, Art of This Century gallery, Surrealist
Room, 1942.

an alternative architectural criticism emerge, one that is frank about the spatial and disciplinary confusion inherent in architectural practices and attentive to the peculiar kinds of flatness and space that occur in architecture. The artists of the 1960s obsessed upon and exploited architectural conventions. In their attempts to evade opticality as the primary category of experience, and in their efforts to confuse the reductiveness of visual flatness with literal structure and surface, literalist sculptors such as Donald Judd and Robert Morris became explicitly engaged with architecture. They made no effort to consign space, structure, or architecture to the background. Their work and their thinking can be confused effectively with the architecture (figs. 2.16, 2.17).

Symptoms of these problems, or complexes, which are fundamental to literalism, make at least one appearance in Greenberg's writings of the 1960s. In a 1965 essay on the work of Anthony Caro, the sculptor whom both he and Michael Fried considered to be the single most important modernist sculptor after David Smith, Greenberg's language implies a connection to architecture. After first praising Caro for avoiding strictly pictorial composition, Greenberg's remarks seem to suggest that he sees Caro's work as architectonic (fig. 2.18): "That the ground plan will at times echo as well as interlock with the superstructure or elevation (as in the superb *Sculpture Two* of 1962) only renders the unity of a piece that much harder to grasp at first. Yet just those factors that make for confusion at first make most for unity in the end."[81] Such passages suggest that Bois is right to not simply dismiss or oppose Greenberg. Rather, by scrutinizing his thoughts in detail, the flatly confused tenor of his early writings can be recovered. Eventually, an awareness of the similarity between Greenberg's early concerns and the problems that would preoccupy 1960s artists and their art criticism opens a way to an explicitly architectural criticism and an architectural approach to flatness.

An early, and well-known, formulation of this critical alternative is Leo Steinberg's notion of the "flatbed picture plane," which he first introduced in 1968 as a direct critique of Greenberg. Steinberg proclaims the emergence of what is neither collage nor montage but a "radically different … pictorial surface that let the world in again. Not the world of the Renaissance man who looked for his weather clues out of the window; but the world of men who turn knobs to hear a taped message … electronically transmitted from some windowless booth."[82] Thus Steinberg refigures Greenberg's characterization of abstract painting as "a more or less opaque window pane."[83]

But, once again, Greenberg's early writings also offer a more intriguing approach than the formulations he advanced in the 1960s. A 1947 passage (which he rewrites and repeats in another essay three years later) offers two other alternatives to the window metaphor that vividly portray the problem of the flatly confused by reasserting the same dichotomy he identifies between Mondrian and Newman and discerns in Kiesler's Gallery of the Twentieth Century—the pictorial flattening of space and surface, text and image, or architecture and painting.

Picasso asks you to construct rather than invent, to survey the terrain of your emotion more consciously and build upon it the largest and most substantial edifice possible—not like Klee, to send up demountable tracery and momentary mists of color. This does not mean that Picasso is more "intellectual" or more deliberate than Klee; he works, in fact, faster than Klee did, and with less meditation. It is simply that he sees the picture as a wall where Klee sees it as a page, and when one paints a wall one has to have a more comprehensive awareness of the surroundings and a more immediate sense of the architectural discipline—though Klee's sense in that respect, if slighter in scale, should not be discounted.[84]

If Greenberg truly believed that Klee should not be discounted, it should follow that the page requires no less of an "immediate sense of the architectural discipline" than the wall. In fact, the tension between the wall and the page is precisely the tension that is elaborated by Steinberg, by literalist criticism, and by the practices that can be flatly confused with that criticism (figs. 2.19–2.26).

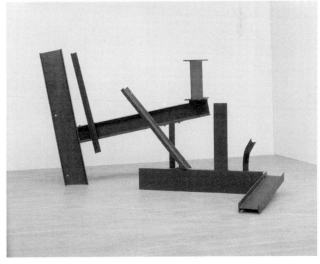

2.16 Donald Judd, installation at Green Gallery, 1963.

2.17 Robert Morris, installation at Green Gallery, 1964.

2.18 Anthony Caro, *Sculpture Two,* 1962. Painted steel, 87 ×
142 × 102 in.

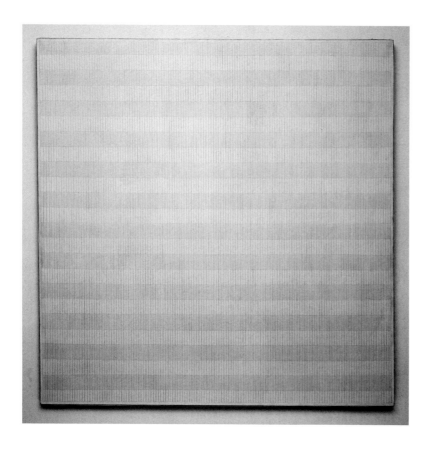

2.19 Agnes Martin, *The Tree*, 1964. Oil and pencil on canvas, 72 × 72 in.

2.20 John McCracken, *Ranger,* 1997. Polyester resin, fiberglass, and plywood, 112 × 19.5 × 2.875 in.

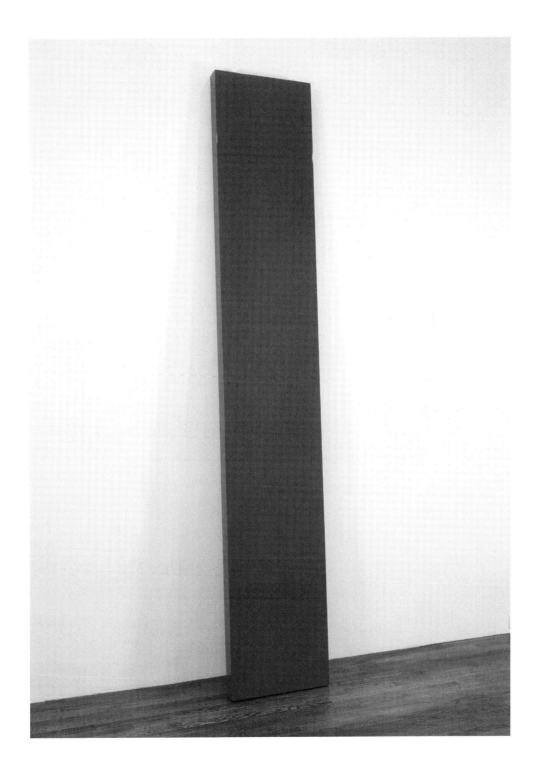

2.21 William Anastasi, *Six Sites (West Wall Dwan Gallery)*, 1967. Photo silkscreen on canvas, 85.5 × 157 in.

2.22 Will Insley, *Wall Fragment 66.2*, 1966 (in foreground, installed at Museum of Contemporary Art, Chicago, 1976). Acrylic on masonite and wood, 96 × 96 × 2 in.

2.23 Robert Mangold, *Red Wall*, 1965. Oil on masonite, 96.5 × 96.5 in.

2.24 Robert Mangold, *Gray Wall*, 1965. Painted wood, 96 × 96 in.

2.25, 2.26 Mel Bochner, *Measurement Room* (at Galerie Heiner Friedrich, Munich), 1969. Tape and Letraset on wall, dimensions determined by installation.

3

Chapter 3

Incredibly Convincing: Michael Fried's Denial of Architecture

Over the course of five years, beginning in late 1965, Michael Fried published thirteen essays in *Artforum* that build on Clement Greenberg's model and simultaneously render it obsolete.[1] Whereas Fried's earlier criticism had implicitly accepted Greenberg's judgments, his *Artforum* essays are nothing less than an ambitious redefinition of modernism that recuperates some of the seemingly "confused" aspects of Greenberg's criticism while contesting the concepts that came to dominate Greenberg's writing in the sixties, such as the ideal of "purity" and the notion of "the modernist 'reduction.'" Most important, Fried not only challenged Greenberg's view of modernist painting but initiated an analysis of sculpture that distinguishes its medium from painting's. In doing so, Fried confronted architectural questions—about objects, space, physicality, structure, inhabitation, and scale—more fundamental than those Greenberg had addressed tentatively in the 1950s. But unlike Greenberg, who at times seemed to find those "confusing" questions intriguing even though he left them largely unexamined, Fried identified architecture as a distinct threat to his conception of modernism.

The formal questions and proposals that would lead to Fried's ultimate denial of a relationship between modernist art and architecture can be traced in all of his *Artforum* essays, including "Art and Objecthood," his infamous 1967 polemic against the "theatricality" of "literalism"—that is, a "concern with the actual circumstances in which the beholder encounters literalist work."[2] Fried's declaration of a "war" between theatricality and "art as such," it turns out, is also a battle against any relationship between architecture and modernist art.[3] This becomes explicit in 1968 and 1970 in two *Artforum* essays on the sculpture of Anthony Caro in which Fried proposes that Caro's sculpture is a "radical abstraction" of architecture. In the 1968 essay, he suggests that Caro's work "explores possibilities for sculpture in various concepts and experiences which one would think belonged today only to architecture," the most poignant of which is a "preoccupation with the fact, or with the implications of the fact, that men have bodies and live in a physical world." However, Fried ultimately concludes that Caro's sculpture is not architectural at all. Instead, it overcomes its seemingly architectural character "by rendering it *anti*-literal or (what I mean by) *abstract*. Caro's genius is that he is able to make radically abstract sculpture out of concepts and experiences which seem … inescapably literal and therefore irremediably theatrical."[4] Two years later, Fried would all but equate literalness with architecture in his bald denial of "any literal or architectural relationship between structure and beholder" in Caro's *Deep North,* a large sculpture with a gridded rectangular form (resembling a canopy or roof) perched horizontally some eight feet above the viewer (fig. 3.1).[5] According to Fried, the fact that "an apprehension of … a kind of roof or ceiling under which we can stand dominates our experience of the sculpture as a whole" is not architectural because "even when we place ourselves directly beneath the massive grid we do not feel that we have entered or that we are inside the sculpture." Instead it is "experienced as a special instance of the limitations inherent in *any* point of view."[6]

Whether or not we accept Fried's argument, it is this writing on Caro's work that fully separated his criticism from Greenberg's. By claiming in 1970 that Caro's sculpture employs a mode of visuality that is at once "anti-literal" and "un-pictorial," Fried proposes an understanding of the abstraction of modernist sculpture that distinguishes it from literalist modes of abstraction as well as from Greenberg's "modernist 'reduction'"—the idea that "sculpture has turned out to be almost as exclusively visual in its essence as painting itself.… The literalness that was once its handicap has now become its advantage."[7]

3.1 Anthony Caro, *Deep North*, 1969–70. Painted steel,
cadmium steel, and aluminum, 96 × 228 × 114 in.

> Caro on the one hand has frankly avowed the physicality of his sculpture and on the other has rendered that physicality unperspicuous to a degree that even after repeated viewings is barely credible.

Michael Fried, "Two Sculptures by Anthony Caro" (1968)

Fried's concepts of shape, conviction, radical abstraction, acknowledgment, and presentness, as well as his arguments against literalism, theatricality, and objecthood, amount to a new theorization of the work of the artists that both he and Greenberg considered to be central to the ongoing legacy of modernism—primarily the sculpture of Caro and the painting of Jackson Pollock, Jules Olitski, Kenneth Noland, and Morris Louis (figs. 3.2, 3.3). But it was the painting of Frank Stella, whom Greenberg hardly mentioned, that initiated Fried's effort to develop an alternative mode of criticism (fig. 3.4).[8] Fried's first significant divergence from Greenberg occurred in early 1965. His catalog essay for "Three American Painters: Kenneth Noland, Jules Olitski, Frank Stella," an exhibition he curated at Harvard's Fogg Museum, concludes with this claim: "the aspiration of modernist painters such as Noland, Olitski, and Stella are not toward purity, but toward quality and eloquence: and … these inevitably resist both prescription and paraphrase, and can be found only in one's experience of the best paintings of one's time, or of any other."[9] While subtle, the differences with Greenberg that Fried articulates in that sentence are significant, and his *Artforum* essays would elaborate their implications, eventually leading to his concern with sculpture in "Art and Objecthood" and, soon after, to his explicit denial of any architectural implications in Caro's work. Yet the less subtle, even overt, announcement of Fried's break with Greenberg was simply his decision to group Stella with Olitski and Noland. Greenberg had written a great deal on Olitski and Noland (as a curator he had included both in the 1964 show "Post Painterly Abstraction"), but had found less worthy of mention in Stella's striped, structured, or shaped canvases. Since 1959, when Stella's black paintings were included in "Sixteen Americans" at the Museum of Modern Art, he had been a contested figure. Fried saw the divergent interpretations and evaluations of Stella's painting as emblematic of the condition faced by modernist painting and criticism in the 1960s. As he noted at a symposium held at Brandeis one year after the opening of "Three American Painters," "what ultimately is at stake in a disagreement … about, say, Frank Stella's paintings is, or may be, nothing less than the meaning of the great paintings and the identities of the great painters of the past 20 or 60 or 100 or 180 years."[10] Fried believed that he and his generation were forced to confront "a new type of disagreement among critics … that occurs when two or more critics agree, or say, that the work of a particular artist or group of artists is good or valuable or important, but when the terms in which they try to characterize the work and its significance are fundamentally different." Thus Fried could say,

"I feel more desperate about what seems to me bad or meretricious criticism written in praise and, ostensibly, in elucidation of art I admire than I do about bad or meretricious art."[11] Certainly Fried did not see Greenberg's criticism as "bad or meretricious," and the audience at Brandeis likely assumed that Fried was referring to his disagreement with literalist artist-critics such as Donald Judd and Robert Morris, who were hostile toward Greenberg and who understood Stella's work in literalist terms.[12] Yet Fried also was becoming increasingly aware of his own disagreement with Greenberg not only about the quality of Stella's work, but also about the implications his work had for the "enterprise of modernism."[13]

In a long footnote to the published proceedings of the Brandeis symposium (almost one half the length of the essay and presumably written after the conference), Fried explains that what is "at issue" in the new kinds of disagreements (or seeming agreements) is

> each critic's view or version or interpretation of the history—at any rate, the *modern* history—of painting and sculpture.... Or to put it another way: one's conception of the enterprise of painting in our time simultaneously depends on and entails a particular interpretation of the history of painting.... Moreover, to the extent to which critics come to accept this responsibility, their disagreements will ... tend more and more to look like disputes among historians rather than like our traditional picture of disputes among critics.[14]

Compelled by this historical imperative, Fried's *Artforum* essays developed his alternative view of modernism and its implications for contemporary art. Fried believed that Greenberg's approach to the genealogy of modernism as a series of technical innovations could not be sustained unless a more convincing account of the historicity of painting—its particular evolution as a "cognitive enterprise"—could be articulated.

Fried's emerging disagreement with Greenberg was also a challenge to his notion of an empirical "consensus of taste": Fried was entirely opposed to any notion of pluralism or even consensus that was not based in a broader critical and historical agreement.[15] While he shared Greenberg's belief that the test of aesthetic quality always lay in experience, he did not share Greenberg's characterization of the critic as a reporter with superior taste, or of criticism as limited to description, judgment, and consensus. Fried's critical project was more ambitious; his presentation of detailed formal evaluations of specific series of works aspired to demonstrate "how modernism works."[16] As the advocate of a constructive role for the critic, Fried was participating in a pervasive theoretical trend exemplified not only in the writings of his generation of critics, but also by the new generation of artists, particularly those opposed to Greenberg and Fried. As Kynaston McShine wrote in 1966 in his introduction to the catalog for "Primary Structures" (the first major exhibition of literalist sculpture): "Most of the sculptors are university-trained,

3.2 Kenneth Noland, *17th Stage,* 1964. Acrylic resin on canvas, 84 × 80 in.

3.3 Jules Olitski, *Tin Lizzie Green,* 1964. Alkyd and oil/wax crayon on canvas, 130 × 82 in.

3.4 Frank Stella, installation of black paintings in "Sixteen Americans," Museum of Modern Art, 1959.

have read philosophy, are quite familiar with other disciplines, have a keen sense of history, express themselves articulately and are often involved in dialectic."[17] Fried's *Artforum* essays rely explicitly on philosophical sources, including the writings of Wittgenstein, Merleau-Ponty, and, increasingly, his friend Stanley Cavell.[18] In the 1960s Greenberg also increasingly turned to philosophy, but to undermine the use of theory in art criticism. In a 1961 essay addressed to a popular audience, Greenberg wrote: "Quality in art can be neither ascertained nor proved by logic or discourse. Experience alone rules in this area—and the experience, so to speak, of experience. This is what all the serious philosophers of art since Immanuel Kant have concluded. Yet, quality in art is not just a matter of private experience. There is a *consensus* of taste. The best taste is that of the people who, in each generation, spend the most time and trouble on art, and this best taste has always turned out to be unanimous, within certain limits, in its verdicts."[19] For Fried, the obligation of the modernist critic is not only to identify quality, but to persistently reconsider and explain "what *painting* is" (or what sculpture is) in relationship to the history of its conventions. In other words, taste is necessary but not sufficient to settle questions of quality, which are pursued by artists in their attempts to pose the question of painting through painting (or sculpture through sculpture), while critics adjudicated what Fried would call "the politics of conviction."[20]

Fried's use of the term "conviction" derives from Cavell's claim "that the dangers of fraudulence, and of trust, are essential to the experience of [modernist] art," and that as a result even modernist artists "themselves do not quite know who is and who is not rightly included among their peers, whose work counts and whose does not."[21] In this situation, art's "immediate relevance depends upon a willingness to trust the object, knowing that time spent with its difficulties may be betrayed." Most important, modernist art demands "trust" of one's own perceptions and understanding, but also requires critical engagement with others'—artists', critics' and observers'—efforts to articulate what they see, think, or claim to know. Cavell concludes: "One often does not know whether interest is elicited and sustained primarily by the object or by what is said about the object. My suggestion is not that this is bad, but that it is definitive of a modernist situation."[22] For Cavell, to understand modernist art and to make aesthetic judgments mean that "you have reached conviction, but not about a proposition; and consistency, but not in theory. You are different, what you recognize as problems are different, your world is different."[23]

Fried applies Cavell's point to his own criticism and argues that modernist art "is capable of compelling conviction" through a constant reinvention of its conventions, and that "the task of the modernist [artist] is to discover those conventions which at a given moment *alone* are capable of establishing his work's identity as painting [or as sculpture]."[24] The critic's task, on the other hand, is to discern those conventions and to explain their historical significance.

> The object of [the modernist painter's] enterprise is *both* knowledge and conviction—knowledge *through,* or better still, *in,* conviction. And this knowledge is simultaneously knowledge of *painting* … and of *himself* … apprehended not as two distinct entities, but in a single, inextricable fruition.
> Michael Fried, "Shape as Form" (1966)

Fried's emphasis on the historical evolution of art's conventions distinguishes his critical model from Greenberg's, and his own retrospective account of those differences with Greenberg is both lucid and misleading. At a 1987 symposium held to reassess the art world events of 1967 (the foremost of which was the publication of "Art and Objecthood"), Fried explained: "I was deeply influenced throughout the sixties by the art criticism of Clement Greenberg.… But by 1966 I had become unpersuaded by his theorization of the way modernism works (as put forward, for example, in essays like 'Modernist Painting' and 'After Abstract Expressionism'), in particular by his notion that modernism in the arts involved a process of *reduction* … a view that seemed to me ahistorical."[25] In his 1982 essay "How Modernism Works," Fried had offered an elaborate account of his departure from "Greenberg's reductionist and essentialist conception of the modernist enterprise" as a lineage that "has evolved by a process of … casting off, negating, one norm or convention after another in search of the bare minimum that can suffice."[26] Whereas Greenberg viewed the course of modernist painting since Manet as an inexorable process in which the formal devices of "the flat surface, the shape of the support, [and] the properties of pigment"[27] became increasingly evident even as the technical means of exploring them evolved, Fried proposed a more fluid modernism in which the conventions of painting themselves are constantly redefined. Looking back in 1982, Fried claims that he first "took issue with" reductionism in "Shape as Form: Frank Stella's New Paintings," his third essay in *Artforum.* In a footnote he writes:

> I take a reductionist conception of modernist painting to mean this: that painting since Manet is seen as a kind of cognitive enterprise in which a certain quality (*e.g.,* literalness), a set of norms (*e.g.,* flatness and the delimitation of flatness), or core of problems (*e.g.,* how to acknowledge the literal character of the support) is progressively revealed as constituting the *essence* of painting—and by implication of having done so all along. This seems to me gravely mistaken, not on the grounds that modernist painting is *not* a cognitive enterprise, but because it radically misconstrues the *kind* of cognitive enterprise modernist painting is.… What the modernist painter can be said to discover in his work—what can be said to be revealed to him in it—is not the irreducible essence of *all* painting, but rather that which, at the present moment in painting's history, is capable of convincing him that it

can stand in comparison with the painting of both the modernist and pre-modernist past whose quality seems to him beyond question.[28]

But, as already noted, Fried had first acknowledged his move away from Greenberg not in his critique of reductionism in "Shape as Form," but nearly two years earlier in *Three American Painters*. Even though Fried explicitly establishes his argument on the basis of Greenberg's writings in the first section of that ambitious catalog essay, the second section carefully but decisively distinguishes his formalism from Greenberg's. When that section of *Three American Painters* was republished as "Jackson Pollock"—Fried's first *Artforum* essay—it appeared with a slight editorial alteration that emphasized Fried's one explicit point of disagreement with Greenberg. Of the eight footnotes that had originally appeared in the excerpted portion of the catalog essay, only one remained in *Artforum*.[29] Conspicuous in its singularity, the footnote politely challenges Greenberg's analysis of Pollock.

It was apparently *Artforum*'s editor, Philip Leider, who recognized and magnified the footnote's significance. In his introductory article to the issue, Leider makes much of the fact that a version of "Three American Painters" was then being shown at the Pasadena Art Museum while at the Los Angeles County Museum of Art a show was up titled "The New York School: The First Generation: Paintings of the 1940s and 1950s." The coincidence of the two exhibitions in California of two generations of New York painters provided a pretext and the context for Leider to examine Fried's motives. Quoting from Fried's catalog essay, Leider implies that Fried's essay aims not only to legitimate the work of the second generation, but to establish the terms of a new discourse on "formal intelligence" that was emerging among contemporary painters and critics.

That this might indeed be Fried's intention is most strongly indicated in the sentence in "Jackson Pollock" that contains the conspicuous footnote: here Fried claims that "the formal issues at stake" in Pollock's paintings of the late 1940s "cannot be characterized in cubist terms."[30] Clarifying his point in the footnote, Fried quotes and challenges Greenberg's assertion that Pollock "took up Analytical Cubism from the point at which Picasso and Braque had left it, when, in their collages of 1912 and 1913, they drew back from the utter abstraction for which Analytical Cubism seemed headed."[31] Fried follows the quotation with this remark: "One is always ill at ease disagreeing with Greenberg on visual grounds; however I cannot help but see Pollock's all-over painting of those years in radically different terms."[32] To sustain his disagreement, Fried builds the remainder of "Jackson Pollock" on Greenberg's notion of opticality, to construct an equally formalist but fundamentally different understanding of Pollock's abstraction as one in which "line is used in such a way as to defy being read in terms of figuration."[33] In his effort to devise a more robust conception of abstraction, Fried proposes an understanding of space more sophisticated (and reductive) than any ever presented by Greenberg. According to Fried, in Pollock's paintings the effect of line is wholly "optical because it addresses itself to eyesight alone. The materiality of his pigment is rendered sheerly visual, and the result is a new kind of space—if it still makes sense to call it space—in which conditions of seeing prevail rather than one in which objects exist, flat shapes are juxtaposed or physical events transpire."[34] Instead, Pollock represents "a space to which eyesight gives access but which somehow denies even the possibility of literal, physical penetration by the beholder."[35]

In other words, in the late 1940s Pollock achieved a version of what Fried, in "Art and Objecthood," would call "presentness": his paintings transform the spatial and temporal relationship between the spectator and the object into timeless subjectivity, a "continuous and perpetual present" constituted by the visual apprehension of form. As Fried writes, "It is this continuous and entire presentness, amounting … to the perpetual creation of itself, that one experiences as a kind of *instantaneousness:* as though if one were infinitely more acute, a single infinitely brief instant would be long enough to see everything, to experience the work in all its depth and fullness, to be forever convinced by it."[36]

In support of his claim that Pollock achieves this effect without recuperating cubist modes of abstraction (facet planes, sheer flatness, figuration), Fried offers a strikingly original analysis of two atypical paintings of 1949—*Cut Out* and *Out of the Web*—in which Pollock cut out oddly shaped portions of the painting to reveal a stained but "mostly blank canvas-board behind it" (fig. 3.5). Fried then attempts to explain why "Pollock did not repeat his remarkable solution," and instead began to experiment with "staining thinned-down black paint into unsized canvas." He suggests that the shapes that appear as cutouts in 1949 become stains in 1951, and with that staining technique (which not by chance resembles the use of paint in the 1960s by Noland, Louis, Olitski, and others), "Pollock seems to have been on the verge of an entirely new and different kind of painting, combining figuration with opticality in a new pictorial synthesis of virtually limitless potential" (figs. 3.6, 3.7).[37]

In Fried's account, the potential lay in staining rather than cutting,[38] and his analysis of why this is so is (literally) spectacular. He rationalizes that Pollock "abandoned the solution [of using cutouts] because it could not be improved upon or developed in any essential respect and because to repeat the solution would have been to debase it to the status of a mere device."[39] But perhaps Fried should have written "a merely *literal* device," because it is precisely the literalness of cutting the shape that seems to prevent Fried from imagining its improvement or development, despite the fact that Stella and other painters had already achieved just that (figs. 3.8, 3.9).[40]

The holes in Pollock's paintings constitute not figures but what Fried calls "a kind of blind spot, a kind of defect in our visual apparatus." Questions of support and literalness are posed only

3.5 Jackson Pollock, *Out of the Web,* 1949. Oil and enamel paint on masonite, 48 × 96 in.

3.6 Jackson Pollock, *Number 7, 1951,* 1951. Oil on canvas, 56.5 × 66 in.

3.7 Morris Louis, *Aurora,* 1958. Acrylic on canvas, 93 × 175 in.

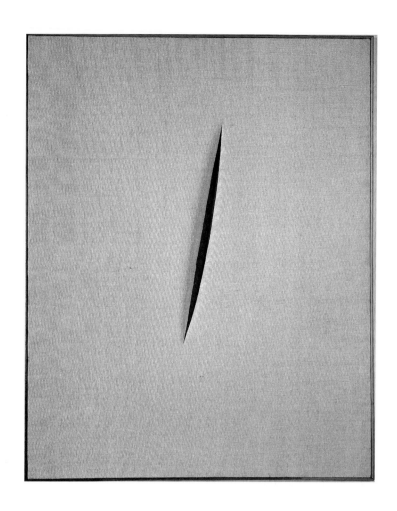

3.8 Frank Stella, installation (portrait series) at Castelli Gallery, 1964.

3.9 Lucio Fontana, *Concetto spaziale attesa (Waiting)*, 1960. Water-based paint on canvas.

negatively, as "the absence, over a particular area, of the visual field.... The figure is something we *don't* see—it is, literally, *where* we don't see—rather than something, a shape or object in the world, we do see." Thus Fried proposes that the physical cuts in the surface as well as the literal spaces they produce and in which they appear are sublimated as pure subjectivity: "In the end, the relation between the field and the figure is simply not spatial at all: it is purely and wholly optical: so that the figure ... seems to lie somewhere within our own eyes, as strange as this may sound."[41] Fried's reading of Pollock is a strange version of a Gestalt figure-ground reversal, in which the effect is not an equivocal oscillation between figure and ground but a dialectical opposition of abstraction and absence.

Thus there is an intriguing parallel between Fried's combination of literal figures with sheer opticality and Colin Rowe's fascination with the blank walls of Villa Schwob and La Tourette, as well as his subsequent application of figure-ground analysis of space in architecture.[42] Like Rowe's uses of figure-ground analysis to represent (and design) urban space as positive figures, or shapes, that are seen against the background texture of built form, Fried's notion of abstraction values the visual effects of a formal device over the artifacts (the paintings or the buildings) that produce the effect. In Pollock's work, Fried dissociates the figures from the painting, the holes in the canvas, and its support; similarly, with the blank walls, Rowe finds that the figures are at once "without intrinsic interest" and "the problem in terms of which the whole building is stated." With figure-ground analysis however, while the figures are not actually visible in the city, they reappear as figural space.[43] So while Rowe saw figure-ground analysis as a representation of "real" space, his reading of the blank panels is closer to Fried's reading of Pollock, in which the shapes are purely mental, operating at a limit of visuality that implies spatiality. But unlike Rowe's analysis, Fried's reading of Pollock is quite distinct from Greenberg's explanation of cubist collage as an ambivalent combination of illusion and representation. Whereas Greenberg maintained that Picasso and Braque used "utterly literal means to carry the forward push of the collage (and of Cubism in general) *literally* into the literal space in front of the picture plane,"[44] Fried represses "literal space" altogether and thus evades the sort of spatial confusions that perplexed Greenberg and tantalized Rowe. Fried imagines that in Pollock's paintings of 1949 the picture pushes forward even more radically (and phenomenologically) to seem "on the verge of dancing off the visual field or of dissolving into it and into each other as we try to look at them."[45]

Fried's evasion of "space" is a brilliant alternative to Greenberg's (and Rowe's) interpretation of the figure of the blank surface or empty canvas. Fried swerves from Greenberg's model, because Fried's sublimation of space requires an experience of blankness (or the empty canvas) that is simply and literally a kind of blindness—not a reduction or negation of painting's conventions. Pollock's cutouts are a willful and skillful negation of opticality itself.[46] In effect, and in wholly new terms, Fried revises not only the figure of the empty canvas, but also the problems Greenberg had analyzed in Picasso's and Braque's experimentation with the dialectic between material and illusion in collage. Fried does not contest Greenberg's narrative leading from analytic cubism through collage to construction sculpture, but he sees those precedents as sublated (or sublimated) in Pollock's new dialectic of opticality with its absence. Whereas Greenberg concludes his essay "Collage" by identifying the "monumental unity" of cubist collage with "the self-evident self-sufficiency of architecture," Fried can be understood to be claiming that Pollock recuperates collage in "a new pictorial synthesis" that is "simply not spatial at all: it is purely and wholly optical."[47]

Needless to say, such a radical model of visuality could have nothing less to do with architecture. But it has everything to do with Fried's understanding of Caro's sculpture. In "Two Sculptures by Anthony Caro," Fried writes of Caro's "conversion to radical abstraction around 1959" (a shift often attributed to the influence of Greenberg) and explains that Caro "has frankly avowed the physicality of his sculpture" and at the same time "has rendered that physicality unperspicuous to a degree that even after repeated viewings is barely credible." In other words, the abstraction of Caro's sculpture is *incredibly convincing:* it "compels us to believe what we see rather than what we know, to accept the witness of the senses against the constructions of the mind."[48] Here again, there are similarities with Rowe. Fried's understanding of Caro identifies, but sublimates, the same duality Rowe had applied to La Tourette: "this elaborate divorce of physical reality and optical impression."[49] Fried's approach to sculpture is also a purer version of Rowe's and Slutzky's conception of phenomenal transparency in architecture. Fried not only identifies and ranks what Rowe and Slutzky call the "continuous dialectic between fact and implication":[50] his key innovation in regard to Greenberg's modernism is to conceive pictorial "space" as a phenomenal apperception that is *sustained* by the literal support of the canvas (or of the steel, in Caro's case), but is achieved only in *acknowledging* and *defeating* it.[51] That is, modernist painting and sculpture must "proclaim the contradiction" between illusion and support, and at the same time *resolve it visually.* In this way, Fried's writings of the 1960s amount to an increasingly sophisticated and rigorous effort to expunge spatiality from modernist art, beginning as early as 1962 with his description of Richard Chamberlain's sculpture as exhibiting "a sense of the space within it circulating effortlessly across its surface also: as if the distinction between inside and outside were not much more useful than talking about a Klein's bottle."[52] This effort became overt in *Three American Painters,* where he credits Barnett Newman with "rendering *spatiality itself* sheerly optical."[53]

Ultimately, it is Fried's conception of sculpture that reconfigures the "confusing" spatial notions that occur at different moments in Greenberg's criticism. The first is Greenberg's understanding of "easel painting" as "the vehicle of an imagined equivalent" or "an illusion of the same kind of space as that in which our bodies move."[54] The second is his notion of abstract painting as always *implicitly* a mural, "a kind of picture that, without actually becoming identified with the wall like a mural, would *spread* over it and acknowledge its physical reality."[55] The third is his notion of the "modernist 'reduction,'" and the paradoxical claim that sculpture's literalness provides the basis for a more complex pictorialism. In "Jackson Pollock" Fried manages to recuperate all three notions, while rejecting any confusion they may imply: the spatial confusion of the first and the confusing conflation of literalness and abstraction implied by the second and third. Eventually, in "Art and Objecthood" and in his essays on Caro, Fried would extend a version of his argument to sculpture, thus completing his revision of Greenberg's formalism and, in the process, insisting upon architecture's irrelevance to modernist art.

Stella's new paintings, by making literalness illusive, not only come to grips with but actually *resolve* … the conflict … between a particular kind of pictorial illusion—i.e., addressed to eyesight alone—and the literal character of the support. And … for the first time since the late 18th century sculpture is in a position to inspire painting; and in Stella's recent paintings this has actually begun to happen.

Michael Fried, "Shape as Form" (1966)

Stella is the hinge figure in Fried's move toward sculpture. In "Shape as Form," Fried detailed how Stella's painting is an advance on Pollock's. Rather than a dialectic of abstraction and absence, Stella employs a new visual dialectic between literal shape (the canvas and its support) and depicted shape (the use of color on the canvas's surface). That dialectic would be central to the notion of modernist painting and sculpture that Fried developed in his subsequent *Artforum* essays, and, although Fried does not make reference to it, that dialectic is based in significant ways on Greenberg's 1961 essay "Collage."[56] But while Greenberg saw the tension.between literalism and illusion as the engine that produced modernist sculpture, Fried argued in "Shape as Form" that Stella had reclaimed it for painting: "Frank Stella's new paintings investigate the viability of shape as … a medium in which choices about literal and depicted shapes are made mutually responsive. And by the viability of shape, I mean its power to hold, to stamp itself out, and *in*—as verisimilitude and narrative and symbolism used to impress themselves—compelling conviction.… These are powers or potentialities—not to say responsibilities—which shape never until now possessed."[57]

Fried's innovation was to identify shape as the salient formal issue of the 1960s, a pursuit that involved rethinking the importance of both literalness and shape in Greenberg's criticism.[58] In "Shape as Form," Fried claims that "shape has become something different than it was in traditional painting or, for that matter, in modernist painting until recently. It has become, one might say, an object of conviction, whereas before it was merely … a kind of object" (18).[59] Stella's achievement was to have overcome, or "resolved," the dialectic between literal and depicted shape. The crucial event was Stella's "discovery shortly before 1960 of a new mode of pictorial structure based on the shape, rather than the flatness of the support…. In general the development of modernist painting during the past six years can be described as having involved the progressive assumption by literal shape of a greater—that is, more active, more explicit—importance than ever before, and the consequent subordination of depicted shape" (18–19). While Stella's "stripe paintings represent the most unequivocal and conflictless acknowledgment of literal shape in the history of modernism," an even more important development occurs in Stella's shaped canvases of 1966: "In Stella's new paintings … the relation between depicted and literal shape seems nowhere near as straight forward in its declaration of the latter as in the stripe paintings" (22, 24) (fig. 3.10). The new strategy "does not affirm the dependence of the depicted on literal shape so much as it establishes an unprecedented *continuity* between them…. It is as though in a painting like *Moultonboro III* there *is no* literal shape and, therefore, no depicted shape either; more accurately, because none of the shapes that we experience in that painting is wholly literal, there is none that we are tempted to call merely depicted" (24).

Ultimately, Fried claims in "Shape as Form" that literalness is dissociated from the support in Stella's new paintings and becomes a property of "the individual shapes themselves": "what is rendered illusive … is nothing less than literalness itself" (24). It is "as though one's experience of literalness is above all an experience of the literalness of the *individual shapes themselves*" (24). Thus Fried explains that Stella does with shape what Pollock had done with the figure and what Caro does with "physicality." The connection between Fried's theory of shape and his later discussion of Caro's sculpture is direct, and it is in "Shape as Form" that Fried first contrasts the (proper) modernist uses of literalness with the (degraded) modes of sheer literalism. Fried sets up this contrast by introducing the negative example of

> certain younger artists to whose sensibilities all conflict between the literal character of the support and illusion of any kind is intolerable, and for whom, accordingly, the future of art lies in the creation of works that more than anything else, are wholly literal—in this respect going beyond painting…. But it ought to be observed that the literalness isolated and hypostatized in the work of artists like Donald Judd and Larry Bell is by no means the same

literalness as that acknowledged by advanced painting throughout the past century: it is not the literalness of the support. Moreover, hypostatization is not acknowledgment.... Their pieces cannot be said to acknowledge literalness; they are simply literal. (22)[60]

Fried introduces the discussion of literalist art at this point in his essay because his analysis of Stella's painting hinges on a distinction between the striped paintings, which "are among the *last* paintings that literalists like Judd are able to endorse more or less without reservation," and his newer "shaped canvases," which "repudiate—not literalist taste or sensibility exactly—but the literalist *implications* … which his stripe paintings appear to carry" (24).[61]

Armed with this philosophically sophisticated, historically based, and technically rigorous "post-Cubist critical vocabulary,"[62] Fried would promote his revised version of modernist art and eventually, in "Art and Objecthood," declare "war" against the literalists, a war he waged on two fronts: more or less covertly against Greenberg's modernist criticism, and very publicly against an entirely new type of critic: artists who write criticism as part and parcel of their work. Considered in terms of the legacy of modernist art and formalist criticism, the publication and impact of "Art and Objecthood" comprise the core of the pivotal "event" of the 1960s New York art world— an event that documents, condenses, and reconfigures interdisciplinary conflicts. "Art and Objecthood" gathers and bundles the strands of an art world knot coupling recent painting and sculpture, the California and New York art worlds, various modernist and avant-garde legacies, modernist critics and literalist artist-critics, and the methods of a new generation of formalist critics with the increasingly intractable views of Greenberg.[63] On each count, "Art and Objecthood" aimed to clarify the terms of the opposition between Fried's innovative and precise notion of modernist art and the alternatives and challenges formulated by others.

Fried's attitude toward architecture—disguised in his rhetoric as "literalism" or "theatricality"—makes several appearances in "Art and Objecthood" as the enemy of "art."[64] Compared with Greenberg, who periodically struggled with architecture or asserted its significance for modernism, Fried employs much more extreme and exclusionary polemics, casting architecture in an antagonistic role as the discipline that both sustains and impairs the potential of modernist painting and sculpture. Architecture is implicit in Fried's definition of the term "literalism" in the first paragraph of "Art and Objecthood": "Literalist sensibility is theatrical because, to begin with, it is concerned with the actual circumstances in which the beholder encounters literalist work.... The experience of literalist art is of an object *in a situation*—one which, virtually by definition, *includes the beholder*" (15). Simply put, literalism involves architectural effects: "literalist art [objects] must confront the beholder—they must … be placed not just in his space but in his way" (15–16). To be literal is to project "presence" or, as Fried writes later in "Art and Objecthood," "a kind of *stage*

3.10 Frank Stella, installation (irregular polygons) at Castelli
Gallery, 1966.

presence."[65] Literalness is the very criterion of objecthood. Opposed to the literalist work in Fried's equation is the "work of modernist painting and sculpture [which is] in some essential respect *not an object*" (15),[66] a formulation Fried attributes to Kant, via Cavell.[67] For Fried, modernism overcomes presence (the obdurate literalness of objecthood) by maintaining the *propriety* of the relationships between the arts and the resulting specificity of each medium. To those premises Fried adds his polemical claim that anything that "lies *between* the arts is theater" (21), and his proposal that the demand for "art" to "defeat or suspend its objecthood is at bottom the imperative that it *defeat or suspend theater*. And *this* means that there is a war going on between theater and modernist painting, between the theatrical and the pictorial" (20), between objecthood and art, or, as I propose, between architecture and art. A detailed reading of "Art and Objecthood"—one that traces the sources of his claims—reveals that architecture, disguised as theater, plays the role of antagonist in Fried's drama.

Fried introduces theatricality as a capacious and negative term. The closest he comes to positively defining it is near the end of the "Art and Objecthood" in the assertion that "at bottom, theater addresses … a sense of temporality," and in a footnote to that passage where he writes: "There is, in fact, a deep affinity between literalist and Surrealist sensibility … ; both tend to deploy and isolate objects and persons in *situations*—the closed room and the abandoned artificial landscape" (23). Fried thus vaguely identifies architecture not only with theater, but with all interdisciplinary artworks. The war Fried declares against objecthood and theatricality is a conflict over disciplinary boundaries, and its battles are waged on terrain that is implicitly architectural (between the arts). In other words, the war between art and objecthood was not exactly between modernism and literalism, but between those who wanted to maintain the (mythical) autonomy of art and those who identified opportunities in accepting and acknowledging (or at the very least, no longer denying) architecture's role in sustaining that myth.[68]

Without intending it, but as a result of the sheer ambition of his effort to codify a new formal agenda for modernist painting and to extend its conclusions to sculpture, Fried touches upon profound architectural conventions. It is not surprising that the role of architecture in covertly sustaining the premises of Fried's modernism emerges in "Art and Objecthood": the essay marks a turning point in Fried's interests, from developing a theory of painting to a preoccupation with sculpture.

"Art and Objecthood" is primarily Fried's interpretation and critique of five recent articles that present the views of Donald Judd, Robert Morris, and Tony Smith, all of whom explicitly refused modernist criteria: an edited radio discussion published in *Art News* as "Questions to Stella and Judd," Judd's "Specific Objects," Morris's "Notes on Sculpture" and "Notes on Sculpture: Part 2," and Samuel Wagstaff's "Talking to Tony Smith."[69] Two motives lie behind the vehemence of

Fried's attack. First, he wanted to maintain the distinction between the production of art and the function of criticism. As much as he might disagree with other critics, he never attacked them so publicly or specifically as he did Judd, Morris, and Smith. Second, even more than the critics who supported their work, Morris, Smith, and especially Judd explained their work as a rejection of the incapacities and limitations of modernist painting and sculpture. In 1966, Morris specifically refuted Greenberg and Fried in his assertion that "the concerns of sculpture have been for some time not only distinct but hostile to those of painting" because "the sculptural facts of space, light, and materials have always functioned concretely and literally."[70] One year earlier, Judd bluntly wrote in the opening sentence of "Specific Objects": "The best new work in the past few years has been neither painting nor sculpture."[71] In contrast to Fried's sublation of "space—if it still makes sense to call it space," Judd maintained: "Almost all paintings are spatial in one way or another. Yves Klein's blue paintings are the only ones that are unspatial, and there is little that is nearly unspatial, mainly Stella's work. It's possible that not much can be done with both an upright rectangular plane and an absence of space."[72] Judd suggests that artists should embrace space, engage architecture, and reject painting:

> Three dimensions are real space. That gets rid of the problem of illusionism and of literal space, space in and around marks and colors—which is riddance of one of the salient and most objectionable relics of European art. The several limits of painting are no longer present. A work can be as powerful as it can be thought to be. Actual space is intrinsically more powerful and specific than paint on a flat surface. Obviously, anything in three dimensions can be any shape, regular or irregular, and can have any relation to the wall, floor, ceiling, room, rooms, or exterior or none at all.[73]

Acutely aware of the threat to modernism posed by Morris's and Judd's work, Fried's aim was to undermine the appeal of its improprieties. Unlike Greenberg, he did not dismiss the new sculpture as simply non-art, but saw it as a devious reconfiguration of the terms of modernist criticism. As he writes in "Art and Objecthood," the new artists' "seriousness is vouched for by the fact that it is in relation to both modernist painting and modernist sculpture that literalist art defines or locates the position it seeks to occupy" (12). In the first half of the essay, Fried constructs a coherent and explicit polemic from the scattered writings of Judd, Morris, and Smith, ignoring their differences as well as the specific contexts of their remarks.[74] Fried saw the need to construct his version of the literalist position not primarily because he was interested in contesting it, but because he recognized that in order to extend Greenberg's discourse he needed to offer more than a revised notion of modernist painting; he also needed to conceive that revision in such a way as to extend its implications to sculpture.

Following Greenberg's notion of a "strict and radical separation of the art" while also insisting on the inseparability of the pictorial and the aesthetic, Fried insists that "the concepts of quality and value—and to the extent that these are central to art, the concept of art itself—are meaningful, or wholly meaningful, only within the individual arts" ("Art and Objecthood," 21). Both Fried and Greenberg repress architecture's role in sustaining the conditions of the pictorial, but Fried's more consistent formulation constructs an implicit characterization of architecture not just as a problem or agent of confusion (as in Greenberg's criticism) but as a diametrically opposed medium. Architecture is necessarily identified with theatricality and literalism in Fried's polemic and is thus itself inevitably "between the arts" and "corrupt." In Fried's version of modernism, architecture is, quite simply, not an "art" but an "object." This gives new significance to Fried's claim in "Art and Objecthood" that literalism is "a response to the *same* developments that have compelled modernist painting to undo its objecthood—more precisely, the same developments *seen differently*" (20). Those developments, Fried claims, reached a critical juncture "around 1960" when "the risk, even the possibility, of seeing works of art as *nothing* more than objects" emerged: "modernist painting has come to find it imperative that it defeat or suspend its own objecthood, and that the crucial factor in this undertaking is shape, but shape that must belong to *painting*—it must be pictorial, not, or not merely, literal" (12, 15).

This attempt to contrast the role of shape in the literalist sensibility with its role in modernist painting first emerged in "Shape as Form" and was reformulated in "Art and Objecthood" as an attack on the literalists, not simply because their use of shape is literal (as Fried argues in "Shape as Form"), but because it advances a fraudulent (unconvincing) projection of shape *as objecthood.* As Fried explains in "Art and Objecthood," "For both Judd and Morris ... the critical factor is shape.... The shape *is* the object: at any rate, what secures the wholeness of the object is the singleness of its shape" (12).

About two-thirds of the way through "Art and Objecthood," as Fried's argument reaches its crescendo, architecture emerges in an explicit way for the first time.[75] Moving beyond the general assertion that "the experience of literalist art is of an object in a situation," he claims that, ultimately, it is "as though the object is needed only within a room (or perhaps in any circumstance less extreme [than an abandoned or empty area]" (19). In a footnote remarking on his use of the word "room" (a term that had also appeared earlier in the essay in a quotation of Morris), Fried reveals his aversion to architecture: "The concept of a room is, most clandestinely, important to literalist art and theory. In fact, it can often be substituted for the word 'space' in the latter: something is said to be in my space if it is in the same *room* with me (and if it is placed so that I can hardly fail to notice it)" (23).

In constructing his argument around an opposition between the words "space" and "room," Fried himself "fails to notice" the dialectical and historical relationship between the rise of the art "object" and the modern art gallery and art museum: that is, a specific genre of architecture that Brian O'Doherty later allegorized as "the white cube."[76] Only with the emergence of the white-walled, bare, high-ceilinged art gallery as a common type of "room" could modernist painting and sculpture maintain the myth of autonomy. Of course this is a well-known dialectic, yet it was not architects but the literalists who explicitly scrutinized and confronted the question of autonomy in their work, and thereby the dominance (even the tyranny) of pictorial aesthetic values and Kantian modes of reception.

But in some cases the literalists were also wary of architecture.[77] For example, Fried quotes Morris's expression of the desire to avoid any confusion between the literal, spatial, and temporal qualities of sculpture and those same qualities of architecture. While Morris explained that "one's awareness of oneself existing in the same space as the work" requires acknowledging "the space of the room," he was quick to add that this "does not mean that an environmental situation is being established" (see fig. 2.17). To drive home that point, Morris claims: "Ideally, it is a space without architecture as a background and reference" which would be the best for his sculpture. Thus he seems to fall into the same trap as Fried, who is quick to identify the contradiction in his opponent's position: "Unless the pieces are set down in a wholly natural context, and Morris does not seem to be advocating this, some sort of artificial but not quite architectural setting must be constructed" (20).[78]

This "artificial but not quite architectural setting" is precisely what Fried means by the word "theater," which is clear in his contention that there is an inverse relationship between art and theater: "the more effective—meaning effective as *theater*—the setting is made, the more superfluous the works themselves become" (20). In other words, in "Art and Objecthood" Fried has identified a continuum leading from the "presence" of the "object" to its involvement in its architectural context, a slippery slope toward theatricality that threatens the autonomy of art.

But why doesn't Fried go all the way past "theater" and address the literalism of architecture? How can he profess alarm at "theater's profound hostility to the arts" and not recognize that his argument leads ultimately to a confrontation with architecture? Clearly, if objecthood is not defeated, art must recognize its "presence" in a "situation," and such a recognition, if taken to an extreme, leads to the dominance of architecture—as exemplified in Fried's fear of what might happen if "the concept of a room" were to replace the implicitly abstract modernist concept of "space." In his brilliantly oblique manner, Fried ends up where Greenberg found himself in the late fifties. Both confronted the fact that any assertion of literalness is a corruption of autonomy in which architecture necessarily emerges and ultimately threatens the sanctity of the optical

3.11 Anthony Caro, *Deep Body Blue*, 1967. Painted steel, 58.5 × 101 × 124 in.

3.12 Robert Morris, *Untitled* ("L's"), 1965. Painted plywood, each 96 × 96 × 24 in.

basis of modernism. The war Fried declared was defensive, and "art," as he conceived it, would survive this war only by dominating, or defeating, architecture.[79]

Fried directly addresses the connection between architecture and literalness in the two essays on Caro published in 1968 and 1970. Both begin by making analogies between architecture and Caro's work, but advance arguments for how Caro defeats any architectural implications (specifically, of "scale" or "entry") by addressing them in "abstract" terms. "Two Sculptures by Anthony Caro" opens with a description of *Deep Body Blue* as "open as wide-spread arms and then as a door is open" (fig. 3.11). The "arms" (two long steel elements on the floor) "*gather* the beholder into a far more compelling embrace than could be achieved by literally embracing him—the way, for example, one is embraced by Bernini's colonnades in front of St. Peter's" or the way one is confronted by literalist sculpture (fig. 3.12).[80] Having thus compared and contrasted the sculpture with architecture in two analogies, Fried spends the remainder of the article rendering the work "radically abstract."

In "Caro's Abstractness," Fried applies his notion of abstractness to the issue of scale. Fried discusses Caro's table sculptures, and claims that "by tabling, or precluding grounding, … Caro was able to establish their smallness in terms that proved virtually independent of actual size."[81] Thus, in describing Caro's *Deep North,* Fried is able to argue that it

> allows, but does not compel, the beholder to position himself beneath it.… Even when we place ourselves beneath the massive grid we do not feel that we have entered or that we are inside the sculpture.… None of this is to deny that an apprehension of the grid as overhead, as a kind of roof or ceiling under which we can stand, dominates our experience of the sculpture as a whole. What must be insisted upon is that this is true whether or not we choose to station ourselves beneath the grid: it is a function, not of any literal or architectural relationship between structure and beholder, but of the internal relations (or syntax) of the sculpture alone, relations which are deeply grounded in the nature and potentialities of the human body.[82]

All of this reiterates (and, Fried would surely claim, defeats) the questions raised in an early essay, published in 1965 in the *Lugano Review,* where Fried addresses not the architectural character of the object, but the literal relationship between the object, the artist, the beholder, and the room in which it is produced or viewed. In "Anthony Caro and Kenneth Noland: Some Notes on Not Composing," Fried makes his first attempt (which he would later disavow) to compare the formal conventions of modernist painting and sculpture. Writing before his focus on shape occurs, Fried proposes that "both Caro's sculptures and Noland's paintings are not composed,"[83] but while Noland avoids composition through the exploration of "deductive structure" (a theory elaborated in *Three American Painters*), "Caro has no positive alternative to traditional composition."[84] Instead, Caro resists composition by preventing himself from stepping back from his work. Quoting Caro from a previously published interview, Fried notes that Caro insists on "working indoors in a restricted space," which prevents him from viewing his sculptures "from a distance." Thus he achieves what Fried calls "a point of *no* view."[85] Fried even suggests that "there are affinities I hope to explore between Caro's situation and Pollock's."[86] Presumably this comparison would extend beyond their similar choices to work in small spaces, on the floor, in a kind of active bodily sympathy with their work, to include a relationship between the blind spots achieved by Pollock's cutouts and the up-close visual relationship between surface, color, space, and shape in Caro's open sculptures. Yet, just as Fried shied away from the literalness of the cutting, so here he avoids seriously considering the literal obstacles to viewing imposed by "a restricted space," even as he suggests that "as beholder, one occupies (or ought to occupy) a position in relation to Caro's finished sculptures analogous to that occupied by Caro in relation to his work in progress."[87]

If the first overtly architectural moment in "Art and Objecthood" was Fried's mention of "rooms," the second (and less overt) is his description of objecthood as "not … entirely unlike … the silent presence of another *person*,"[88] an image that he derives from Cavell's assertion that by "emphasizing the experience of fraudulence and trust as essential to the experience of art, I am in effect claiming that the answer to the question 'What is art?' will in part be an answer which explains why it is we treat certain objects, or how we *can* treat certain objects, in ways normally reserved for treating persons."[89] But Fried so reconfigures this proposition that it has entirely different aesthetic implications than Cavell's *philosophical* point.

Furthering the notion of objecthood as "a kind of *stage* presence," Fried implies that the literalist object is thus both historically regressive and aesthetically illegitimate. It is regressive, for example, in its attitude toward scale. Using Tony Smith's six-foot steel cube *Die* as an example, Fried claims that literalist sculpture is no less than a "surrogate person—that is, a kind of *statue*." Further, its wholeness as well as its hollowness make it analogous to a human body and suggest a "latent or hidden naturalism, indeed anthropomorphism."[90]

This is Fried's version of Cavell's comparison of the ways we encounter works of art with the ways we treat "other persons" who, of course, are not objects, but subjects.[91] The deficiency of literalism, Fried implies, is that it objectifies this subjective relationship. Literalism, theatricality, or objecthood each "*distances* the beholder—not just physically but psychically. It is, one might say, precisely this distancing that *makes* the beholder a subject and the piece in question … an object."[92] In this way, Fried's new understanding of modernist sculpture, based in his notion of compositional "syntax," might be termed *analogous and abstract anthropomorphism.* As Fried wrote as early as 1963: "The three-dimensionality of sculpture corresponds to the phenomenological framework in which we exist, move, perceive, experience and communicate with others. The corporeality of sculpture, even at its most abstract, and our own corporeality, are the same."[93] In 1968 he would characterize this analogous condition in terms of "radical abstraction"[94] which, he claims, is "not a *denial* of our bodies and the world: it is the only way in which they can be saved for high art in our time."[95] Architecture plays a role in this discussion, if only negatively, to clarify the necessity for "art" to divest itself of any direct relationship to concerns that are traditionally proper to the architectural discipline: for example, spatial recession, scale, duration, literalism, theatricality, and, most important, objecthood—that is, not only a simple awareness of the physical "presence" of an artwork but, more important, awareness of the physical presence of one's own body in "beholding" the work of art.[96]

But Cavell proposes an entirely different relationship, one that is not anthropomorphic but radically intersubjective in its skepticism—toward other persons, one's world, and works of art: the "truth" of those encounters is that identifying

> vanishes exactly with the effort to *make* it present.... How do we learn that what we need is not more knowledge but the willingness to forgo knowing? ... We think skepticism must mean that we cannot know the world exists, and hence that there isn't one (a conclusion some profess to admire and others to fear). Whereas what skepticism suggests is that since we cannot know the world exists, its presentness to us cannot be a function of knowing. The world is to be *accepted;* as the presentness of other minds [or an artwork] is not to be known, but acknowledged.[97]

The result of this condition, for Cavell, is that "survival" in any "modernist" practice "depends upon constantly eluding, and constantly assembling, critical powers." As a consequence, modernist practices inevitably involve negotiating a triangulated discourse: "the oblique and shifting relations between an art, and its criticism, and philosophy."[98] Therefore, contrary to Fried's denunciations, the literalists are in fact modernists in Cavell's sense, precisely because they venture impropriety in their work and their writings. By adapting architectural concepts and devices in practice, criticism, and theory, the literalist legacy—including conceptual, performance, installation, and earthworks—challenges our understanding of art and at the same time plays a role in establishing new forms of discursive legitimacy. As Cavell makes explicit, "you often do not know which is on trial, the object or the viewer," and the only resolution of that ambivalence lies in building "trust," which is a very different thing from Fried's "conviction."[99] Fried constantly conceives of art as a matter of puritan faith, whereas Cavell insists it involves (literally) "coming to terms" with the "truth of skepticism."

Near the end of "Art and Objecthood," Fried remarks that to accept theatricality is to be swept up in the misguided belief that "the arts are sliding toward some kind of final, implosive, hugely desirable synthesis."[100] Cavell would likely point out that the forms of art driven by productive improprieties stand no danger of achieving "synthesis," and could in no way lead to a "final" condition. Rather, each of the various arts would interact as dependent disciplines endlessly deriving insight from the others by acknowledging precisely what Fried abhors: "the *inclusiveness* of [the] situation."[101] Yet the arts also bear the burden of asserting distinct identities. That is the legacy of literalism, a success achieved only by critically engaging specific aspects of architecture, and a legacy architects have only begun to recuperate.

Chapter 4

Non-sitely Windows: Robert Smithson's Architectural Criticism

In the early 1960s, a poignant and paradoxical image became almost a fixture of formalist discourse, in effect announcing a crisis, or at least a peculiar impasse, in modernist criteria and claims for transparency, advance, and accessibility. Critics as different as Colin Rowe, Clement Greenberg, Donald Judd, and Michael Fried each explored the formal irony of an empty framed surface, either a wall or a canvas.[1] Each offered an interpretation of a "blank" picture to support their divergent attitudes toward space, surface, materiality, vision, and anthropomorphism. Each attempted, with varying degrees of explicitness, to reinvent the Albertian trope of painting as a window in a wall by recombining that figure's three elements: window/wall/picture.[2]

A few years later, those concerns reached a simultaneously metaphorical and formal sublation, or translation, in the work and writings of Robert Smithson.[3] His attack on the formalist conventions of pictorial space, from Alberti to Fried, led him to propose versions of what he variously called "three dimensional physical perspective," "enantiomorphic perspective," or "crystalline and collapsible space."[4] Most important, Smithson arrived at his reconfiguration of formalism through an engagement with architecture, a transdisciplinary exchange that has largely been overlooked in the numerous accounts of his artwork, writings, and intellectual significance.[5]

Like many of the literalist artists in his circle, Smithson had been increasingly interested in architecture since the early 1960s.[6] Beginning with allusions in his earliest writings to curtain walls, movie houses, suburban developments, and "science-fiction-type architecture," through his subsequent curatorial and critical conflations of architecture and language, to his own quasi-architectural projects in 1969 and 1970—including *Partially Buried Woodshed,* the *Hotel Palenque* lecture, and his proposals for a "Cinema Cavern" and "dearchitectured" sites—Smithson's writing and then his work became increasingly involved with specifically architectural concerns. In the process, he not only devised a wholly original form of art—the non-site—but introduced new modes of *architectural* criticism.

Thus it is not a coincidence that Smithson emerged as a major figure in the New York art world at the same time as he participated in a unique architectural collaboration. More or less simultaneously, in the latter half of 1966, Smithson not only began a prolific, eighteen-month period of writing and staged his first one-man exhibition of sculpture, but on July 1 began what would be a one-year contract as an "artist-consultant" to Tippetts-Abbett-McCarthy-Stratton Engineers and Architects (TAMS), one of the firms responsible for the initial planning and design of the new Dallas–Fort Worth Airport.[7] The opportunity to work on the airport project came on June 17, 1966, when Smithson appeared at the Yale School of Art and Architecture in a symposium titled "Shaping the Environment: The Artist and the City."[8] Walther Prokosch, a partner at TAMS, was in the audience and approached Smithson about the possibility of working with his firm. As spelled out one month later in a letter of agreement from Prokosch, Smithson received $400 per month plus expenses for "rendering consultation and advice" and was expected to "be available from time to time for discussions with members of our staff [and] for field trips to the site."[9]

While the collaboration with TAMS was sporadic and something of a marketing ploy on the part of the architects, it seems nonetheless to have been a catalyst for Smithson's development. Smithson had begun to exhibit what he called his "mature" sculpture in 1966,[10] but the concerns of those and previous works—artificial materials, critiques of vision and perspective, crystalline forms, and the "new monumentality"—while implicitly architectural, do not explicitly engage the issues of site, scale, interior space, the basic conventions of architectural representation, or building elements and processes that would begin to characterize his thinking during and after his role as an artist-consultant. This period is bracketed by his two most famous essays: "Entropy and the New Monuments" (published in June 1966, the same month he met Prokosch) and "The Monuments of Passaic" (published in December 1967).[11] Smithson's imaginative understanding and increasing knowledge of architecture—whether of "the slurbs," Park Avenue, Central Park West, or the specific proposals he made for the Texas "air terminal site"—were fundamental to his reconfiguration, and evasion, of what he called "the rational categories of 'painting, sculpture and architecture.'" Smithson's work and writings trace an intensive effort to relate or combine incommensurable modes of representation—primarily perspective, photography, and mapping, but also an increasingly competent use of plans and occasionally sections—to portray spatial ideas that were specifically excluded or repressed in the then-dominant pictorial formalist discourse of Greenberg and Fried.

From the dooms of "modernism," something cries out for the Missing Dust, then fades into the printed word and photograph. The Dust is leaving us with "pop" art and Clement Greenberg's visual Puritanism. Soon there will be nothing to stand on except the webs of manufactured time warped among throbbing galaxies of space, space, and more space.
Robert Smithson, "The Iconography of Desolation" (1962)

Each of Smithson's first three published writings contains references to architecture. In May 1966, Smithson published "The Crystal Land" in *Harper's Bazaar*. Illustrated with a single photograph of one of his "mirrored crystal structures" of 1965 (fig. 4.1), the essay describes the suburban architecture, landscape, and infrastructure of New Jersey in terms of crystalline repetitions of form,[12] in a narrative that leads from his first encounter with Donald Judd's "pink-plexiglass box" of 1965 (which "suggested a giant crystal from another planet") to the artists' joint "excursion" with Nancy Holt and Julie Judd to New Jersey where "the entire landscape has a mineral presence. From the shiny chrome diners to glass windows of shopping centers, a sense of the crystalline prevails."[13] Acting out what could be described as a version of Dalí's paranoid-critical method, Smithson encounters crystals everywhere, from the ice in his ice cream to the car radio's "row of five plastic buttons in the shape of cantilevered cubes," and finally in the "countless cream colored square tiles on the walls" of the Lincoln Tunnel as the four artists reentered New York City. Yet Smithson was on the lookout not only for the "abstract" architecture of "crystalline structures," but for ordinary buildings that caught his imagination, including "a gray factory" in the Great Notch Quarry that "looked like architecture designed by Robert Morris" and the New York City skyline and "high-tension towers" juxtaposed against the quarry's "cracked, broken, shattered" cliffs.

In various interviews, Smithson explained how "crystalline structures" inspired his first sculptures, and how later, during his work as an artist-consultant, that interest "gradually grew into" a

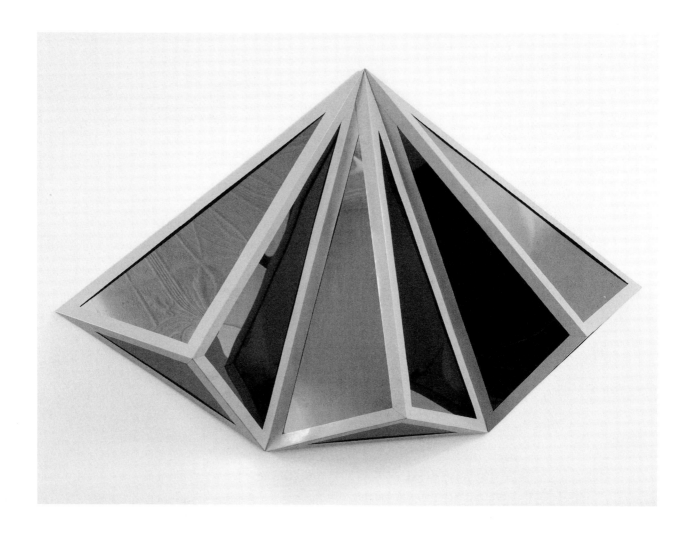

4.1 Robert Smithson, *Untitled* (mirrored crystal structure), 1963.
Painted metal and mirrored plastic, 50 × 40 × 18 in. © Estate of
Robert Smithson.

4.2 Robert Smithson, *Enantiomorphic Chambers,* 1964. Steel
and mirrors, each 34 × 34 × 34 in. © Estate of Robert Smithson.

concern with the crystal-like grids of cartographic "mapping structures."[14] In a 1969 interview, Smithson traced an autobiographical path from dealing with "the scale of a raw crystal" to "drawing lines and grids over the world" to the non-sites, which "return to the raw material where the abstract lattices and grids encompass the raw material."[15] Speaking in 1972 about his wall-mounted mirror sculpture of 1964, *Enantiomorphic Chambers* (fig. 4.2), he says: "I was dealing with grids and planes and empty surfaces. The crystalline forms suggested mapping…. In other words, if we think of an abstract painting, for instance, like Agnes Martin's, there's a certain kind of grid there that looks like a map without any countries in it…. So I began to see the grid as a kind of mental construct of physical matter, and my concern for the physical started to grow."[16]

However, it was only in retrospect that Smithson claimed to have begun to think in terms of abstract mapping systems *before* the airport project. Crystals did serve as the pretext of his earliest sculptures and published writings, but the interest in maps would come later, through his involvement with the airport project. Architecture had also emerged as a subtext in his thinking before his contract with TAMS. For example, one year before publication of "The Crystal Land," in a catalog essay on Donald Judd's work, Smithson described his friend's early "plywood and aluminum structures" as "Mannerist" manipulations of "matter" and "mass," and concluded: "By such means, Judd discovered a new kind of 'architecture,' yet his contrary methods make his 'architecture' look like it is built out of 'anti-matter.'"[17] That same year, in an artist's statement in the catalog of the art show at the American Express Pavilion at the New York World's Fair, Smithson struck a similar tone and suggested that his own plastic painting, *Quick Millions,* "might be an anti-parody of science-fiction-type architecture, or slippery forms and spaces, but I doubt it."[18]

Smithson's "doubt" may have been somewhat disingenuous, or at least intentionally ironic. "Entropy and the New Monuments," written only months later, begins with wry references to science-fiction architecture—this time with no disclaimer. The essay's opening sentence offers an intriguing assertion: "Many architectural concepts found in science-fiction have nothing to do with science or fiction, instead they suggest a new kind of monumentality which has much in common with the aims of some of today's artists."[19] An example appears in the article's epigraph (taken from Eric Temple Bell's science-fiction novel *The Time Stream*), which describes a desert filled with "thousands" of inscribed cylindrical monuments: "broad, low pillars" that formed "long parallel avenues." Further into the essay, Smithson offers several contemporary architectural images of the "new monumentality," including "the slurbs, urban sprawl, and the infinite number of housing developments," "the discount centers and cut-rate stores with their sterile facades," "the 'moderne' interior architecture of the new 'art-houses' like Cinema I and II," and the much denigrated architecture of Park Avenue known as "cold glass boxes," along with the Manneristic modernity of Philip Johnson. The Union Carbide building best typifies such architectural entropy. In its vast lobby … the sleek walls and high ceilings give the place an uncanny tomb-like atmosphere. There is something irresistible about such a place, something grand and empty. This kind of architecture without "value of qualities," is, if anything, a fact. From this "undistinguished" run of architecture, as Flavin calls it, we gain a clear perception of physical reality free from the general claims of "purity and idealism."[20]

Art is sometimes put in the lobbies of office buildings.... Everybody loves the Seagram Building and hates the Pan Am Building.
Robert Smithson, "Untitled (Site Data)" (1968)

To recuperate the architectural aspects of Smithson's work is also to revise the standard story, advanced in part by Smithson but especially by those who followed him—critics, artists, and landscape architects—which maintains that the primary importance of his work on the airport project is that it launched the practice known as earthworks. A different path can be traced, however, which reveals the intricate and specific architectural concerns that are fundamental to his art and his criticism. In six major essays[21] published in the eighteen-month period from just before until five months after his year as an artist-consultant, Smithson reconceived the representational and spatial possibilities of the Albertian trope as both *an aesthetic figure and an architectural problem.*[22] He had begun this pursuit as early as 1964 with the "split and reversed vanishing point"[23] of his *Enantiomorphic Chambers;* it would culminate near the end of 1967 or in early 1968 with his invention of the non-site—a composite artwork that he described as "a three dimensional logical picture that is *abstract,* yet *represents* an actual site" (fig. 4.3).[24] Smithson acknowledged that the non-sites were a direct outgrowth of his involvement in the airport project and, more specifically, his concern with the design of the terminal *building:*

> I was interested in capturing the sense of expanse and remoteness outside of the room space. The experience of my work had to take place both indoors and outdoors. I got interested in the earthworks as a result of that airport project. The non-sites came as a result of my thinking about putting large-scale earthworks out on the edge of the airfield, and then I thought, how can I transmit that into the center? The terminal was there, yet there was no evidence of these things out there, so I thought of putting television out there and transmitting these things back in, and telescopes. That became a kind of miniature

4.3 Robert Smithson, *Non-Site,* Oberhausen, Germany, 1968.
Steel, slag, maps with photographs.

universe, that sort of fit into my concerns of mapping. And the converging lines, the polar-ities led into an interest in three-dimensional physical perspective.[25]

The non-sites (all produced in 1968) are Smithson's most elegant and complex version of a re-configured formalism. Each non-site "represents" an actual site in a "backwater" or "fringe" area, and consists of three parts: documents (maps, photographs, descriptive text) of the site; mineral samples (sand, rocks, slag) from the site; and a fabricated, compartmentalized bin that "contains" the samples and functions as an index of their position on the site. First, Smithson selected an actual site, based on his own recollections and supplemented by geographical and geological research; he then traveled to the site, gathered the samples, and placed them in the bin. Finally, the documents, the bin, and the samples would be installed in an otherwise empty gallery on both the wall and the floor.[26]

The name "non-site"—like the title of Smithson's recently published 1967 essay, "The Artist as Site-Seer"—uses the term "site" as the double of "sight" (that is, the pure visuality that in Green-berg's and Fried's criticism ultimately entails the complete erasure of architecture's efficacy and effects). In another recently published text, "A Provisional Theory of Non-Sites" (written in 1968), Smithson explains that he considers his non-sites as an alternative to the pictorial tradition and describes his work in terms of a shift to the production and construction of "logical pictures": "By drawing a diagram, a ground plan of a house, a street plan to the location of a site, or a topo-graphic map, one draws a 'logical two dimensional picture.'"[27] A logical picture "differs from a nat-ural or realistic picture in that it rarely looks like the thing it stands for. It is a two-dimensional analogy or metaphor—A is Z." The non-sites extend this application of technique into the third dimension and can be understood as a reconfigured "window" that is both vertical and horizon-tal, more a map than a picture, more material than visual, more diagrammatic than pictorial, and as architectural as it is sculptural. Smithson's interest in the window is not simply as a metaphor for a picture, but as a literal "architectural detail" which, if also understood *abstractly* as a (non) site, potentially combines line and letter, text and image, space and time, art and architecture, art and criticism into a kind of "building." Thinking in architectural terms allowed Smithson to evade not only the limitations of the medium of painting, but also what he saw as the reduction of space in pictorial art to a perceptual phenomenon. Persistently critical of the understanding of space that he discerned in Greenberg's criticism (one in which space is "represented" visually through pictorial illusion), Smithson suggested that space in the non-sites is a matter of linguistic and formal structures or, more provocatively, a structure of linguistic and formal *matter*. The window-structure of the non-site invokes perspective, but it is not pictorial. Rather, it is "a three dimen-sional picture which doesn't look like a picture."[28] Whereas a pictorial window—for Alberti as well as Greenberg—connects an "inside" with an "outside" through the devices of perspective, framing, and/or flatness,[29] the non-site provides a more specific, and more abstract, connection between the "outskirts" (the actual site) and the "interior" (the gallery) (figs. 4.4, 4.5).[30] Smithson explained: "In a sense, my non-sites are rooms within rooms."[31] In other words, the non-site is involved in a dialectic with the actual site that it documents, indexes, samples, and contains: "There's a central focus point which is the non-site; the site is the unfocused fringe where your mind loses its boundaries and a sense of the oceanic pervades, as it were.... This is a map that will take you somewhere, but when you get there you really won't know where you are. In a sense the non-site is the center of the system, and the site itself is the fringe or edge."[32]

Smithson began to think of space in this way early in his involvement in the design of the Dallas–Forth Worth air terminal building:

> The terminal complex might include a gallery (or aerial museum) that would provide visual information about where these aerial sites are situated. Diagrams, maps, photographs, and movies of the projects under construction could be exhibited—thus the terminal complex and its entire airfield site would expand its meaning from the central spaces of the terminal itself to the edges of the air fields.[33]

Clearly, the conceptual apparatus for the non-sites emerged while working on the airport project. But the non-sites also achieve an aspiration Smithson had articulated as early as 1965. In a brief explanation of his plastic crystal sculptures, or as he called them, "mirrored crystal structures," Smithson claimed: "The commonplace is transformed into a labyrinth of non-objective abstractions."[34] Three years later Smithson would make a similar claim for the non-sites, but in a less enigmatic and more sophisticated form, explaining that the dialectic of site and non-site produces "a space of metaphorical significance. It could be that 'travel' in this space is a vast metaphor. Everything between the two sites could become physical metaphorical material devoid of natural meanings and realistic assumptions."[35] In other words, Smithson conceived of the space of the non-sites as "fictional," and opposed it to the "natural," "realistic," and "mythical" space of pictorial art.[36] The same could be said of his criticism, which not only was full of references to science fiction but mimicked its narrative modes. In essays such as "The Crystal Land," "The Iconography of Desolation," and "The Shape and the Future of Memory," he attempted to construct a kind of fictional space by combining diverse cultural references—skylines and quarries, factories and sculpture, the museum and the strip—and by assembling seemingly unconnected technical terms, statistics, religious symbols, literary references, quotations, and popular images.[37] In this way Smithson could make literal connections across assumed or familiar categories of information to portray a surprisingly encompassing and strange fictive world.

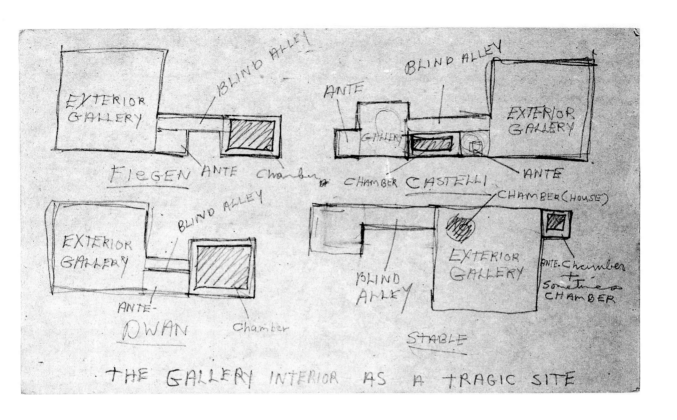

4.4 Robert Smithson, *Gallery Interior as a Tragic Site,* c. 1966.
Pencil on cardboard, 8 × 14 in. © Estate of Robert Smithson.

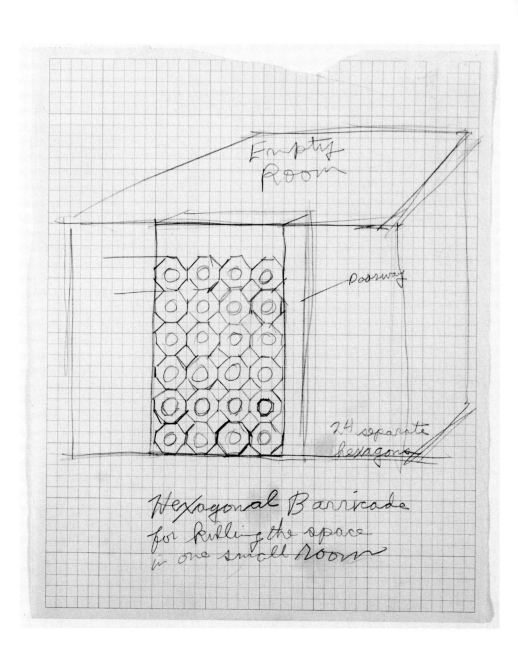

4.5 Robert Smithson, *Hexagonal Barricade for Killing the Space in One Small Room*, n.d. Pencil on graph paper, 8 × 10 in. © Estate of Robert Smithson.

Architecture appears constantly in those early writings, but his criticism would first become literally window-like several months after he began working as an artist-consultant. "Quasi-Infinities and the Waning of Space," published in November 1966, consists of four carefully designed pages (fig. 4.6).[38] In the center of each is a framed "block of print." The main text scrolls through those four blocks, with the footnotes to that text and various epigraphs appearing as smaller (usually unframed) blocks in the "ultramundane margins": the intermediate (fringe) zone between the central blocks and the edges of the page. These notes and epigraphs range from conventional annotations to photographs ("reproduced reproductions") and mathematical ratios ("indeterminate information"), all of which operate as windows not only to the outside of the article (like all footnotes), but also to its inside—the central blocks of print—by offering partial views and "glances" into Smithson's often opaque text.[39] The page becomes a kind of bin, containing visual and textual samples and operating as a fictional index of fictive space. Smithson's interest in architecture is obvious in the first few footnotes of "Quasi-Infinities," which include architectural drawings and small photographs of buildings or parts of buildings.[40] But the significance of the essay lies as much in its graphic architecture of quasi-windows as in the meanings of its images and words.

"Quasi-Infinities" predates Leo Steinberg's lecture at the Museum of Modern Art on his notion of "the flatbed picture plane" by only four months. Using Rauschenberg and Warhol as examples, Steinberg theorized the flatbed as a new mode of representation based on the printing press that abandons the humanist implications (sight) of the Albertian picture on the wall as a kind of "window" opposite our bodies that offers views of *nature*. It is replaced with a horizontal "bed" that receives reproduced *cultural* images and information (site). Steinberg's ultimate claim is that the flatbed announces a "radical shift in the subject matter of art, the shift from nature to culture," an idea with numerous affinities to Smithson's thinking and practices. Not only did both write their criticism in explicit opposition to Greenberg's notion of modernism, but Steinberg offers some very Smithsonian examples to illustrate his position.

Steinberg argues that prior to modernist abstraction and the emphasis on the flatness of the canvas, the humanist picture represented the world as an interior space in which one might "juxtapose a doorway or window view with a framed painting, and next to that, a mirror filled with reflection. These three kinds of image serve as an inventory of the three possible roles assignable to the [vertical] picture plane."[41] Each produces a distinct type of space: one exists behind the picture plane, the second is integral to it, and the third appears before it. The modernist notion of painting has limited what were once three possibilities to just one, and has banished the representation of a world from among painting's aims. But Steinberg discerns a return of the world on the flatbed picture plane, arguing that "post-Modernist" artists have "invented ... a pictorial surface that let[s] the world in again. Not the world of the renaissance man who looked for the weather out of the window; but the world of men who turn knobs to hear a taped message, 'precipitation probability ten percent tonight,' electronically transmitted from some windowless booth."[42]

Smithson's "Quasi-Infinities" exemplifies Steinberg's model, not by being windowless but by treating the printed page as a peculiar kind of window or, perhaps, even a hyperwindow not unlike the relatively recent conventions established for the computer screen (which Smithson would certainly be excited to learn now takes its typical form as a flat liquid crystal display). As "printed-matter,"[43] Smithson's criticism is unabashed about its status as a flatbed picture plane. But it also constructs an extreme abstraction and invites a radical spatial confusion: it is an attempt to portray "visual time" and to configure "mixed media." Smithson deploys a radically different pictorial logic, but in this case it is a radically different pictorial logic of the essay.[44] As an implicit window, "Quasi-Infinities" is one of the first instances of a particular kind of architectural criticism that is not simply about architecture but is implicitly architectural in its media, its content, its siting, and its form.

All language becomes an alphabet of sites, or it becomes what we will call the air terminal between Dallas and Fort Worth.
Robert Smithson, "Towards the Development of an Air Terminal Site" (1967)

Eight months after publication of "Quasi-Infinities," in the same issue of *Artforum* as Fried's "Art and Objecthood," Smithson published "Towards the Development of an Air Terminal Site," the first of two significantly different articles in art magazines recounting his role as an artist-consultant. In his later, much shorter article, "Aerial Art" (1969), Smithson's account is more descriptive than in the earlier essay, which by comparison seems a rambling and eclectic collection of ideas. But if understood in terms of the kinds of textual combinations that are made so explicit by the graphic structure of "Quasi-Infinities," the seemingly awkward writing and idiosyncratic illustrations in "Towards the Development" begin to structure an intricately interrelated context for Smithson's startling and ambitious remarks (which might otherwise be dismissed as hyperbolic metaphors). The most significant of those remarks is his statement of an "aim" as an artist and a writer "to reconstruct a new type of 'building' into a whole that engenders new meanings." An awareness of Smithson's fictive modes allows an understanding that he is proposing a general approach—"building"—that, conceivably, could be applied equally to art, architecture, or criticism: "What is needed is an esthetic method that brings together anthropology and linguistics in terms of 'buildings.' … Art at the present is confined by a dated notion, namely 'art as a criticism

Quasi-Infinities and the Waning of Space

1 The Amiens Labyrinth
(France)

2 Built for Fabricus at the
University of Padua

For many artists the universe is expanding; for some it is contracting.

By
ROBERT SMITHSON

AROUND FOUR BLOCKS of print I shall postulate four ultramundane margins that shall contain indeterminate information as well as reproduced reproductions. The first obstacle shall be a labyrinth[1], through which the mind will pass in an instant, thus eliminating the spatial problem. The next encounter is an abysmal anatomy theatre[2]. Quickly the mind will pass over this dizzying height. Here the pages of time are paper thin, even when it comes to a pyramid[3]. The center of this pyramid is everywhere and nowhere. From this center one may see the Tower of Babel[4], Kepler's universe[6], or a building by the architect Ledoux[6]. To formulate a general theory of this inconceivable system would not solve its symmetrical perplexities. Ready to trap the mind is one of an infinite number of "cities of the future"[7], Inutile codes[8] and extravagant experiments[9] adumbrate the "absolute" abstraction[10]. One becomes aware of what T. E. Hulme called "the fringe . . . the cold walks . . . that lead nowhere."

In Ad Reinhardt's "Twelve Rules for a New Academy" we find the statement, "The present is the future of the past, and the past of the future." The dim surface sections within the confines of Reinhardt's standard (60" x 60") "paintings" disclose faint squares of time. Time, as a colorless intersection, is absorbed almost imperceptibly into one's consciousness. Each painting is at once both memory and forgetfulness, a paradox of darkening time. The lines of his grids are barely visible; they waver between the future and the past.

George Kubler, like Ad Reinhardt, seems concerned with "weak signals" from "the void." Beginnings and endings are projected into the present as hazy planes of "actuality." In *The Shape of Time; Remarks on the History of Things*, Kubler says, "Actuality is . . . the interchronic pause when nothing is happening. It is the void between events." Reinhardt seems obsessed by this "void," so much that he has attempted to give it a concrete shape—a shape that evades shape. Here one finds no allusion to "duration," but an interval without any suggestion of "life or death." This is a coherent portion of a hidden infinity. The future criss-crosses the past as an unobtainable present. Time vanishes into a perpetual sameness.

Most notions of time (Progress, Evolution, Avant-garde) are put in terms of biology. Analogies are drawn between organic biology and technology; the nervous system is extended into electronics, and the muscular

3 The Pyramid of Meidum

4 The Tower of Babel

5 Kepler's model of the universe

6 Claude-Nicolas Ledoux
(1736-1806)

10 Ad Reinhardt installation
(March 1965) Betty Parsons
Gallery

9 From Edgar Allan Poe's
Eureka

```
        0
        0   0
        1   0
        1   1
    2   2       2
    0   1   2   0
    3   3       3   3
    3       2       3
4   4   4       4   4
0   1   2       3   4
```

8 A. *Discrete Scheme Without
Memory* by Dan Graham

```
HGFEDCBA
GHFEDCBA
FGHEDCBA
EFGHDCBA
DEFGHBA
CDEFGHBA
BCDEFGHA
ABCDEFGH
```

B. Non-code based on *The
Ars Magna* of Ramon Lull

7 "City of the Future"

---

12 Plate probably drawn by
Spigelius (1627?)

13 Willem deKooning

```
nowhere
,
η
nowhere,
,
,
),
the pleasure
nowhere.
let him go to sleep
η
```

John Cage: *Silence.*
Cambridge: M.I.T. Press

system is extended into mechanics. The workings of biology and technology belong not in the domain of art, but to the "useful" time of organic (active) duration, which is unconscious and mortal. Art mirrors the "actuality" that Kubler and Reinhardt are exploring. What is actual is apart from the continuous "actions" between birth and death. Action is not the motive of a Reinhardt painting. Whenever "action" does persist, it is unavailable or useless. In art, action is always becoming inertia, but this inertia has no ground to settle on except the mind, which is as empty as actual time.

THE ANATOMY OF EXPRESSIONISM[1]

The study of anatomy since the Renaissance lead to a notion of art in terms of biology[2]. Although anatomy is rarely taught in our art schools, the metaphors of anatomical and biological science linger in the minds of some of our most abstract artists. In the paintings of both Willem deKooning[13] and Jackson Pollack[14], one may find traces of the biological metaphor[15], or what Lawrence Alloway called "biomorphism[16]." In architecture, most notably in the theories of Frank Lloyd Wright, the biological metaphor prevails[17]. Wright's idea of "the organic" had a powerful influence on both architects and artists. This in turn produced a nostalgia for the rural or rustic community or the pastoral setting, and as a result brought into aesthetics an anti-urban attitude. Wright's view of the city as a "cancer" or a "social disease" persists today in the minds of some of the most "formal" critics and critics. Abstract expressionism revealed this visceral condition, without any awareness of the role of the biological metaphor. Art is still for the most part thought to be "creative" or in Alloway's words "phases of seeding, sprouting, growing, loving, fighting, decaying, rebirth." The science of biology in this case, becomes "biological-fiction," and the problem of anatomy dissolves into an "organic mass." If this is so, then abstract-expressionism was a disintegration of "figure painting" or a decomposition of anthropomorphism. Impressionistic modes of art also suffer from this biological syndrome.

Kubler suggests that metaphors drawn from physical science rather than biological science would be more suitable for describing the condition of art. Biological science has since the nineteenth century infused in most people's minds an uncosncious faith in "creative evolu-

14 Jackson Pollack

B. Guggenheim Museum

4.6 Robert Smithson, opening spread of "Quasi-Infinities and the Waning of Space," *Arts Magazine*, 1966.

of earlier art.' … Criticism exists as *language* and nothing more."[45] One example of this approach involves the "problem" of the "actual meaning of an air terminal and how it relates to aircraft" which, when sited on the "enormous runways," turn "into 'buildings' for short spaces of time, [and] then these 'buildings' will disappear." Near the end of the article, Smithson examines the window as another example of such a "building": "The rational category of 'painting' was derived from the visual meaning of the word 'window' and then extended to mean 'wall.' The transparency of the window or wall as a clear 'surface' becomes diseased when the artist defines his art by the *word* 'painting' alone.… 'Painting' is not an *end*, but a *means,* therefore it is linguistically an out-of-date category."[46]

By making that explicit connection between painting and windows, Smithson implies that architecture, like art, is "confined by a dated notion"—the window in the wall as a kind of picture. Furthermore, it is significant that Smithson's rejection of painting is not primarily formal or aesthetic but "linguistic." For Smithson, it is "language problems" that prevent the integration of fields such as "art, engineering or architecture."[47] He was preoccupied with the effects of what he called "diseased words and outmoded criteria." Instead of accepting the categorical distinctions between painting, sculpture, and architecture, he chose to view such words as "linguistic details" and maintained that "without linguistic awareness there is no physical awareness," to which he added the Wittgensteinian axiom: "Usage precedes meaning." Wittgenstein is lurking in Smithson's attitude toward language, particularly in his conflation of architectural construction and the construction of meaning: "As one becomes aware of discrete usages, the syntax of esthetic communications discloses the relevant features of both 'building' and 'language.'"[48] Smithson's treatment of words as a kind of building material recalls the parable of the builders near the beginning of *Philosophical Investigations,*[49] and in some fairly general ways his critical approach is similar to Stanley Cavell's version of ordinary language philosophy.[50] All three writers arrive at surprising understandings of ordinary expressions and terms by manipulating seemingly obvious terms. As Cavell explained it, the philosophers of ordinary language (Wittgenstein, G. E. Moore, Gilbert Ryle, and J. L. Austin) asked "what meaning, or use" seemingly "ordinary questions" might have: "The surprising result was that their results were surprising."[51] Smithson seemingly extends the philosophical examination of ordinary language into an artistic use of ordinary artifacts, as though aiming to make art philosophical, to make philosophy literally an art, or to treat artifacts as "linguistic objects." Smithson's friend and dealer, Virginia Dwan, has said that he "had this— call it an uncanny ability to take the most mundane things and make them seem—well, make them seem fantastic and intensely exciting. Like the Golden Spike Motel, for example, that dumpy nowheresville kind of place with linoleum rugs and strange heaters up high on the wall.

To Bob, the Golden Spike was not just a dump, it was an adventure, a place of mystery, so strange and exciting one would swear he was in a science fiction world."[52]

This concern with finding "surprising results" in otherwise ordinary places (whether buildings or language) provides one way to understand Smithson's claim near the end of "Towards the Development of an Air Terminal Site" that painting is implicated in and perpetuates a "world-view [that] imitates that architectural detail—the window." By concluding his essay with a discussion of an "architectural detail," he reveals his interest in applying his "esthetic method" to architecture and demonstrates that he is not satisfied to merely subvert painting. Instead, he identifies a literal element of architecture as the "linguistic detail" that is most deeply infecting "the rational categories of 'painting, sculpture and architecture.'" Most important, it is an ordinary kind of contemporary architecture that inspires Smithson's alternative approach:

> The linguistic meaning of a "wall" or "window," when emptied of rational content, becomes surfaces, and lines. The most common type of window in the modern city is composed of simple grid system that holds panes of clear glass. The "glass wall" is a part of many standard stores and office buildings. By emphasizing the transparent glass we arrive at a total crystalline consciousness of structure, and avoid the clotted patchy naturalistic details of "painting." The organic shapes that painters put on the "canvas-pane" are eliminated and replaced by a consciousness that develops a new set of linguistic meanings and visual results.[53]

This enthusiasm for curtain wall buildings is a reprise of the passage published one year earlier in "Entropy and the New Monuments" in which Smithson wryly praised "the much denigrated architecture of Park Avenue known as 'cold glass boxes.'" But in "Towards the Development of an Air Terminal Site," Smithson not only praises these buildings but proposes that "the surfaces and lines" of curtain wall architecture offer a model for the new art: "'Sculpture,' when not figurative, also is conditioned by architectural details. Floors, walls, windows, and ceilings delimit the bounds of interior sculpture. Many new works of sculpture gain in scale by being *installed* in a vast room.... The walls of modern museums need not exist as walls, with diseased details [paintings] near or on them. Instead, the artist could define the interior as a total network of surfaces and lines."[54] An early draft of "Towards the Development of an Air Terminal Site" is more revealing. It shows how, at first, Smithson saw the window as something so mythical it should be avoided:

> The exact installation of art shows makes one conscious of the actual *walls* rather than any "portable walls" smeared with gas-like color. The actual walls establish a regular limit

that makes the art objects in the site highly distinctive. Through a precision of installation the art objects all but vanish.... This experience does not imitate any architectural detail like "windows" or "walls," but instead makes clear mental and material structures.... It is not the art object we apprehend but the entire site.... This means we do not want "windows" or "walls" in the air terminal. The window like the painting is a diseased detail that has a rational origin. The wall is an oversized version of both. We must see only surfaces and lines.[55]

But then, swerving from the reductive implications of "surfaces and lines," Smithson claims that compared to a painting, "any *actual* window is much better to look at—mainly because most of them are simple grid systems that hold surfaces of transparent glass. So that, even a window really isn't a window. A wall is in effect an opaque window. Thinking about windows evokes an infinite array of window meanings."[56]

Visiting a museum is a matter of going from void to void. Hallways lead the viewer to things once called "pictures" and "statues." Anachronisms hang and protrude from every angle. Themes without meaning press on the eye. Multifarious nothings permute into false windows (frames) that open up onto a verity of blanks.
Robert Smithson, "Some Void Thoughts on Museums" (1967)

The final paragraphs of "Towards the Development of an Air Terminal Site" are by far the most elaborate and explicit instance of Smithson's interest in windows, walls, and pictures. Yet from 1964 to 1968 in both his artwork and his criticism it is possible to trace several themes that involve a critique of "that architectural detail—the window." As early as 1964, Smithson began to pursue a recuperation of perspective not as a perceptual device but as a representational technique.[57] His *Enantiomorphic Chambers* was an attempt to construct "an external abstraction of the eyes" as if literally mapping and "entering the field of vision. It's like a set of eyes outside" of one's body.[58] His motive was to offer a "depersonalization" of sight (or, more enigmatically, to make an "actual structure of two alien eyes").[59] He wanted "to deal directly with the physiological factors of sight as a 'thing-in-itself'" separated from subjectivity as "a stereopticon kind of situation— artificial eyes—that ... establishes ... a point of departure not so much toward the idealistic notion of perception, but all the different breakdowns within perception.... I'm interested in zeroing in on those aspects of mental experience that somehow coincide with the physical world."[60]

In 1965 Smithson constructed several internally mirrored boxes, similar to fixed, table-height kaleidoscopes, each titled *Mirrored Vortex*. Either individually or in aligned sets, these prismatic objects (with three or four sides) produced a kind of *mise-en-abyme* as one gazed down into them and saw one's image reflected in facets to infinity. Other untitled pieces made of mirrorized Plexiglas in 1965 had the opposite structure. Like wall-mounted or prone crystals, these "mirrored crystal structures" produced a fragmented (but not a multiple) image which, if viewed as a unified image (like a painting or an object), would be disorienting in the extreme.[61] A 1964 drawing that depicts a triangular version of the *Mirrored Vortex* as well as two mirrorized Plexiglas sculptures includes annotations that make explicit connections to perspective (fig. 4.7). One of those Plexiglas pieces, made up of two tetrahedrons with a single shared axis of symmetry joined at their bases, is described as having a "double vanishing point—exists as a solid rever[s]al of traditional illusionistic perspective—infinity without space." At the top of the drawing, Smithson writes: "The entire room that the piece is in, is absorbed by the piece." There are also two other explicit connections to architecture in the drawing. Near the bottom of page, Smithson writes: "In the words of Jorge Luis Borges, I have set out 'to design that ungraspable architecture,'" and in the upper right-hand corner is a note that he is "working on a set of 24 blocks or slabs with mirrors on them, with these I can make an endless vari[e]ty of mazes, toy hotels, tiny corridors ect. [sic]."[62] *Cryosphere,* exhibited in 1966 in "Primary Structures," apparently is the result of that work with "blocks" and "slabs" (fig. 4.8). The most complex of his mirror boxes, *Cryosphere* consists of six identical "solid hexagonal modules," each with twelve mirrors. According to Smithson, there are also twelve "invisible" modules and thus "66 2/3% of the entire work is invisible." He invites his audience to "invent your sight as you look. Allow your eye to become an invention."[63]

By 1967, while still writing about and working with mirrors (and glass, but in ways that had more to do with using their reflective surfaces as a material and less to do with perspective),[64] Smithson would conceive and fabricate an entirely nonreflective and opaque fiberglass sculpture titled *Pointless Vanishing Point.* In this piece he seems to have achieved a condensation of the issues and problems of perspective and space that interested him, but without resorting to the interactive effects and didactic purposes of *Enantiomorphic Chambers* or the *Mirrored Vortex* pieces (figs. 4.9, 4.10). In a short contemporaneous essay (not published until 1978), Smithson traces an idiosyncratic set of connections between *Pointless Vanishing Point* and the work of 1964. He begins by characterizing art since Rembrandt (the painter who "spoiled the straight line") as having undergone a gradual loss of the "artificial factor of perspective."[65] In the remainder of the essay Smithson weaves a deliberate confusion of perspective technique with the facts of binocular vision, a conflation which he suggests has been the actual historical consequence of the ways perspective had mediated the logical conflicts between two modern conceptions of space: physiological (or "visual space") and artificial (or "surveyor's space").[66] Smithson explains that our "eyes do not see" the artificial space that the "surveyor imposes ... on the landscape ... and in

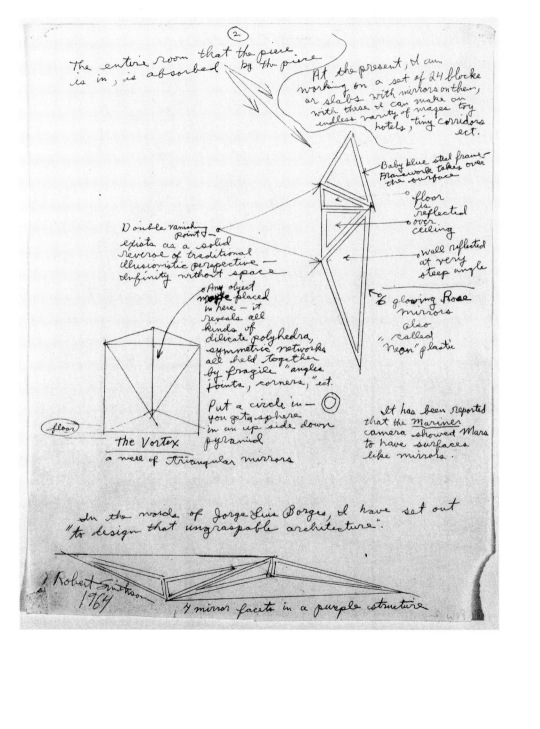

the entire room that the piece
is in, is absorbed by the piece

At the present, I am
working on a set of 24 blocks
or slabs with mirrors on them,
with these I can make an
endless variety of mazes toy
hotels, tiny corridors
ect.

Baby blue steel frame—
Framework takes over
the surface

○ floor
is
reflected
over
ceiling

Double vanishing
point — ○
exists as a solid
reverse of traditional
illusionistic perspective —
infinity without space

○ wall reflected
at very
steep angle

○ Any object
maybe placed
in here — it
reveals all
kinds of
dilicate polyhedra,
symmetric networks
all held together
by fragile "angles
joints, corners," ect.

⟵ glowing Rose
mirrors
also
called
"Neon" plastic

Put a circle in — ◎
you get a sphere
in an up side down
pyramid

It has been reported
that the Mariner
camera showed Mars
to have surfaces
like mirrors.

floor

the Vortex
a well of Triangular mirrors

In the words of Jorge Luis Borges, I have set out
"to design that ungraspable architecture".

Robert Smithson
1967

4 mirror facets in a purple structure

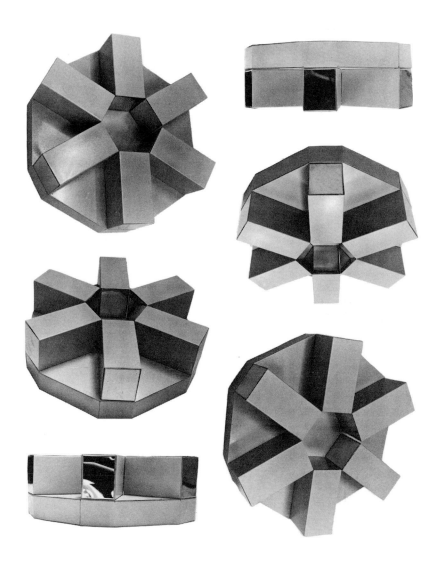

4.7 Robert Smithson, *Three Works in Metal and Plastic,* 1964. ink on typing paper, 8.5 × 11 in. © Estate of Robert Smithson.

4.8 Robert Smithson, *Cryosphere,* 1966. Painted metal, mirrors, each 17.25 × 17.25 × 6.5 in. © Estate of Robert Smithson.

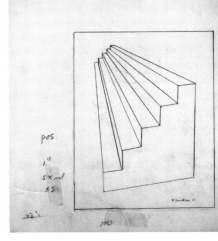

4.9 Robert Smithson, *Pointless Vanishing Point,* 1967. Fiberglass, 40 × 40 × 96 in. © Estate of Robert Smithson.

4.10 Robert Smithson, perspective drawing for *Pointless Vanishing Point,* 1967. Pencil on vellum, 12 × 12 in. © Estate of Robert Smithson.

effect produces perspective projections along the elevations he is mapping. In a very non-illusionistic sense he is constructing an illusion around himself because he is dealing directly with literal sense perceptions and turning them into mental conceptions."[67]

As a consequence of the naturalizing of perspective, the problems engendered by that conflation of two kinds of space tend to be overlooked, and now the act of seeing—which "is mainly three dimensional and dualistic in conception"—has become something that "is two dimensional and unitary." Further, "we tend to forget the actual stereoscopic structure of our two eyes or what I will call 'enantiomorphic vision'—that is seeing double." For Smithson, the virtue of what he calls "enantiomorphic perspective" is that it "negates any central vanishing point" and "abolish[es] the central fused image."[68] *Pointless Vanishing Point* achieves a different objective: rather than denying our habits of vision, it is a literal representation and condensation of conflicting spatial logics.[69]

These are just the most explicit examples that can be found in both Smithson's criticism and his artwork that emulate or operate as models (of various versions) of an abstract window, one that evades pictorialism while, at the same time, reconfiguring certain formal problems posed in Greenberg's and Fried's criticism, from the fundamental notion of the "canvas-support" to Fried's concepts of "deductive structure" and compositional "syntax."[70] One of Smithson's earliest essays ridicules "Clement Greenberg's visual Puritanism,"[71] and his notebooks as well as his published articles include numerous quotations from Greenberg's 1961 book *Art and Culture.*[72] "Quasi-Infinities" offers explicit criticism of Greenberg's "anthropomorphizing of space," and two of Smithson's recently published articles—"The Pathetic Fallacy in Aesthetics" and "What Really Spoils Michelangelo's Sculpture" (both written during the time of his work on the airport project)—are extended critiques of Greenberg and, to some extent, Fried. For example, in "The Pathetic Fallacy," Smithson writes: "All 'formal' criticism and art is based on representational space and its reduction. The latest 'formal advance' to come out of this 'reductive tendency' has to do with the 'framing support.' 'The picture-support,' as it is also called, is interesting as a critical mutation of Greenberg's space speculations, but should not be considered abstract by any stretch of the imagination. Yet, the dubious seriousness and pretended rigor of Fried's criticism tends to keep the 'space' myth going."[73]

Despite his constant and decisive dismissal of Fried and Greenberg, Smithson mentioned in a 1969 interview that he considered Fried "a more interesting adversary" than other writers of his generation.[74] In his 1968 essay "A Sedimentation of the Mind: Earth Projects," Smithson satirizes Fried's articles on the painter Jules Olitski, and suggests that both Fried and Olitski ("the artist or critic with a dank brain") have a predisposition toward "melting, dissolving, soaking surfaces that give the illusion at times of tending toward a gaseousness, atomization or fogginess. The watery syntax is at times related to the 'canvas support.'"[75] Here, as in his other writings, Smithson does not attempt to debate with Fried; rather, he offers a knowing evasion of pictorial formalism by promoting the seeming attraction to "dryness" that characterizes not only his non-sites but the work of his contemporaries for whom, he suggests, the "desert is less 'nature' than a concept" that has replaced the pastoral landscape as both a literal and metaphorical site for artworks.[76] The passage on Fried and Olitski in "A Sedimentation of the Mind" is one of the clearest examples of how Smithson's mode of criticism offers (dry) "fictions" as alternatives to the (fluid) "myths" on which more widely accepted interpretations such as Fried's are based.

To talk constantly "about seeing" is a linguistic problem not a visual problem. All abstract concepts are *blind*, because they do not refer back to anything that has already been seen. The "visual" has its origin in the enigma of blind order— which is in a word, *language*.[77]

Robert Smithson, "The Artist as Site-Seer; or, A Dintorphic Essay" (1966–67)

Both "Sedimentation of the Mind" and Smithson's numerous non-sites of the same year are "physical metaphorical material" and fictive forms that conflate building and language. Both can be seen as summations of the subjects and techniques that he explored in the period that began with the writing of "Entropy and the New Monuments" and ended with the publication of "The Monuments of Passaic," a time when Smithson's architectural thinking grew much more explicit, specific, and deep.[78] While the earlier essay exemplifies the "new monumentality" in terms of architectural *images,* the later not only identifies but represents and elaborates upon specific architectural forms and instances of the new monumentality by "fictionalizing" them. In the case of Passaic, its infrastructural[79] monuments were "made physical" by photographing and writing about them, thus enacting not only Smithson's often-stated conviction that language is a form of matter, but also his less-known and more elusive assertion that "photographs are the most extreme contraction" of matter.[80] Using black-and-white snapshots taken with his cheap Instamatic camera, Smithson illustrated a hybrid narrative—equal parts science fiction, anthropological reportage, and wry travelogue. In other words, in "Passaic" Smithson's fictive criticism achieves the kind of monumentality that he only alluded to in "Entropy and the New Monuments." However striking or lucid his architectural metaphors and images are in "Entropy," they do not become "physical" until after he begins to work with the architects and engineers on the Dallas–Fort Worth project.

Unfortunately, relatively little evidence—models, drawings, meeting notes—remains of Smithson's collaboration with Prokosch, but Smithson's early interest in the terminal building (as opposed to the airport site) is clear from the architects' account of their initial meeting when Smithson "indicated that [he] would probably wish to study the problem in [his] own studio in model form or otherwise."[81] In at least one interview Smithson recounts how initially

> [the] architect … asked me if I would participate in the building of the Dallas–Fort Worth Airport, in terms of trying to figure out what an airport is. They would provide me with all the mapping material, and we had interesting discussions. I made models of possible airports. But I became less and less interested in the actual structure of the building and more interested in the processes of the building and all the different preliminary engineering things, like the boring of holes to take earth samples.… So I was interested in the preliminary aspects of building.[82]

More important, two of the earliest drawings that remain from the collaboration are crude architectural drawings of the terminal (figs. 4.11, 4.12). Both show the central transportation axis unique to that airport's design: one is a plan drawn at the peculiar scale of 1" = 350' showing echelon-shaped terminals strung along the main axis, and the other is a section of a multistory ziggurat drawn on graph paper showing volumes dedicated to "cargo," "concourse," "check in," and "bag claim." But as the project developed, Smithson grew frustrated with what he saw as the burdensome amount of statistics and computer analyses involved in planning the huge project,[83] and he became more interested in the "mapping material"[84] that was provided to him by the architects. This led him to work on the airport site rather than the terminal building.[85]

In this shift of interest from the building to the site lies the opening for those who see Smithson's involvement in the Dallas–Fort Worth project primarily as the origin of earth art. It is true that his retrospective remarks do focus largely on site issues, and in several interviews Smithson explained that the airport experience was the time he "began formulating [his] ideas on earthworks" or that he "got interested in the earthworks as a result of that airport project."[86] Perhaps the most interesting example is the opening paragraph of "Aerial Art," which first refers to the relationship between sculpture and architecture but then slips into a landscape metaphor: "Art today is no longer an architectural afterthought, or an object to attach to a building after it is finished, but rather a total engagement with the building process from the ground up and the sky down. The old landscape of naturalism and realism is being replaced by a new landscape of abstraction and artifice."[87] But as Smithson proposed to "develop" it, this "new landscape" would include the terminal building at its center: the building would relate to the land around it (runways, perimeter fences, parking lots, and so on) in the same way as the non-sites related to their sites. Such a proposal, Smithson claims, "begins to shape an esthetic based on the *airport as an idea*":

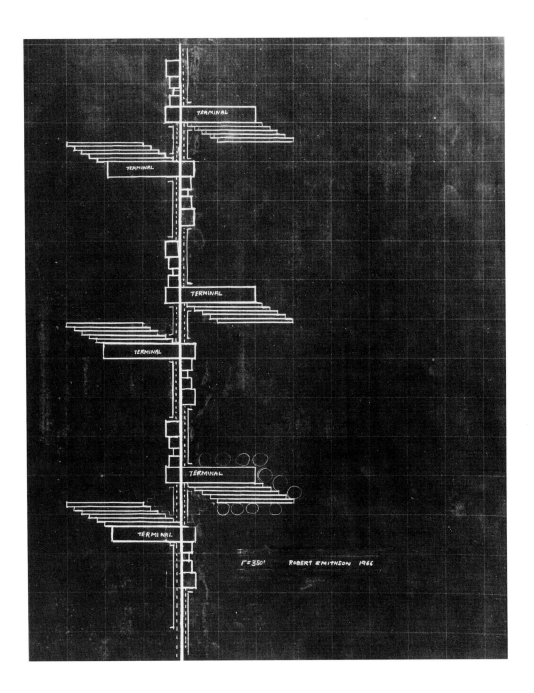

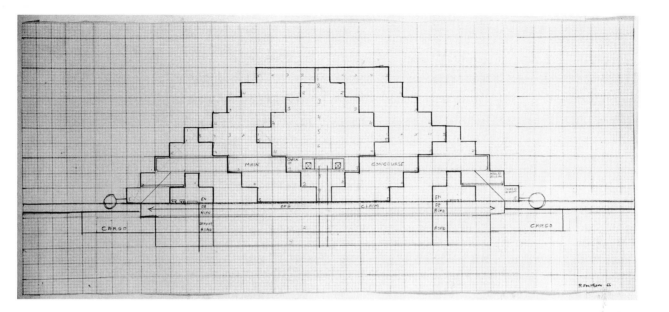

4.11 Robert Smithson, *Terminal: Plans for Dallas–Fort Worth Regional Airport*, 1966. Photostat, 17 × 12 in © Estate of Robert Smithson.

4.12 Robert Smithson, *Airport* (building section), 1966. Pencil, ink, and crayon on paper, 9 × 21 in. © Estate of Robert Smithson.

The straight lines of landing fields and runways bring into existence a perception of "perspective" that evades our conceptions of nature.... The landscape begins to look more like a three dimensional map than a rustic garden.... The rational structures of buildings disappear into irrational disguises and are pitched into optical illusions.... The terminal complex might include a gallery (or aerial museum) that would provide visual information about where these aerial sites are situated. Diagrams, maps, photographs, and movies of the projects under construction could be exhibited—thus the terminal complex and its entire airfield site would expand its meaning from the central spaces of the terminal itself to the edges of the air fields.[88]

Smithson used strikingly similar terms to describe the *Pine Barrens Non-site,* the hexagonal form of which is derived from three intersecting, unpaved, and nearly invisible runways at the center of its site:

Parallactic perspectives have introduced themselves into the new earth-projects in a way that is physical and three dimensional. This kind of convergence subverts gestalt surfaces and turns sites into vast illusions. The ground becomes a map. The map of my *Non-Site #1 (an indoor earthwork)* has three vanishing points that lose themselves in a pre-existent earth mound that is at the center of a hexagonal airfield in the Pine Barrens Plains of New Jersey.[89]

So, less than a year after his contract with TAMS was terminated, Smithson had proposed a "new type of building," but one that is an obvious inversion of the situation in Texas. Rather than the terminal containing the gallery (a room in a building), the terminal has been replaced by the non-site, which is installed in a gallery (a room within a room). Thus, whereas in "Towards the Development of an Air Terminal Site" the conflation of painting, sculpture, and architecture had been contained by "that architectural detail—the window," in "Aerial Art" the window is reconceived in terms of the non-site, which was itself a result of the collaboration on the airport project. "Language" is replaced by "three dimensional logical pictures" made up of "diagrams, maps, photographs, and movies"—that is, a more heterogeneous language that is both literal and abstract.

The architectural sources of the non-sites have been obscured by those who understand Smithson in relation to landscape and landscape painting. Eugenie Tsai, for example, makes no connections to the discipline of architecture, explaining instead that Smithson "grew familiar with aerial photographs, maps and models, and his involvement in the planning process heightened his awareness of potential ways to redefine ... the representation of landscape."[90] But Smithson's artwork and writing make clear that his increasing knowledge of aerial photographs, maps, and models and his involvement in the planning process enabled him to redefine the representation of *architecture:* that is, the peculiar conflation of abstraction and language, artifice and matter, sight and site that occurs in buildings as well as in the models, plans, sections, and other architectural representations that produce them.

Also instrumental in this autodidactic process is Smithson's effort to relate architecture and language. Influenced by writers such as Jorge Luis Borges and Roland Barthes, Smithson thought of writing as a kind of building. In turn, he began to think of artworks as a kind of architectural writing, an approach that becomes explicit during the time of the airport project. Smithson's familiarity with architectural processes and modes of representation clearly helped him to elaborate the terms of the architecture/language analogy, and ultimately contributed to his innovative reconfigurations of architectural concepts such as "site" and "window" in the non-sites and his later building projects. The architectural "precedent" that dominated Smithson's thinking was the Tower of Babel. His transmutation of that mythic image into a kind of "ruined" writing is exemplified by his essays, but is portrayed even more concisely in his famous 1966 drawing *A Heap of Language* (fig. 4.13). Drawn, or written, on graph paper, it arranges a list of 129 phrases and words in the form of a ziggurat with twenty levels, or lines. Each of those phrases and words "represents" an attitude toward the use of language as well as "signifies" building elements which, heaped together, form a monument. At the top of the heap is the word "Language"; at the bottom is a string of several words and phrases: "hieroglyphic neologic word coiner argot billingsgate pidgin English orthoepy terminology theosaurus [sic] cipher." This artwork can be understood in many ways: as a pyramid made of word-bricks (or, a labyrinth of babbling-bricks),[91] a foreshortened perspective of "Language," a geological fiction, or a "section" of a literal Tower of Babel which is at once a source and site of language as well as a commentary on the compacted nature of meaning.[92]

Smithson's commitment to the literal and material aspects of language would only increase over time. In June 1967, the month "Towards the Development of an Air Terminal Site" was published, he helped to curate a show at the Dwan Gallery titled "Language to Be Looked At and/or Things to Be Read."[93] In the press release (which he wrote "anonymously" under the pseudonym Eton Corrasable), Smithson aphoristically explains his interest not only in conflating writing and art, but also in the visual, the material, and the linguistic *in* art. "Here language is built not written.... The scale of a letter in a word changes one's visual meaning of a word. Language becomes monumental because of the mutations of advertising." An early draft is more explicit: "Artists don't write, they build with words."[94] Smithson reiterated his position five years later in a signed, handwritten note (dated June 2, 1972) at the bottom of a copy of that press release: "My sense of language is that it is matter and not ideas—i.e., 'printed matter.'"[95]

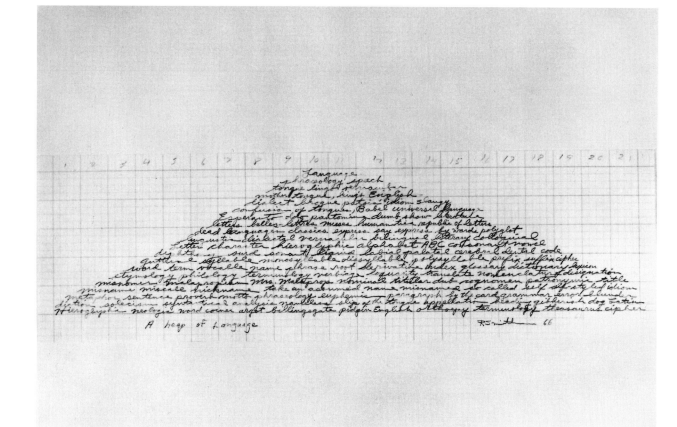

4.13 Robert Smithson, *A Heap of Language,* 1966. Pencil on paper, 6.5 × 22 in. © Estate of Robert Smithson.

A more elaborate example is the opening paragraph of his 1968 essay on the writings of other artists, "A Museum of Language in the Vicinity of Art," which pursues an elaborate mixed metaphor treating art criticism as a kind of linguistic labyrinth with "strange corridors of history" and "full of bottomless fictions and endless architectures and counter-architectures."[96] Smithson pictures criticism as "a mirror structure" with "dangerous stairways or words, a shaky edifice of fictions" where "language 'closes' rather than 'discloses' doors." The paragraph ends with a warning to the reader: "The entire article may be viewed as … a monstrous 'museum' constructed out of multi-faceted surfaces that refer, not to one subject but to many subjects within a single building of words—a brick = a word, a sentence = a room, a paragraph = a floor of rooms, etc. Or, *language becomes an infinite museum, whose center is everywhere and whose limits are nowhere.*"[97]

Smithson's collapsing of architecture and language makes it possible to understand that were it not for the physical and literal limitations of the various sites in which his work appeared—for example, the pages of magazines as opposed to the walls and floors of galleries—there would be no clear distinction between his uses of media in the criticism and in the artworks. An entry in a notebook (c. 1966) plays out this complexity:

A "magazine" is a place that remains unchanged even when distorted. Thin planes of pressed pulp form a stratum a little less than a 1/4 of an inch high. The left edge of the place is pierced normally by two wires, this in turn allows the place to be folded over, thus forming what looks like a stack of "paper" on the right edge. It is possible to mistake the stack for thin glass but this rarely happens. As is most often the case, one becomes accustomed to the "paper" because it is not breakable. Although, if this so-called "magazine" were to be made of metal, chances are someone would mistake it for a geological formation. They might even think of the "pictorial" matter as some sort of fossil. The top or cover for [the] most part is of many colors. Angles in the shape of abstract designs seem to spell out something, for instance in a red rectangle on a certain "magazine," in white marking one sees LIFE.[98]

In a short piece written in 1968, Smithson outlines a similar, explicitly architectural fiction in a rudimentary list of seven "Recent Site Developments," beginning with "the urban apartment" and including "the suburban house," "the art museum (modern)," and "the urban office building." Smithson explains his interest in these sites in a prefatory paragraph:

The following "site data" is an attempt to locate "structural" meanings by observing building sites within a kind of abstract anthropology. Each site should stand entirely as "the critical object at zero degree, a site empty but eternally open to signification." (Roland Barthes—*On Racine.*) How each site pertains to art shall be described according to its physical limits. The definitions are apparent rather than actual, or you might say "reconstructed appearances."[99]

Smithson's final category, "the industrial site," includes five subcategories of which the last is "air terminals." Unfortunately, while Smithson wrote paragraphs elaborating the first categories on the list, he did not complete notes for the last. But it is clear, even in the paragraph on the first category, that his passage on windows in "Towards the Development of an Air Terminal Site" would have been an appropriate conclusion:

> 1. *The urban apartment.* The room configuration is random and largely determined by pictures and windows. As a dwelling place it has its origin in the 19th century. Within this dwelling the occupant attempts to "live" according to the myth of individualism. He decorates it with memory traces of the 19th century notion of "nature" and "reason." For him "painting" is not a linguistic category but something personal, intimate, private. "Painting" is his false window that looks back to "impressionism."[100]

As the scare quotes suggest, what Smithson means by "impressionism" is not a style of painting. Rather, as he explained in various other fragments of writing, "impressionism" means nothing less than the entire ideology of pictorial art. Smithson first introduced his idiosyncratic definition of impressionism in his discussion of windows in "Towards the Development of an Air Terminal Site": "The impressionistic* world view imitates that architectural detail—the window. The rational category of 'painting' was derived from the visual meaning of the word 'window' and then extended to mean 'wall.'"[101] That Smithson expresses his contempt for "impressionism" not only in terms of an "architectural detail" but in the context of some of his most elaborate discussions of architecture reinforces the claim that his development from 1966 to 1968 should be understood as an explicit assimilation of normative aspects of architecture to devise new art forms, namely the non-site.

The Ultramoderne of the 'thirties transcends Modernist "historicistic" realism and naturalism, and avoids the avant-garde categories of "painting, sculpture and architecture."
Robert Smithson, "Ultramoderne" (1967)

In what is perhaps his most architecturally intense essay, "Ultramoderne," Smithson claims (and thus reveals his own aim as an artist) that "many builders in the 'thirties … transformed the window into an art form."[102] Over the summer of 1967, at the end of his contract as an artist-consultant and only months before he would produce his first non-sites, Smithson took the photographs for and wrote the text of a wild excursus on the art deco architecture of Central Park West (fig. 4.14). In the architecture of the thirties he sees the window, partnered with the mirror, as "a privileged post for site-seers of transmodernism." What Smithson terms the "ultraist view through the ultra window" is a reconfiguration of Steinberg's "inventory of the three possible roles assignable to the picture plane" (window/painting/mirror).[103] In effect, Smithson has applied his new "esthetic method" to the windows, mirrors, and brickwork of 1930s architecture. The ingenious details of those seemingly stylized buildings are not "diseased" but linguistically robust. In prose that seems almost to represent an epiphany, Smithson presents the "infinite array of window meanings" he had glimpsed somewhat earlier in curtain wall architecture. He suggests that the art deco architecture of the 1930s is actually more timely than Greenberg's notion of the avant-garde. In Smithson's words: "There are two types of time — organic (Modernist) and crystalline (Ultraist)." As in all his criticism, but perhaps in "Ultramoderne" more than anywhere, the most confusing issue is whether Smithson is explaining his own work or describing his favorite buildings:

> Unlike the realist or naturalist, the Ultraist does not … "make" history in order to impress those who believe in one history.… Repetition not originality is the object. It is not an accident that "the mirror" is one of the more widely used materials of the 'thirties, and that the facades of buildings contained countless variations of brickwork. Repetition and serial order run constantly through the buildings of that paradigmatic period.
>
> The window reminds us that we are captives of the room, by suggesting both flight and confinement. The ziggurated frameworks that contain certain windows show a keen awareness of the window — as a "thing in itself." This is the direct opposite of the International Style where the window has no meaning other than function. Form does not follow function in the Ultramoderne cosmos of fixity and facets. The corner window is a right-angled boundary that involves the idea of the double or a "split-window" from which there is no escape.
>
> The "window" and the "mirror" are secret sharers of the same elements. The window contains nothing, while the mirror contains everything. Consider them both, and you will find it impossible to escape their double identity. The "ultra-window" is a privileged post for those "site-seers" of trans-modernism. The window doubles as an open and closed space, and this is accentuated in many 'thirties buildings. Many builders in the 'thirties such as Helme, Corbett, Harrison, Sugarman and Burger transformed the "window" into an art form.[104]

4.14 Robert Smithson, negative photostat prints of snapshots for "Ultramoderne," 1967. Each 8.5 × 8.5 in. © Estate of Robert Smithson.

But we have to return to Dallas–Fort Worth to find the most direct evidence of Smithson's interest in windows. Of the thirteen drawings that remain from his work on the airport project, three—each dated 1967 and titled *Earth Window* or *Three Earth Windows*—depict in plan and section versions of a construction that would emit light through horizontal squares seemingly cut into the surface of the earth and filled with crushed glass (figs. 4.15–4.17). In *Three Earth Windows*, each square is a different size and composed of a different number of similar units, or panes. Nine, sixteen, and twenty-five smaller squares of glass are illuminated from below with stadium lights. Building on his new knowledge of construction processes, Smithson included concrete foundations in these drawings, including weep holes to drain the flat surface.

Another drawing shows his attempt to install his and others' proposals for the airport project for a 1967 exhibition (fig. 4.18). It is related to the earth windows and itself operates as a proto-non-site. Smithson's perspective depicts maps, objects, and drawings all deployed in a grid or in series on the floor, the wall, and what appears to be a mantle. In this way, Smithson has sited representations in the gallery and fictionalized them as three-dimensional "physical metaphorical material." Thus, by the end of 1967, on the verge of his invention of the non-site, Smithson had reached a point in his thinking and writing where he not only employed architecture in his work and his criticism, but built his work and criticism as a siting of architecture. Through his collaboration with architects on the airport project, Smithson's interest in and understanding of architecture—translated through his criticism and realized in his artwork—enabled him to devise entirely unprecedented modes of representation and a hybrid identity for the artist that would have been inconceivable without the architectural knowledge—from documents to monuments—that he gained as an artist-consultant.

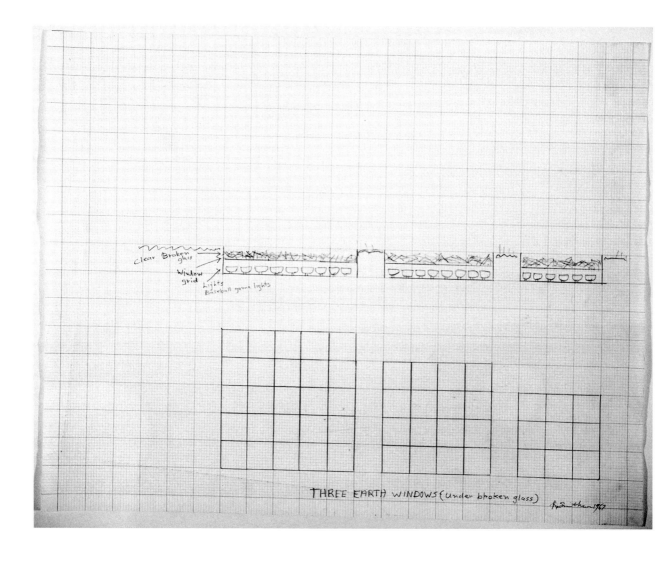

Clear Broken glass

Window grid
lights
Baseball game lights

THREE EARTH WINDOWS (under broken glass)   R Smithson 1967

4.15 Robert Smithson, *Three Earth Windows (under broken glass),* 1967. Pencil and ink on graph paper, 17 × 22 in. © Estate of Robert Smithson.

4.16 Robert Smithson, *Earth Window,* 1967. Pencil on paper, 24 × 19 in. © Estate of Robert Smithson.

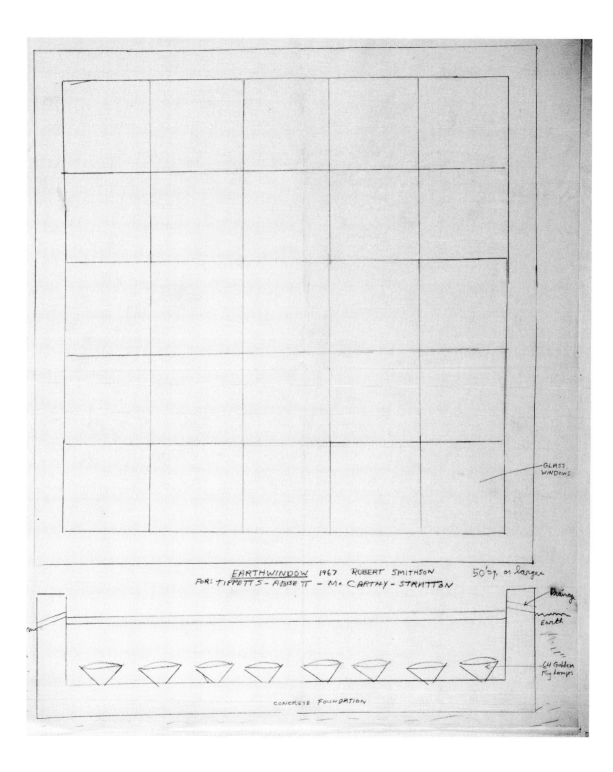

EARTHWINDOW 1967 ROBERT SMITHSON   50'sq. or larger
FOR: TIPPETTS - ABBETT - McCARTHY - STRATTON

GLASS
WINDOWS

Drainage

Earth

64 Golden
Fog Lamps

CONCRETE FOUNDATION

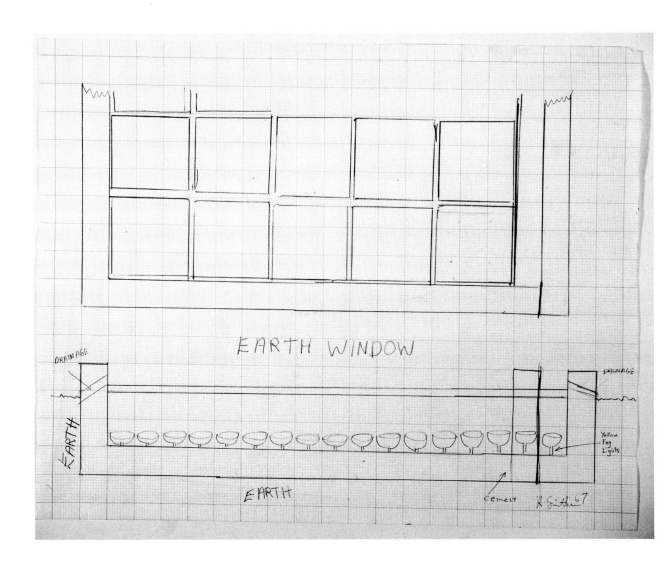

EARTH WINDOW

DRAINAGE

DRAINAGE

EARTH

Yellow Fog Lights

EARTH

cement

R. Smith 67

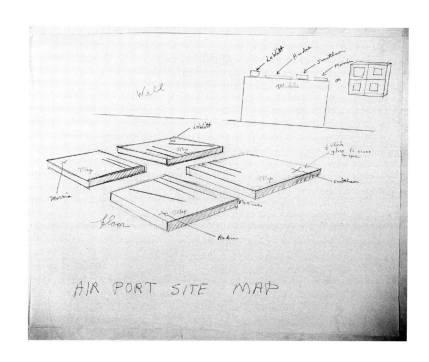

4.17 Robert Smithson, *Earth Window*, 1967. Pencil on graph paper, 17 × 22 in. © Estate of Robert Smithson.

4.18 Robert Smithson, *Airport Site Map,* 1967. Pencil on paper, 19 × 24 in. © Estate of Robert Smithson.

Chapter 5

Obliquely Dense: John Hejduk's Wall House

On one point John Hejduk uncharacteristically agreed with the conventional wisdom about his work. His Wall House of 1970 was "the real break" in his career (fig. 5.1).[1] There is little agreement, however, on how and why the Wall House marks that break. The art historian Richard Pommer, whom Hejduk often cited as a perceptive critic of his projects, understood the Wall House as a product of Hejduk's "modernist faith in the meaning of abstract spatial signals" and as the most cogent example of his concerted attempts, beginning with his Texas Houses (1954–63) and continuing in the Diamond Projects (1962–67), to conflate drawing and building by "match[ing] the conventions of pictorial flatness to the ground plan of architecture" (figs. 5.2–5.3).[2] With the Wall House, those conventions become literalized as a blank *vertical* surface and, according to Pommer, the implied picture plane of the wall, particularly when portrayed in Hejduk's flattened 90-degree axonometric drawings, proposes "an axial precision impossible to achieve in reality. We are forced to imagine the different states of approaching and dwelling, of freedom and containment, of our eventual isolation, which neither perspective views nor the building itself could evoke in the same way."

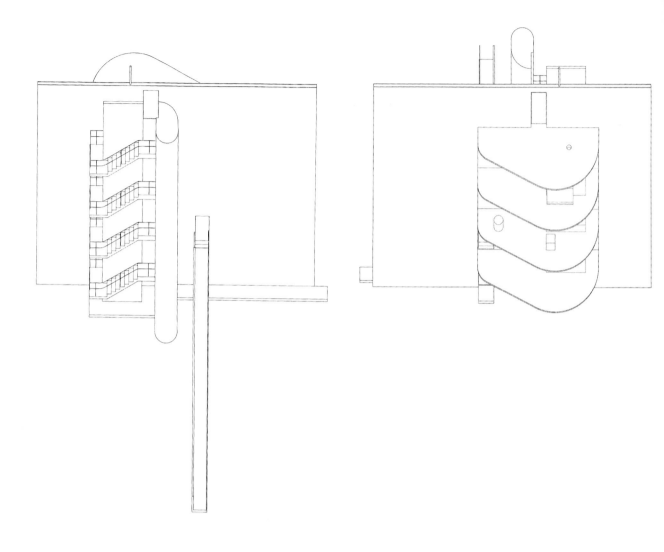

5.1 John Hejduk, Wall House, 90° axonometrics, 1968–70. Ink on paper, each 34 × 36.5 in.

A contrary explanation of Hejduk's work was offered in 1972 by the historian and critic Kenneth Frampton, who argued that the "literally spatial intent" of Hejduk's Wall House distinguishes it from his earlier investigations of pictorial spatial devices. Unlike Pommer, Frampton derided Hejduk's effort to employ pictorial techniques in architecture, labeling it a "quasi-syntheticist viewpoint" that "rework[s] certain European spatial innovations of the '20s and '30s" in the hope that "art and architecture should cease to maintain their independent identities."[3] Frampton's admiration for the Wall House and his critique of the pictorial methods of Hejduk's prior work (and of all "formalist" design methods in general) were motivated by a belief that "the conceivably proper object of a modernist architecture" is a concern not with abstract spatial signals, but with "the significant occupation of space" and "the manifest and consistent creation of literal space." Surprisingly, and ingeniously, Frampton turned to Clement Greenberg's "Modernist Painting" to support his argument for architectural propriety and against the pictorialism of Hejduk's work prior to the Wall House. Even more surprising and insightful is Frampton's claim, near the end of his article, that Hejduk's departure from pictorialism is aligned with "the recent culture of Minimalist art, that critical antithesis of modernism, [which] poses for architecture a challenge which it has yet to take up. Hejduk, amongst the formalists of his generation, has perhaps come closest to answering this challenge. His remarkable wall house project of 1970, ... despite its evident theatricality, ... postulates an architecture which celebrates ... the penetration and occupation of space."[4] Frampton's mention of "theatricality" signals his familiarity not only with Greenberg's writing but also with Michael Fried's. Reiterating Fried's analysis of contemporary art, and recognizing its architectural implications, Frampton argues that even as "modernist painting escapes into film or even into theater, into fields which ... are no longer the proper area of its competence ... architecture, irrespective of modernism, is excluded from such an escape since both literally and metaphorically its domain lies outside the traditional boundaries separating the arts; for, as properly constituted, it either is, or subtends, the 'space of public appearance' in itself." For Frampton, a pictorialist architecture abandons architecture's properly public medium and embraces instead a "hybrid modernist intent" as a means to "escape" into the more private art world of sculpture and painting.[5]

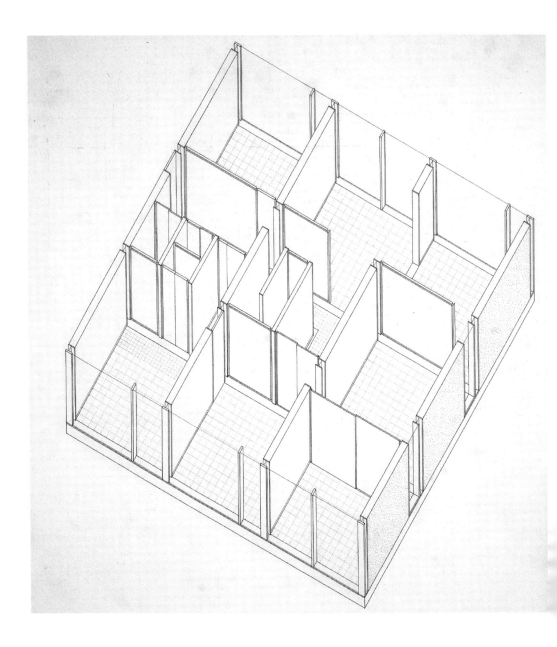

5.2 John Hejduk, Texas House 4, axonometric first floor, 1956–60. Ink on board, 30 × 20 in.

5.3 John Hejduk, Diamond Project B, axonometric first floor, 1962–67. Ink on paper, 29 × 29 in.

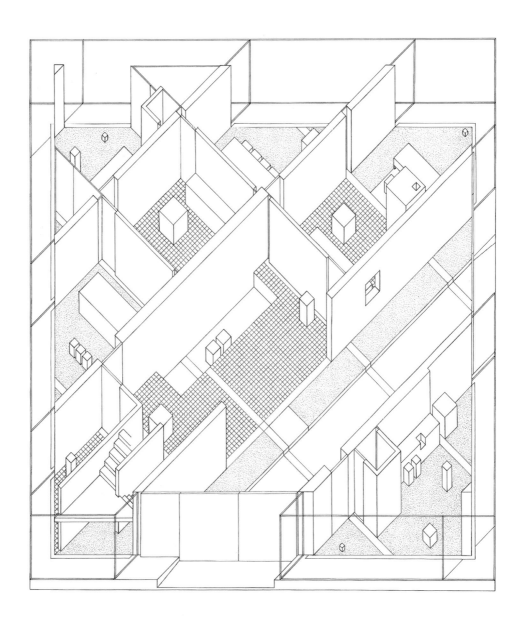

The Texas Houses … were *not modern.* … But the Fourth House, of all those Houses, is the closest to method. … The real break, the Wall House, can be compared to the Fourth House, maybe.

John Hejduk, Mask of Medusa *(1985)*

Frampton suggested that aspects of both literalism and pictorialism appear in Hejduk's work and teaching prior to the Wall House. On the one hand, the "literally spatial" and properly architectural concerns are manifested in Hejduk's seven Texas Houses and the nine-square problem that he, Robert Slutzky, and Lee Hirsche developed when teaching together in Austin—along with Colin Rowe—from 1954 to 1956 (fig. 5.4). On the other hand, the pictorialist approach appears in Hejduk's Diamond Projects and the "Juan Gris problem," which he and Slutzky developed for the program in architecture at the Cooper Union, where Hejduk began as director in 1964 (fig. 5.5). Contrary to Hejduk's later claim that "the Texas Houses … were *not modern,*"[6] Frampton saw the Texas Houses and the nine-square problem as exemplars of modernist propriety in architecture, because both present architecture "solely in terms of consistent three-dimensional spatial operations."[7] Hejduk, however, believed otherwise. He insisted that while his concern in the Texas Houses was with "basic architectonic construction method," it was with "construction at a conceptual level," and that his thinking was "always abstract, not literal."[8] Both the Texas Houses and the Diamond Projects methodically pursue the pictorial impropriety articulated in the writings of Rowe and Slutzky, a pursuit that was instigated during Hejduk's residence in Texas, when he began to "take Corb books and just pour over them."[9] The result was work that engages a wide range of properly architectural issues in pictorial terms, and what ultimately emerged from those explorations, as if forgotten or repressed, was literalism in general and the wall in particular.

For Hejduk, as for Rowe and Slutzky, it is the combination, even confusion, of pictorial and literal intentions that drives modernist architecture. This insistence on ambiguity is clear in the fact that Hejduk and Slutzky continued to use the nine-square as the introductory exercise in their teaching at Cooper, as well as in Hejduk's explicit claim that the initial nine-square models are a means toward drawings, which in turn are a means toward "three-dimensional implications" and "an idea of fabrication." For Hejduk, the intent of the nine-square problem is not "solely" to investigate literal space, but to teach students to "begin to comprehend the relationships between two-dimensional drawings, axonometric projections, and three-dimensional (model) form." Thus the nine-square problem is not, as Frampton claimed, "clearly removed from the intrinsic illusionism of the so called Juan Gris problem." Both problems investigate the potential and difficulties of relating pictorial devices to architectural form, although each engages distinct aspects of that relationship. As Frampton noted, the three-dimensional drawings of the nine-square

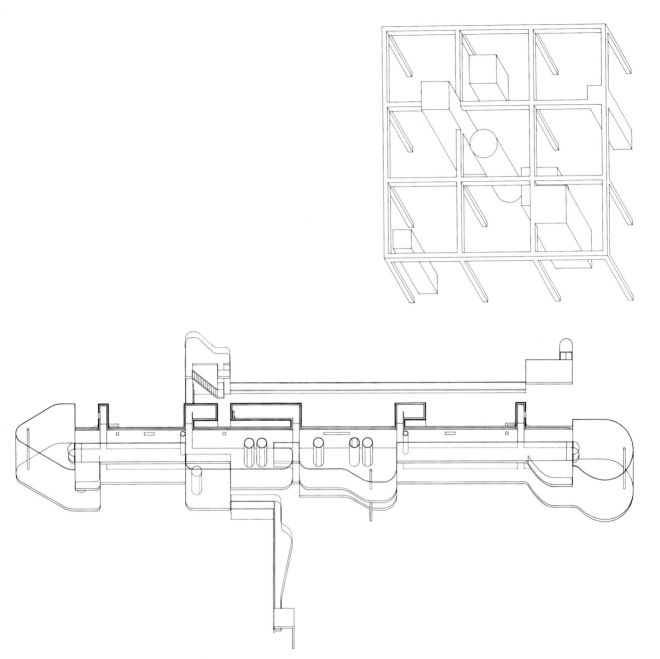

5.4 Edwin Aviles, nine-square grid problem, 1964, from *Education of an Architect: A Point of View* (New York: Cooper Union, 1971).

5.5 Paul Amatuzzo, house (Juan Gris problem), 1969, from *Education of an Architect: A Point of View.*

5.6 John Hejduk, Wall House, model, 1968–70.

problem and the Texas Houses are 45-degree axonometrics, which emphasize volume, whereas the Gris problem and the Diamond Projects employ 90-degree projections in which the elevations and plans appear to flatten into the same plane. Frampton was certainly correct to identify how the different systems of projection are associated with the motives of each of the problems and projects. The difference, however, is less categorical than methodological. The two exercises employ different techniques to initiate related investigations. In Hejduk's own work as well as in the pedagogy he instituted at Cooper Union, the two approaches are practically inseparable and exemplify what Hejduk described as the "two opposing systems of thought" inherent in all architecture: "one dealing with the cube and the other dealing with the plane."[10]

The Wall House is Hejduk's attempt at a synthesis of those two systems and, in effect, of both Pommer's and Frampton's interpretations of his work. The "real break" represented by that highly polemical project lies in its combination and condensation of literal and pictorial understandings of architectural space in a seemingly blank figure: a structural wall that is painted neutral gray on its "public" face and clad in "reflective metal" on the other, "basically private" side (fig. 5.6). All of the house's circulation elements are attached to the front side of the wall but are self-supporting: a long entrance ramp, an open stair spiraling around a smaller, darker wall, and an elevator. On the other side of the wall are four cantilevered slabs supporting three glass-enclosed spaces and a roof terrace. The cantilever is supported by the wall but counterbalanced and stabilized by the circulation elements. The inhabitant, or visitor, approaches the gray wall frontally on the ramp (a minor entrance, or exit, runs parallel and adjacent to the wall on the ground level), then passes through the wall into the lowest of the levels and gains a view of the landscape beyond through the curving glass that encloses the space. In order to proceed to the floors above, one turns around, once again facing the immense wall, but this time the encounter is entirely different. Because the back surface of the wall is reflective, one sees oneself and the landscape that is now behind, as well as a reflected double of the space in which one stands. The wall, which at first appeared as a neutral object—a blank canvas—has now become an encompassing optical device—a mirror. When one leaves each level to use the stairs or elevator, one moves into and past the reflection, through the wall, and occupies for an instant the space, or nonspace, between two vastly different surfaces and the spaces they produce. The entire project is an elaborate device to produce that reiterated moment of passage in which one encounters a confused and condensed combination of literal and pictorial space.

The Wall House structures an allegory of passage not simply from one side to another, or even between two opposed spaces, but between what Hejduk calls "the so called real world" and "abstraction." For Hejduk, that complex passage both characterizes the intention of every architecture project and aligns the pursuits of architecture with those of painting: "A wall is the quickest, the thinnest, the thing we're always transgressing, and … the most surface condition. The painter starts with the real world and works toward abstraction, and when he's finished with a work it is abstracted from the so-called real world. But architecture takes two lines. The architect starts with the abstract world and … works toward the real world. The significant architect is one who, when finished with a work, is as close to that original abstraction as he could possibly be."[11]

The Wall House is thus an ambivalent passage between architecture and a rather constrained conception of art. Presumably, the individual for whom Hejduk intended that passage was himself. The Wall House is literally a construction of architectural identity. Hejduk used a basic architectural device to enact a simulated inhabitation of the "total condition" of literalized pictorial space, and he continued to explore the possibilities of literalist devices in architecture in the several years after completing the Wall House. A didactic example is his *That Is That House,* a conceptual proposal that was part of the group of projects he called *Silent Witnesses* (fig. 5.7). The house is a simple cube containing a single volume. It is sketched both isometrically and orthographically. Two of its six surfaces, one vertical (a "wall") and the other horizontal (the "roof"), are hinged on one of their edges and swing from the house's structural frame. On the horizontal surface is a projection of the plan; it literally folds up to become part of the elevation. On the vertical surface is a projection of the objects inside the volume: it folds down to become an extension of the plan. The very title of the house resembles the mantra of literalism—this is this—and as Stan Allen has noted in regard to Hejduk's Dilemma House (1976), a similarly "mechanical" but more intricate project (which Hejduk has called "the most abstract I ever attempted"), the relationship between its elements is "a concrete series of operations, performed as if the elements were already material.… For all its formal precision, this is not a *geometrical* operation but rather a *plastic* operation."[12] In other words, it exemplifies the simultaneity of "abstraction" and "reality" that Hejduk identified as the essence of architecture. Perhaps one could also call these kinds of operations "literal architectural devices," of which the most literal is the wall in Hejduk's Wall House.

But how did Hejduk arrive at this interest in literalism? How did the wall make its appearance in his work? How did Hejduk come to this "break thru—fresh very fresh" to the "total condition" of "concrete architecture concrete poetry" (see fig. 5.18)? A strictly formal lineage can be traced between the Wall House and Texas House 4 (1956–60) which develops a system of parallel structural walls that appeared first in House 3 (1954–60). But House 4, which is the first in the series to have more than one level, includes an internal stair that is placed adjacent to one of the walls. As one moves up or down the stairs, one engages the wall's vertical surface both frontally and laterally, a possibility that Hejduk considered only after some study. In early drawings of the project, the stair is situated in the center of the plan and is independent of the walls, but as the

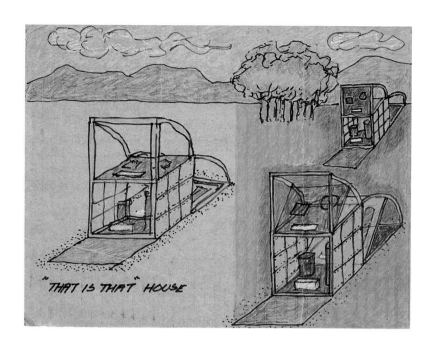

5.7 John Hejduk, *That Is That House,* c. 1975. Felt-tip pen and colored pencil on cardboard, 9 × 12 in.

project developed Hejduk moved the stair to an asymmetrical position against a wall (fig. 5.8). This asymmetry, which is studiously avoided in the first three Texas houses, would become total in the Miesian plan of House 5, then fade in House 6 where the stair is contained in a tower outside the cubic volume of the main house. But both the asymmetry and the relationship between the wall and the internal stair return in House 7, a project with six floors and—like House 4—a basement. In House 7, the stair is not simply adjacent to the wall but circulates around and through it, so that when moving vertically through the building the inhabitant would pass through the wall as many as twelve times (if one were to walk from the basement to the sixth floor or vice versa) (fig. 5.9). Unlike the other walls in the house, which diminish as they rise and gradually transform into piers and then columns (as an index of the decreasing structural load on the upper floors), the segment of the wall that is associated with the stair remains intact as a vertical extrusion throughout the entire height of the house. Thus, embedded in House 7, which was produced in the same year that Hejduk was beginning the Diamond Projects, there is a repetitive passage through a wall that might be seen as a rough prototype for the circulation of the Wall House. Hejduk does not repeat that formal prototype in the Diamond Projects, yet those projects use other means to imagine the complex spatial passage that would be concretized in the Wall House.

From the flattening out internal to the Diamond Houses—the moment at which one perceives the hypotenuse—comes the "Wall" houses. The wall is a neutral condition…. And the wall represents the same condition as the "moment of the hypotenuse" in the Diamond houses—it's the moment of greatest repose and at the same time the greatest tension. It is a moment of passage.
John Hejduk, Works: 1950–1983 *(1983)*

Hejduk elaborates upon the spatial significance of the hypotenuse in two texts. The first is his essay "Out of Time and into Space," first published in 1965, which explains the rotated plan of Le Corbusier's Carpenter Center (1960–63) as an attempt to realize "the idea of cubist space in Architecture."[13] The second is the explanatory text Hejduk wrote for the 1967 exhibition "The Diamond in Painting and Architecture," a collaboration with Slutzky. There Hejduk claims that his Diamond Projects go further than Le Corbusier by pursuing a "post-Cubist" mode of space that is the architectural correlate of Mondrian's diamond paintings (fig. 5.10). Hejduk imagined himself carrying on "Mondrian's prophetic concern for the spatial-architectural dilemma" and investigating its implications for the complex but "intrinsic unity of painting, sculpture and architecture."[14] Unlike Le Corbusier, who was "not able to detach himself from the cubist tradition,"[15] Hejduk

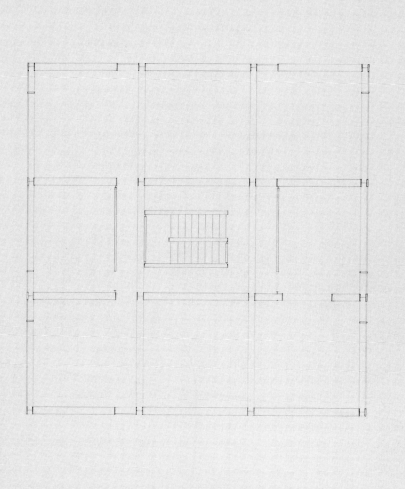

5.8 John Hejduk, Texas House 4, plan showing centralized stair, 1956–60. Pencil on vellum, 18 × 18 in.

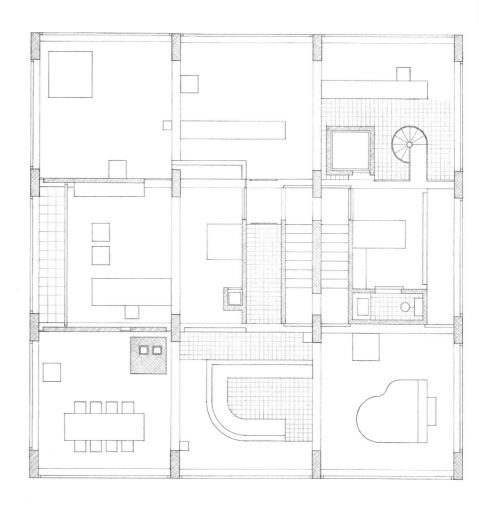

5.9 John Hejduk, Texas House 7, plan level 4, 1962–63. Ink on paper, 30 × 36 in.

characterized his Diamond Projects as an anticipation of a "new projected and exploded space" inspired by Mondrian which he predicted (in a sentence he would excise from the published versions of the text) "is about to become a fact."[16]

Integral to his 1967 text is a series of diagrams that explain how the diamond, if it is drawn using 45-degree isometric projections, is implicitly both flat and volumetric (figs. 5.11, 5.12). If a diamond is conceived as a plan, and it is drawn as an isometric, it will appear to be a square. Then, rather than producing the illusion of volume that is characteristic of isometrics, it appears to be flat, like a 90-degree isometric of a square: "The two-dimensionality of a plan, projected into the three-dimensional isometric, still appears two-dimensional, closer to the two-dimensional abstraction of the plan and perhaps closer to the actual two-dimensionality of the architectural space."[17] A similar flattening of the volumetric occurs in elevation drawings of an extruded diamond: the two perpendicular sides of the diamond flatten into the same surface, thereby turning a cube into a plane. While these effects may seem at first to be simply tricks of projection, or perhaps ironic failings of projective systems, they are for Hejduk profound instances of the difficulties involved in producing, representing, and conceptualizing "actual architectural space." These simple projective operations exemplify "one of the major architectural arguments of today ... the dialectic between the concepts of two-dimensional and three-dimensional space."[18] The question that seems to have intrigued Hejduk is how he could produce an equally simple and profound condition in an actual architectural space.

Hejduk found a possible answer in the "moment of the hypotenuse"—the diagonal plane of the extruded diamond—which, on the one hand, is an internalization of the flattening that occurs in drawing the elevation and, on the other, is the moment when the competing geometries of the diamond and the square reach a tense equilibrium analogous to the resolution of diagonal grids in a cubist painting. But while cubist paintings "attempt to destroy the corporeal experience of volume," architecture requires a more ambivalent mode of abstraction. Its "total effect" requires that "the observer becomes involved with the geometric rules of the game."[19] Hejduk means this literally. The potential of the hypotenuse is to produce actual architectural spaces in which one becomes physically "encompassed by the flattening out of the two sides: we have here the appearance of a coordination of external and internal experience."[20] He discerns this potential in the Carpenter Center. As a result of rotating the building and allowing circulation along the site's diagonal, "two [vertical] planes of operation, the external and the internal" are "co-joined to the same organic system." Elevations and sections, mediated by plans, operate as a "multitude of planes" that constitute the "visual-cerebral mechanism" of architectural space.[21]

Hejduk's spatial proposition, despite its origins in the formal devices of painting—especially that of Gris, Mondrian, and Slutzky—is far from a declaration of the "quasi-syntheticist position"

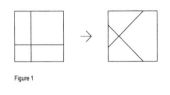

Figure 1

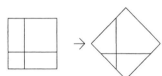

Figure 2

Figure 3

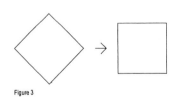

Figure 4

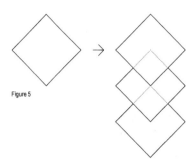

Figure 5

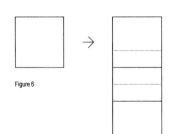

Figure 6

Figure 7

Figure 8

Figure 9

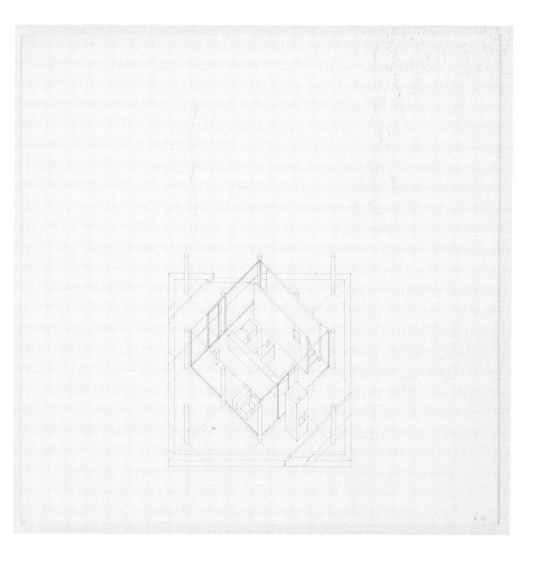

5.10 John Hejduk and Robert Slutzky, installation of "The Diamond in Painting and Architecture," 1967.

5.11 John Hejduk, diagrams from "The Diamond in Painting and Architecture," 1967.

5.12 John Hejduk, Diamond Project A, axonometric first floor, 1963–67. Ink on board, 30 × 30 in.

that Frampton ascribes to it. Rather, the intent of Hejduk's diagrams is specifically architectural, and as such they inaugurate the "real break" that occurs with the Wall House. Hejduk began to work on the Wall House in 1968, soon after completing the Diamond Projects. Although its genesis lies in the very formalist exercises and pictorial methods that Frampton criticized, Hejduk's aim was not to synthesize painting and architecture, but to discern the pictorial devices and effects that are peculiar to architecture. While Frampton's description and analysis of the devices and problems in Hejduk's work display insight into contemporary art discourse that was rare for architectural critics, his insistence on literal space as the proper medium of modern architecture obscures the ways in which Hejduk's trajectory, from the nine square of the Texas Houses to the systematic pictorialism of the Diamond Projects, is a transdisciplinary effort to engage "post-cubist" painting (exemplified by Mondrian's and Slutzky's diamond canvases) as a means to surpass Le Corbusier's (and Rowe's) mode of pictorialism. The Texas Houses, the Diamond Projects, and the Wall House all are motivated by Hejduk's desire to "realize" the significance of abstract painting for architecture, especially that of Mondrian, who Hejduk claimed "is not as abstract as you might think he is. He is a realist."[22]

Some questions come up: What is the reality of architecture? What are architectural representations of reality? Is architecture's realization absolutely necessary? The re-presentation of an actuality is most important: how the so-called reality can, in fact, represent itself in architecture—as perhaps, in a non-objective Mondrian painting.... In a Mondrian painting, reality is conceived, reality is represented, reality is realized. All are one in the same thing.
John Hejduk, "The Flatness of Depth" (1980)

Hejduk's realization of abstraction is most powerfully evident in his foundation plans, especially that of House 7. That drawing has a strong relationship to the diagram and foundation plan of Diamond Project A, which—like House 7—was begun in 1962 (figs. 5.13, 5.14). In the Texas Houses as well as the Diamond Projects, it is the foundation drawings that are simultaneously the most literal, most abstract, and most diagrammatic representations of architectural space: the foundation plans depict the spaces that are most literally constrained by walls, but they also most effectively distill the formal logic of the projects. They are the clearest manifestation of Hejduk's desire to integrate the literal structure of the building with "construction at a conceptual level."

Not surprisingly, diagonals are lurking not only in those drawings but also in almost all of the Texas Houses, ranging from the programmatic relationships in House 3 to the volumetric scaling of cubes in House 6. Although neither Pommer nor Frampton mentions the significance of the diagonal for the Wall House, Frampton does discuss Hejduk's fascination with the Carpenter Center which, in Frampton's analysis, is the prototype for the pictorial devices of the Gris problem. In both, the conflation of literal and pictorial frontality is abandoned in favor of an "extravagant solution … to treat the surrogate picture plane as a corridor of movement."[23] One engages these vertical surfaces by moving along and through them, similar to the way the stair works in House 7, but in this case the aim is to attenuate the surface's visual effects. Frampton suggests that this collapse of pictorial space into a *promenade architecturale* allowed Hejduk to evade "the dilemma of cubist sculpture" in which three-dimensionality is constrained by the need for frontality (fig. 5.15). Hejduk, however, explains the direct engagement with the picture plane in the Gris problem and the Wall House not as an evasion of frontality but as its intensification.[24] What *is* evaded, however, is the dialectic of center and periphery that characterizes cubist painting. What replaces that dialectic is "encompassing lateral extension": a sense of immersion in an all-over field condition analogous to the space depicted in Mondrian's painting.[25]

For Hejduk, this architectural encounter with flatness is a reconfiguration of the normative condition of frontality in architecture—epitomized in the Renaissance facade—which both alters and preserves that norm's salient traits. Like a facade, the moment of the hypotenuse operates as a threshold that mediates inside and outside, but most important, it can be experienced as a passage through *or* along the hypotenuse, and thus it not only maintains but also clarifies a fundamental distinction between architecture—which always involves the "physicality of moving"—and painting—in which "you are always the observer."[26]

Hejduk's "moment of the hypotenuse" is to architecture what the blank canvas is to painting: a critical codification of disciplinary conventions and a reconfiguration of crucial concepts. Rather than painting's "flatness and the delimitation of flatness" (Greenberg), the moment of the hypotenuse is an interplay of both two- and three-dimensional formal devices. Yet, like the blank canvas, the moment of the hypotenuse shifts the focus of pictorialism from visual effects to technical means—from transparency to opacity—and as a result "expands the possibilities of the pictorial."[27]

In the Diamond Projects this "moment" remains a conceptual possibility produced by architectural drawing, but in the Wall House its appearance becomes literal. The wall obviously presents a pictorial surface, yet it is entirely unlike the affinity in Hejduk's previous work with the mode of architectural pictorialism presented in Rowe's and Slutzky's reading of the villa at Garches. Hejduk, who had taught with Rowe and Slutzky at Texas at the time they wrote "Transparency," and who coauthored an essay with Rowe the following year, adopted the pictorialist practice of transferring the devices of painting to the "art" of plan-making.[28] Hejduk's Diamond Projects and his reading of the Carpenter Center are exemplary instances of contemporary

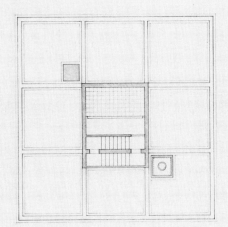

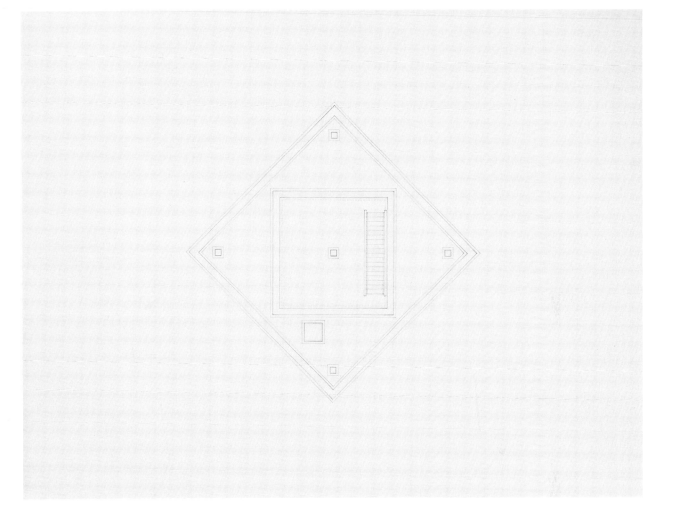

5.13 John Hejduk, Texas House 7, foundation plan, 1962–63.
Ink on paper, 30 × 36 in.

5.14 John Hejduk, Diamond Project A, foundation plan, 1963–67.
Ink on board, 30 × 30 in.

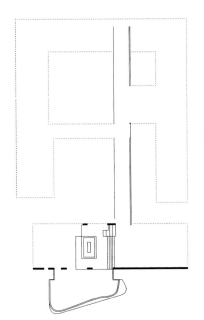

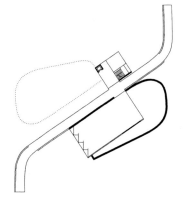

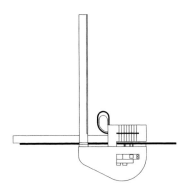

5.15 Partial plans of Le Corbusier, La Tourette, 1960, and Carpenter Center, 1964, and plan of John Hejduk, Wall House, 1968–70. Drawing by Richard McCann.

formal investigations in architecture in which, as Rowe and Slutzky write, even though "a floor is not a wall and plans are not paintings," "the ground is conceived of as a vertical surface."[29] That transfer and interplay between walls and floors generated the tension in Rowe's analyses of projects such as Villa Schwob, the villa at Garches, and La Tourette. But Hejduk's Wall House offers an entirely new kind of "pictorial impropriety" that extends and surpasses Rowe's fascination with the blank surfaces of Villa Schwob and La Tourette. The Wall House takes Rowe's readings of the "internal space" of Le Corbusier's villa at Garches and the "megaron" of La Tourette to their limit. Its wall is not accompanied by a similar pictorialism in the plan, and in the end the Wall House has little in common with either Garches or Schwob. Even an analogy to the blank wall of La Tourette is inadequate. There, the denial of a frontal encounter with the wall leads to its surface being used for "pictorial and sculptural opportunism."[30] The anxiety Rowe experienced at La Tourette, and its sublimation into readings of pictorial effects, was the result of an encounter with a building that has no front. Hejduk reconfigured that condition in the Diamond Projects, where the "facade" is abstracted and embedded within the building as its hypotenuse. But the uneasiness provoked by Hejduk's Wall House derives from the fact that it has two (false) fronts. More troubling yet, it has no "body." The building is all wall and (almost) no floor. Yet paradoxically it is all about interiority. This Hejduk learned from the Carpenter Center.

If La Tourette fails to offer a frontal flat condition and instead offers two pictorial spirals activated by a megaron volume comprised of vertical and horizontal sandwiches, at the Carpenter Center there is an involuted picture plane. The Carpenter Center also does not present itself frontally but folds its elevation into its interior. The effect, unlike the horizontal openness of La Tourette, is to produce an equivocal interplay of a field and its center. While Hejduk has described his essay "Out of Time and into Space" as "a spin-off from Rowe and Slutzky's Transparency #1 article,"[31] his reading of the pictorialist potential of Le Corbusier's Carpenter Center follows more from the protoliteral moments in Rowe's "La Tourette." Curiously, Rowe's unwittingly Lacanian description of his "painful" experience of "tragic insufficiency" in approaching the blank wall of La Tourette also could be applied to the Wall House: "the visitor … is so placed that he is without means of making coherent his own experience. He is made the subject of diametric excitations; his consciousness is divided; and, being both deprived of and also offered an architectural support, in order to resolve his predicament he is anxious, indeed obliged—and without choice— to enter the building."[32]

But while the experience of La Tourette is an anxious encounter with a denial of literal frontality in favor of an oblique and sublimated encounter with a wall's literalness, Hejduk's Wall House, which emerges out of an investigation of pictorial devices in architecture, is actually a refusal of pictorialism in architecture. Unlike Rowe's experience and description of La Tourette, the Wall

House is analogous to neither a collage nor a construction sculpture. Rather, it is a conversion of pictorial conventions into a literalist device that emphasizes the objecthood, presence, and theatricality of architectural space. As Michael Fried feared, this wall "is not just in one's space but in one's way." But unlike Fried's identification of "the concept of a room" as the substitute for "space" in literalist art and theory, Hejduk pursues a transdisciplinary analogy between the wall and the blank canvas as literalist spatial devices.

When one "enters" Hejduk's project, space is neither a continuation of the promenade nor a volume produced by floors and walls. Hejduk not only reconfigures Le Corbusier's combination of horizontal and vertical "sandwiches," he forces a repeated frontal encounter with the blank, literal surface. Hejduk's space is as anxious as that at La Tourette, but the "insufficiency" is not that the frontal relationship is infinitely deferred and sublimated as pictorial effect. Instead, the frontality is both emphatic and without culmination. It is also dichotomous. The blank canvas turns out to be the support for its obverse: the reflective cladding. The back of the wall turns out to be its front, and that "front" appears to be both insubstantial and reflexive—a "mirror" mounted on the back of a "painting." This is not what Rowe and Slutzky theorized as "a divorce of physical reality and optical impression," but a radically literal deployment of pictorial devices *as physical reality*. It is not an architecture that takes pictorialism as a means for the production of optical effect, but an architecture that deploys the devices of pictorialism as literally spatial strategies.

Hejduk did not begin the Wall House project with those concerns, however. In his earliest developmental sketches, Hejduk seems less concerned with pictorial devices than with the visual properties and effects of different construction systems. Those sketches, which clearly derive from the Gris problem, show various arrangements of three types of long parallel walls: transparent glass, translucent glass block, and opaque (and perhaps reflective) stainless steel (fig. 5.16). Living spaces occupy the space between the walls, while service programs are contained in bulbous "tea-cup" forms (including a "john") that are accessed by passing through openings in the walls.[33] One sketch suggests an intent to produce a spatial "inversion": presumably this would occur when the inhabitant passes, for example, through an opaque wall into a transparent container, or encounters the outside of an opaque container in the space between a translucent and a transparent wall.

In subsequent sketches, the walls become taller, with living spaces suspended on one side. Together the walls form a cube (and in some cases a four square in plan) (fig. 5.17). In these iterations, each wall separates services and circulation on one side from habitable spaces on the other, and as a result, in the two spaces between the three walls, services and habitation are juxtaposed across a void. In still later sketches, the three walls are placed in a single line with three program spaces side by side (a configuration that would return in *Silent Witnesses*), and

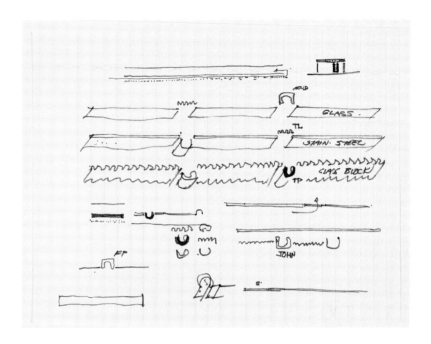

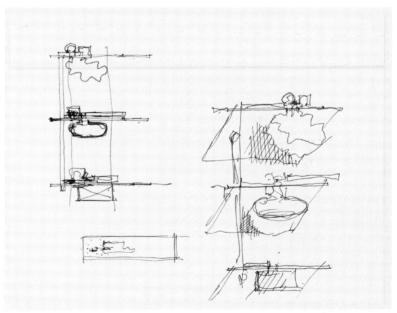

5.16, 5.17 John Hejduk, Wall House sketch, c. 1968. Felt-tip
pen on lined paper, 8.5 × 11 in.

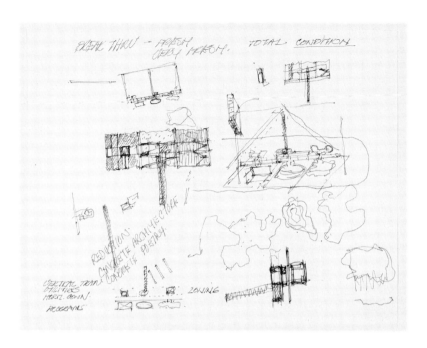

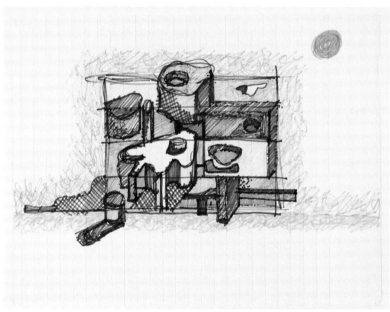

5.18, 5.19 John Hejduk, Wall House sketch, c. 1968. Felt-tip pen on lined paper, 8.5 × 11 in.

ultimately, as in the final project, the spaces are stacked and suspended on a single, nearly square surface (figs. 5.18, 5.19).

Hejduk later explained the Wall House as a "centralized relief on a tableau" or a search for "the elusive still life in architecture" in which "the vertical wall plane becomes the table."[34] But that explanation obscures the literalism of the Wall House and, in turn, the nature of the "real break" that the project represents, a break that is entirely clear in Hejduk's *Fabrications* projects (1968–72), many of which rework earlier projects in post–Wall House terms (fig. 5.20). The sources for that break lie not only in the sophisticated pictorialism of the Diamond Projects, but also in Hejduk's 1962 design for the Dag Hammarskjöld memorial, a forty-foot black cube that is entered on the diagonal (fig. 5.21). The memorial was conceived precisely at the moment when the Texas Houses and Diamond Projects overlap, and within a year of Tony Smith's *Black Box* and *Die* (see figs. 0.1, 1.24). Hejduk's memorial begins to conceive architecture as a device for "combining a geometric theory with an actual physical environment," in this case the island of Manhattan.[35] In sketches related to both that project and the Diamond Projects, Hejduk proposes that Manhattan might be considered as "an abstract city as far as an all-over visual form is concerned."[36] Hejduk conceives the Dag Hammarskjöld memorial as an architectural "Homage to Boogie" that, when placed in its site, would have real spatial effects at the urban scale similar to those represented in Mondrian's famous paintings *Broadway Boogie Woogie* and *Victory Boogie Woogie*. But unlike Mondrian's paintings, and like Tony Smith's *Die,* the memorial's relationship to landscape is entirely literal. Hejduk's work is remarkable for the way it proceeded in parallel to emerging discourses in art, even if direct influences or relationships remain elusive.

When we rode along the roads which moved through the tulip fields I began to understand Mondrian. I always thought him to be an international painter; I found him to be a Dutch painter. It was not the color of the tulips but the density of the sand and earth where the bulbs were planted that reminded me of Mondrian. It was the atmosphere of opacity. The place, the land, the earth was dense opacification.

John Hejduk, Mask of Medusa *(1985)*

Hejduk's persistent investigation of the architectural potential of pictorial space was both a process of formal research and, ultimately, a personal passage from that project into his "art": the work following the Wall House that seems to break entirely with his modernist roots. That passage is realized through the literalization of a sophisticated formal diagram in the form of the Wall House. Through that literalization Hejduk achieves both a return to the traditional modernist

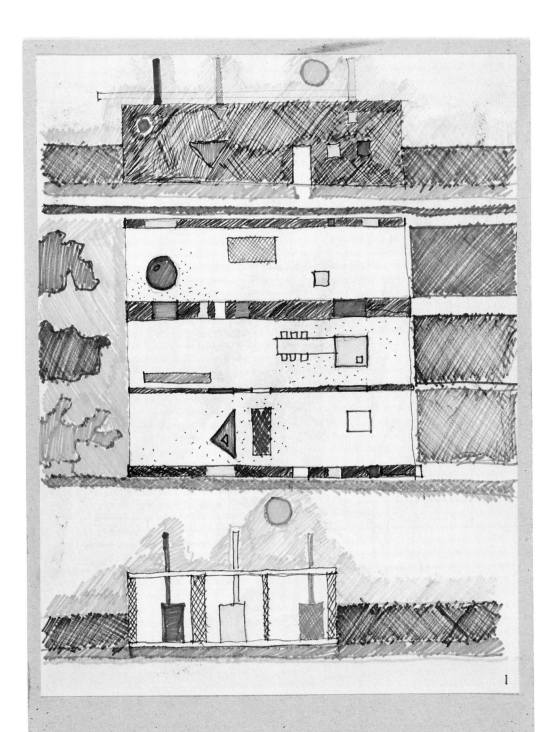

1

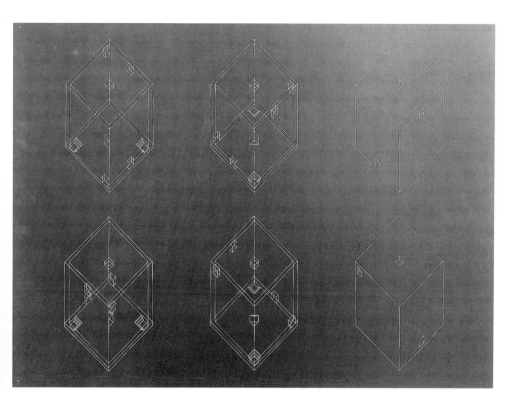

5.20 John Hejduk, *Fabrications,* c. 1970. Felt-tip pen on paper
mounted on cardboard, 10 × 8 in.

5.21 John Hejduk, Dag Hammarskjöld Memorial Competition,
axonometrics, 1962. Internegative, 14.5 × 20 in.

idioms of his early training (materials, structure, program, space) and a symbolic translation of the formal and pictorial vocabulary through which he saw himself (and Slutzky and Rowe) as continuing the Corbusian legacy. This collapse of autobiographical and disciplinary knowledges is the theme of a book by Jay Fellows with which Hejduk identified deeply. Fellows's *The Failing Distance* is a sophisticated reading of the evolving spatial concepts in the writings of John Ruskin as an autobiographical account of the "decline of an optical self."[37] Opposed to the optical self is what Fellows calls the "autobiographical impulse": "a reflexive, spatial heresy of mirrors, as opposed to the orthodox space of windows" produced by the "desire for the emergence of the first person from a condition of voyeuristic invisibility, from an optical system without a sense of self, to a condition of density and opaqueness."[38]

Hejduk was fascinated with Fellows's allegorical formulation of this divided self in terms of the pictorial space of perspective. For Fellows, the vanishing point is a "point of transcendental release" and a pure exteriority that represents the future. Its mirror image is the station point (the observer's location of selfless "voyeuristic invisibility"), which is situated in the past: the already seen, already known, already settled. But the autobiographical occupies a much more difficult and dense condition analogous to the compacted space of the picture plane itself. It is an immersion in the present and the immediate, a pure interiority or "inside-out" mode of visuality that gradually emerges in Ruskin's work and which Fellows imagines as an "optical apocalypse of self and world."[39] For Ruskin, perspective epitomizes the failing of post-Renaissance pictorial space to engage time or self. In perspective, the future (the distance, or vanishing point) can be brought into conciliation with neither the present (the foreground, or picture plane) nor the past (the station point, or the world of the observer). In a chapter of *Modern Painters* (1843) titled "The Truth of Space," Ruskin writes: "if in painting our foreground is anything, our distance must be nothing, and *vice versa;* for if we represent our near and distant objects as giving both at once that distinct image to the eye … we present that as seen at once which can only be seen by two separate acts of seeing, and tell a falsehood as gross as if we had represented four sides of a cubic object visible together."[40]

Sixteen year later, in *The Elements of Perspective* (1859), which Fellows calls "Ruskin's Bible of Perception," Ruskin introduces his subject through a didactic presentation of Alberti's notion of perspective as a window in the wall.[41] He then proceeds to show its faults. Ruskin invites the reader, as student, to perform an exercise: "sit down very near the window" and imagine "what you see through it, as painted on its surface.… But, to do this, … you must not move … ; if you move your head forwards, you will see *more* of the landscape through the pane and, if you move it backwards, you will see *less*." He then launches a fanciful image of how to draw a perfect perspective of a landscape. He asks the student to imagine standing before an "unbroken plate of crystal … so vast (suppose a mile high and a mile wide) … and that you had a brush as long as you wanted (a mile long, suppose)." First you stand close to the glass and paint what you see, then you step back "a quarter of a mile, perhaps" and the perspective "would be all wrong." The lesson ultimately is that to paint properly one is forced to retreat into the optical self and assume a viewpoint that will match an ideal observer's. But as if to suspend that "decline," Ruskin decides to "keep the size of the picture entirely undetermined. I consider the field of the canvas as wholly unlimited and on that condition determine the perspective laws." It is not difficult to imagine Hejduk's Wall House as a realization of Ruskin's fanciful exercise.

Fellows's book appeared in 1975, after the Wall House was completed and exhibited. Yet it offered a confirmation of Hejduk's own identity in both a disciplinary and an autobiographical sense. Hejduk began to see the Diamond Projects and the moment of the hypotenuse as a failed and futile effort to see "four sides of a cubic object visible together" but, more important, as the initiation of a personal transformation in which the problems of pictorialism were the means to their own abandonment. The Wall House was nothing less than the literalization of Hejduk's passage from the optical to the autobiographical self, and from work that was nothing but architecture to work that was that as well as a redescription of himself as an architect.

Chapter 6

Dumby Building: Frank Gehry's Architectural Identity

In 1981, the architect Frank Gehry and the sculptor Richard Serra collaborated on a hypothetical project for a colossal suspension bridge joining the World Trade Center and the Chrysler Building (figs 6.1–6.2).[1] Each man designed one of its immense piers. While Serra proposed a rectilinear pylon not unlike his numerous slab sculptures, Gehry depicted a figure unprecedented in his own work: a giant fish rising out of the Hudson holding the bridge's cables in its mouth as though caught by a woven metal fishing line. For the next several years, the fish appeared regularly in Gehry's work, either as an enigmatic notation in his drawings or as a figural object in various projects, from a series of Formica lamps to a twenty-meter-tall "monument" in front of a restaurant in Japan. Today, the appearance of Gehry's fish is virtually forgotten—superseded by talk of CATIA and titanium—and its significance as an event in architectural discourse remains underexamined and undervalued. While the fish is certainly a peculiar affect of Gehry's identity, it also may be the most compelling evidence of a deep connection between his architecture and the art practices of the

6.1, 6.2 Frank Gehry and Richard Serra, Bridge Project, 1981.

6.3 Frank Gehry, Benson House, 1981.

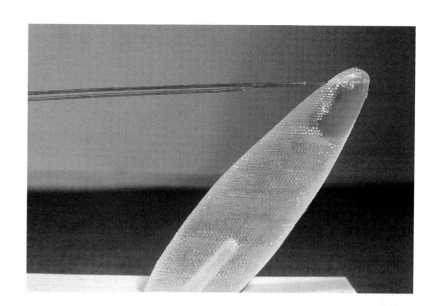

sixties. It may even mark a significant moment in the course of modern architecture, not because Gehry has made a canonical contribution, but because his play with the fish exemplifies a trans-disciplinary mode of architectural thought that recuperates the legacy of literalism and reconfigures the disciplinary identity of the architect.

Such a reading of the fish would run counter to the more common autobiographical or iconographic interpretations. The fish could instead be understood as a truly enigmatic figure: the architectural analog to the pictorial problematic of the blank canvas. This analogy is by no means obvious, yet its possibility is suggested by Gehry himself, who has often characterized his task as an architect as being like "the painter confronting the white canvas." The equivalent architectural problem, according to Gehry, is what he calls the "one room building"—or the "dumb box"—which is "as close as I could get to that pure problem in which the functional issues are so simple that you are faced with only the formal gesture" (fig. 6.3).[2] The fish, then, might be conceived as Gehry's particular version of that "pure problem," one that provokes serious architectural questions. Just as the blank canvas represents a degree zero condition of the conventions of painting—an empty pictorialism in which visuality is forced into a relationship with objecthood—Gehry's fish evades (or obscures) the presumed primacy of function and the limits of the discipline by foregrounding, and seemingly trivializing, conventional architectural relationships between, for example, form and structure, function and space, or image and object.

Yet Gehry's own (dissimulating) explanations of the fish have done much to discourage serious discussion of his persistent experiments. A 1984 interview is typical: "When I was a kid I used to go to the market with my grandmother on Thursdays. We'd go to the Jewish market, we'd buy a live carp, we'd take it home to her house in Toronto, we'd put it in the bathtub and I would play with the goddamn fish for a day until the next day she'd kill it and make gefilte fish. I think maybe that has something to do with it."[3] Such sentimental and decidedly unheroic talk has encouraged critics and architects to view the fish as marginal to Gehry's work. On the one hand, the fish has been dismissed as wholly subjective—an idiosyncratic and highly personal symbol. On the other, it has been treated as an "artistic" compulsion—a distraction from the properly architectural sophistication displayed in his work. Thus Gehry and his critics have played out an economy of dismissal and dissimulation that is as intriguing as it is suspicious, as is evident in the anxiety that the fish provokes among those critics and architects who otherwise so readily discuss Gehry's approach. Perhaps we should be critical of this relationship which manifests both positive and negative transference, what Jacques Lacan has differentiated as "when you have a soft spot for the individual concerned, [or] when you have to keep your eye on him."[4]

Such ambivalences are typical of transdisciplinary projects. In this case, the fish challenges the stability of the distinctions that delimit the normative yet evolving relationship between architecture and sculpture. It is no mere coincidence that Gehry first depicted the fish in a collaboration with a sculptor on a hybrid architectural project—a suspension bridge. In purely semiotic terms, the bridge can be read as a series of differential equations: on each side a boxy form—the World Trade Center or Serra's pylon—is paired with an articulated, figural shaft—the Chrysler Building or Gehry's fish. Thus Serra's pylon (in the East River) identifies with the World Trade Center (on the shore of the Hudson) and Gehry's iridescent fish (in the Hudson) mimics the glittering Chrysler Building (near the East River). Yet this inversion seems to contradict the more obvious duality: because the architect's fish is coupled structurally with a pylon proposed by a sculptor, the fish is something other than sculpture. But even this opposition fails: the fish also appears to be something other than architecture. Whereas Serra's pylon is an obvious repetition of his work as a sculptor, Gehry has broken character. In other words, whereas the bridge might easily be read as an allegory of the workings of collaborative exchange—with each collaborator imagining the other as "other"—the fish seems to put Gehry in collaboration with himself. He has not presented us with something that we recognize as architecture: we are asked to consider other possibilities.

In short, … desire finds its meaning in the desire of the other, not so much because the other holds the key to the object desired, as because the first object of desire is to be recognized by the other.
Jacques Lacan, "The Function and Field of Speech and Language in Psychoanalysis" (1956)

We might take Gehry at his word when he says that the fish represents "a kind of perfection that I couldn't achieve with my buildings."[5] This statement, coupled with his other statements about minimizing problems of function, tempts architects and critics to test the horizon of the discipline. When a fish is unapologetically proposed as a "perfect" architectural form, not only do fundamental assumptions about architecture's obligation to express (or signify) function come under question, but we also cannot simply explain away the fish as (nonfunctional) sculpture or "not-architecture." Such a reductive distinction is apparent in Joseph Giovannini's assertion that "although the [Formica fish] lamps may issue some light, they hardly qualify as usable lamps. They are works of art first and only minimally lamps."[6] Gehry insists that he is first an architect and in that role collaborated with artists. To label him as an artist is to overlook the architectural intentions and implications in all of his work. If Gehry's fish is considered as an *architectural* project, it cannot be dismissed as "art," regardless of his apparent desire to seek the counsel and camaraderie of artists. But the dynamic of those relationships, particularly his desire for the recognition of others outside of the architectural discipline, provides a clue to his work. The fish is a ploy that lures us, and Gehry himself, into another version of the architect's identity.

The otherness of the fish derives both from its challenge to the limits of the architectural discipline and from the way it reconfigures the discipline itself. In both obvious and devious ways, the fish critiques the complex and seemingly inescapable history of the anthropomorphism of architecture. This critique provides one of the deeper connections to literalism. Accusations of anthropomorphism—and attempts to evade its conventions—were at the center of the debates between modernists and literalists, with each believing the other embraced a secretly anthropomorphic, and thus not fully abstract, sensibility. Among the literalists, Robert Smithson satirized Greenberg's formalism for "anthropomorphizing space," while Donald Judd described modernist sculpture as allusive to the human figure: "A beam thrusts; a piece of iron follows a gesture; together they form a naturalistic and anthropomorphic image."[7] Michael Fried's discussion of anthropomorphism in "Art and Objecthood" was a direct retort to Judd: "a kind of latent or hidden naturalism, indeed anthropomorphism, lies at the core of literalist theory and practice."[8] Beyond the charges and countercharges lie concerted efforts by all parties to reconfigure the relationship between abstraction and the human body. While the literalists used direct, physical relationships between objects and individuals to expand the field of abstract thinking to include all manner of everyday conditions, Fried's concepts of "presentness" and "radical abstraction" attempted to convert the human form and its occupation of space into a variety of visual relationships that could "defeat" all literal awareness of the body.[9] This is true of his conceptualization of both painting and sculpture, and in each case it involves a simultaneous refusal of literalness and contained space.

Fried's discussion of the paintings of Jules Olitski offers the most interesting example. In a 1965 essay in *Artforum,* Fried makes the surprising and unelaborated claim that Olitski's use of color makes his paintings appear less like artworks and "more like natural objects to be contemplated, enjoyed or embraced or possessed; most of all they are like the human body." Some inkling of what Fried means is revealed later in the essay when he discusses the "function of the framing edge" in Olitski's work. At issue is whether the surface of the painting appears like a "background"—as in "traditional painting"—or whether it achieves a more "structural" relationship in which "the entire 'contents' of a given picture relate as an integral entity to the framing-edge conceived and experienced as a whole."[10] On the one hand, Fried is attempting to explain how Olitski's work participates in "one of the most crucial formal problems thrown up by the development of advanced painting over the past decade: namely, that of finding a self-aware and strictly logical relation between the painted image and the framing edge."[11] On the other hand, in raising the issue of the human body, Fried is engaging an entirely new issue in his criticism which, in Olitski's case, is addressed through his attention to proportion and scale. Fried argues that, as a result of Olitski's ability to unify the surface and the framing edge, he could produce successful modernist paintings of a size and proportion similar to the human body without lapsing into anthropomorphism: "Structural considerations of this kind must lie behind Olitski's extraordinary success in a number of paintings … whose dimensions—roughly, between six and eight feet high by no more than two feet wide—have never until now been made to yield work of comparable quality" (fig. 6.4).[12]

The following year, in "Shape as Form," Fried would return to this issue of anthropomorphism and clarify his observations and claims. In addition to refusing to allow the painted surface to appear as background, Olitski refuses to allow the framing edge to "mark the limits of a spatial *container*."[13] Again Fried suggests that Olitski's success is in part due to the "narrow vertical format" which makes the painting—or its appearance—"self-sufficient, a presence, like that of a human figure, instead of a void wanting to be filled." Thus Olitski uses pictorial devices to "acknowledge" and "defeat" anthropomorphism. This approach distinguishes his work from that of the literalists which, according to Fried, is unable to achieve a similar effect. Instead, Tony Smith's six-foot cube, *Die* (1962), seems to Fried "something like a surrogate person—that is, a kind of *statue*."[14] Even more objectionable to Fried is the cube's "hollowness"—it has an "inside"—which is precisely the kind of contained space that modernist painting and sculpture overcome through "radical abstraction."

I may try minimalism again. I still like minimalism, whether you believe it or not.
Frank Gehry, from "Conversations with Frank Gehry" (1995)

Gehry's fish repeats this problematic of anthropomorphism, structure, shape, and space in architectural terms, and in doing so disturbs a long, collectively repressed concern with anthropomorphism and humanist iconography in architecture. The fish plays this out as a game of abstraction and refusal on several levels. First, it assumes many of the traits that Greenberg and Fried attribute to modernist art. For example, the inside of the fish is not "contained" by its skin (or scales). Nor is the fish intended to be occupied. It is an "empty" shape. Like painting or modernist sculpture it is "all outside" or "all surface."[15] Compared to Gehry's buildings, the fish is hardly an object. Second, the fish suggests neither of the two postmodernist tropes that were pervasive in the 1980s: neither the humanist inscription of the whole body nor the fragmented body of deconstructivism.[16] Formally and symbolically, a fish establishes an ironic (anti-)humanism; fish are deficient in almost every human attribute, from their subaqueous

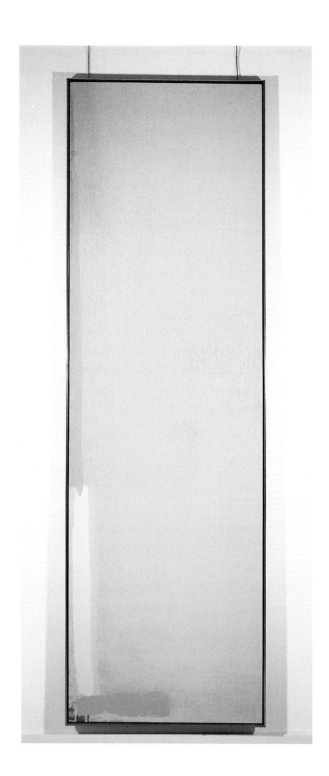

6.4 Jules Olitski, *Suspension*, 1967. Acrylic on canvas, 102 × 30 in.

environment to their lack of limbs, frontality, or expression. Further, the fish connotes an ambiguous sexuality, being simultaneously phallic and feminine, as is clear in an entry in one encyclopedia of symbols, which lists these primary meanings for fish: "Phallic, fecundity; procreation; life renewed and sustained; the power of the waters as origin and preservation of life; the watery element; associated with all aspects of the Mother Goddess as genetrix and with all lunar deities."[17]

Perhaps, then, the fish's perfection derives from the ways it mimics modernist art as well as from its evasion of both functionalism and anthropomorphism. Experimenting with the fish allows Gehry to assume other identities and opens an unusual transdisciplinary dimension in the design, construction, and understanding of architectural form and space. The appearance of the fish-as-architecture can be explained in psychoanalytic terms as an experiment in the redescription of the architect-as-subject and of architecture's subjective effects. Design could be understood in Freudian terms as a process of "working through" *(Durcharbeitung)* an other and a presentation of ever-provisional "constructions" *(Konstruktionen)*. Freudian interpretations of Gehry's fish have been offered by many critics and architects, yet they have focused solely on the role that the fish plays in Gehry's own memories and drives. Those biographical readings, which treat the fish as a screen memory from his childhood that reemerges as a fetish and as a substitute for a yet to be constructed architecture, do not proceed beyond the particular facts of Gehry's own persona and consequently do not exploit the theoretical potential of his work or speculate on how his design process relates to Freudian theories of the psychology of the artist or the psychology of art.[18] To the contrary, Gehry's persistent use of the fish is peculiarly apt to provoke general questions about the limits and possibilities of Freudian and post-Freudian psychoanalytic understandings of architecture.[19]

Freud often described the "work" of psychoanalysis as a kind of edifice. In his 1937 essay "Constructions in Analysis," he explained that the work of the analyst involves two modes of assembling the various kinds of "raw material" (dreams, ideas, actions) supplied by the subject. "Interpretation," which requires making sense of an individual bit of material, is a weaker synthetic act than "construction," which involves the assembly of multiple materials. The analyst's work "is a 'construction' when one lays before the subject a piece of his early history that he has forgotten."[20] The analyst's

> work of construction, or if it is preferred, of reconstruction, resembles to a great extent an archaeologist's excavation of some dwelling-place that has been destroyed and buried or of some ancient edifice.... But just as the archaeologist builds up the walls of the building from the foundations that have remained standing, determines the number and position of

the columns from depressions in the floor and reconstructs the mural decorations and paintings from the remains found in the debris, so does the analyst proceed when he draws his inferences from the fragments of memories.[21]

Thus Freud does not imagine himself as an architect but as an archaeologist.[22] Yet having offered the archaeological analogy, he then asks us to fully suspect it because it implies a wholly different process and conclusion from that of psychoanalysis: "for the archaeologist the reconstruction is the aim and end of his endeavors while for analysis the construction is only preliminary labor."[23] Freud then offers the construction of a house (which proceeds in a planned or linear manner) as a countermetaphor to the complicated progress of analysis: "[Analysis] is not preliminary labor in the sense that the whole of it must be completed before the next piece of work can be begun, as, for instance, is the case with house-building, where all the walls must be erected and all the windows inserted before the internal decoration of the rooms can be taken in hand."[24]

Freud's qualification of his role as an analyst thus establishes a set of identity relationships that are analogous to Gehry's architectural identity as acted out with the fish in the bridge project. Freud constructs, but he is not an architect; he reconstructs, but he is not an archaeologist. Nevertheless he identifies with both roles. Through these mistaken identifications, Freud leads us back and forth along an "alternating" path of understanding. Between assembly and disassembly is dissembling, or what is more commonly called a "put-on." Dissembling is related to both simulation and dissimulation: on the one hand it implies the potential to put on a false appearance, to mimic; on the other, the need to conceal itself. This is not a conscious act of expression, control, or technique, but, by turns, a dis-play, a mis-take, or an acting out.

To borrow the words of Polonius, our bait of falsehood has taken a carp of truth.
Sigmund Freud, "Constructions in Analysis" (1937)

Truth for the psychoanalytic subject is not overtly similar to truth for the architect, yet just as there is a split between the analysand's personal recollections and his or her affects (reconstructions in fantasy, acting out, or speech), there is also a split between the architect's personal recollections and the possible social reconstructions that take the form of architecture. This similitude between architecture and analysis becomes more evident near the end of Freud's essay where he introduces the notion of "historical truth." According to Freud, the therapeutic work of analysis develops upon the "common ground" of a "remote past" outside of personal experience.[25] Freud was interested in establishing an objective datum upon which he could address the common charge that the analyst's construction is authoritative and thus cannot be contested, but only denied, by the subject. Sarah Kofman explains this dilemma as a difficulty in establishing the difference between recollection (memory) and misrecognition (what Jacques Lacan would call *méconnaissance*): "Because recognition can imply misrecognition and bad faith, the analyst can merely construct a plausible historical truth. Verification of the construction is a practical rather than a theoretical matter, for 'truth' in this situation can be known only through its effects on the patient."[26] Those effects are in fact the test of the construction, for unless the construction leads to further recollections by the subject—that is, if it is accepted without denial yet remains incapable of provoking additions to the edifice—the construction will be considered benign, and new ones must be initiated in order for the process to continue. As Freud writes, "Only the further course of the analysis enables us to decide whether our constructions are correct or unservicable."[27]

Stability and reassurance are not the favored attributes of these constructions. They must be "serviceable" or "true"; that is, they must produce positive effects. The psychoanalytic conception of effective construction spurs a number of questions. What could it mean for an architectural design to be a "true" recognition? Do some works of architecture "imply misrecognition and bad faith"? Can transference occur in architectural design without speech? Or does speech play a role in the analysis of architecture? Is architectural design distinct from other arts as they have been examined in the discourse of psychoanalysis?

If architecture, like psychoanalysis, does not conceive of construction as its "aim and end," and if, like psychoanalysis, the process of architectural construction is not linear but "alternating," then architecture too should seek its "verification" in its effects upon the subject, not in its objective appearance. A "true" construction is verified in its being put to use. That is, it will produce further revelations in the mind, and alter the behavior (or symptoms) of the subject. It is possible to recognize the similarity between Gehry's and Freud's concepts of construction if only because Gehry has commented on his own affection for unfinished buildings, an interest that has been interpreted as a fascination with movement or a modernist predilection for structure and transparency. But Gehry seems to have a different interest. As he said of his own house after he had moved into it, "I'm not sure if it's finished. . . . It's confusing. I was wondering the other day what effect this had on my family. I've noticed my wife leaves papers and stuff around … [and] I was beginning to think this had something to do with her not knowing whether I'm finished or not."[28] Gehry is not simply, as one critic has written, "a poet of the temporary."[29] His architecture is intricately involved with what Lacan called "the function of time in the realization of the human subject."[30]

Following Freud's lead, Jacques Lacan puzzled over the tension between development (*Entwicklung*) and history (*Geschichte*—"that within which the subject recognizes himself") and warned against conflating the "times" of individual and collective memory: "The precise reliving—that the subject remembers something as truly belonging to him, as having been truly lived through, with which he communicates and which he adopts—we have the most explicit indication in Freud's writings that that is not what is essential. What is essential is reconstruction, the term he employs right up until the end…. when all is said and done, it is less a matter of remembering than rewriting history."[31] Any thorough psychoanalytic understanding of the fish thus entails not only the recollection of biographical facts, but the reconstruction of historical context.

Gehry has implicated himself in questions of memory and history in one of his well-known explanations of the fish: "I had a fantasy with fish and snakes. The fish became an obsession when people started rebuilding Greek temples. I was very annoyed with Post-Modernism. In the early beginnings I felt that we were just starting to find a way to deal with the present so why did we have to go backwards? I got very angry and I said: 'Well, if we're gonna go backwards, we can go back to fish which are 500 million years before man.'"[32] This seemingly flip remark suggests a movement away from Gehry's individual case toward collective memories and historical truth.[33] The fish is offered as a more "true" recollection than the postmodernist revival of past styles and images of architecture. In Gehry's anti-postmodern story, the source for his material is not only his own memory but that of collective memory as allegorized in the narrative of Darwinian evolution: "I think that the primitive beginnings of architecture come from zoomorphic yearnings and skeletal images, and you know, the fish preceded man on this earth. So there's historic content to it too."[34] Gehry is proposing the fish as a less delusive recollection than that of neoclassicism. However disingenuous or simple his remarks, he is appealing to historical truth in the same way that Freud claims that the collective psychoanalysis of an entire society is possible: "If we consider mankind as a whole and substitute it for the single human individual, we discover that it too has developed delusions which are inaccessible to logical criticism and which contradict reality. If, in spite of this, they are able to exert an extraordinary power over men, investigation leads us to the same explanation as in the case of the single individual. They owe their power to the element of *historical truth* which they have brought up from the repression of the forgotten and primaeval past."[35]

Lacan's concepts provide the technique to demonstrate that the story of Gehry's architecture is inseparable from broader questions of the history of the design discipline. Gehry's investment in the fish, begun in 1981, enacts a peculiar version of transference, involves a kind of mimicry, and manifests an "effect" and "repetition" of the temporal dialectic of the mirror stage. Lacan describes the mirror stage as "the original adventure" of the human subject, in which a child (age six to eighteen months) for the first time recognizes the image of its own body as "mirrored" in another body. This recognition gives the subject "an imaginary mastery over its own body, one which is premature in relation to real mastery" and which occurs before the acquisition of the symbolic means to express or understand its insufficiency.[36] This "drama" of identification precipitates a shift from "insufficiency to anticipation—and manufactures for the subject, caught up in the lure of spatial identification, the succession of phantasies that extends from a fragmented body-image to a form of its totality that I shall call orthopaedic—and lastly, to the assumption of the armour of an alienating identity."[37] After the mirror stage (which is never quite over),[38] the subject is ever seeking to fulfill its lack through identification with others, a process that attains its most acute successes and frustrations in transference, both in and outside of the analytic situation.[39]

When I speak to you of the unconscious as of that which appears in the temporal pulsation, you may picture it to yourselves as a *hoop net (naisse)* which opens slightly at the neck and at the bottom of which the catch of fish will be found.
Jacques Lacan, The Four Fundamental Concepts of Psycho-Analysis *(1964)*

Lacan's complex explanation of transference presents a structure—a "temporal pulsation" of identity, body image, space, time, language, and desire—that conceivably operates in Gehry's design thinking: the fish, as symbolic other, functions in the manner of what Lacan calls the "dummy" [*le mort*] analyst. In such a transferential mirroring event, one that has applications and implications beyond Gehry's personal recollections, the architect projects his or her own incapacities onto a body (the fish) that paradoxically represents both a deficient (antihumanist) image and an image of perfection, performing an imaginary act that inverts and involutes the narrative of Lacan's infantile mirror stage. Instead of the architect's recognizing or constructing his or her image as a complete, orthopaedic double (or an anthropomorphic architecture), the fish serves as a dummy that is more perfect, powerfully (but ironically) phallic, sexually ambiguous, sensuously detached from its own body (unable to see or touch itself), and less human (lacking emotion or expression). Through this act of projective mimicry the architect models a potential transference that may also be enacted in the production of works of architecture. In Gehry's case the dummy is a fish, but we can imagine it taking many other forms, for example the pyramid/tomb mythologized by Adolf Loos or the billboards that Robert Venturi and Denise Scott Brown "found" in the Nevada desert.[40]

Architectural design can be conceived in this way as a psychoanalytic process; drawings and models serve as Freudian "constructions" through which the architect recollects or remembers past or primal architectural events. While those constructions, according to Freud, are offered by the analyst in psychoanalytic practice, they are effectively produced by the architect in the process of design. The dummy plays a crucial role because, as Lacan insists, unconscious thoughts emerge only in "the presence of the analyst." Otherwise there is no transference, but merely "repetition of the same missed encounter."[41] Therefore, if design is to produce transference, either it follows the model of a self-analysis (like Freud's work on his own dreams) or transference is spurred by a dummy, in Gehry's case the virtually silent fish. Either way, the fish is not a construction in Freud's terms. Rather, it is a bit of unconstructed material that lends itself to reconstruction, perhaps in what Gehry has called "dumb buildings." Admittedly, Gehry hesitated to "build" fish, and the fish need not be a mimetic representation of an architecture or even itself an architecture in order for it to work its effects. But if it is conceived as a "dummy" that promises to provoke a new architecture through transference, it would be neither a construction nor a cryptic symbol. It is a quasi-subject that substitutes for (or mimics) several missing figures: analyst, father, benevolent patron, primal form, and the desire of the other. Lacanian models of psychoanalysis and its terms—mimicry, transference, mirroring (doubling), and what he calls *la formation de l'analyste*[42]—demonstrate the possibility of the production of an other architecture:

> At the most elementary level, the silent "neutrality" of the analyst (his role as "dummy") enables the subject to project onto him the image of the significant other to whom the subject is addressing his *parole vide.* … But the analyst himself is neither an object nor an *alter ego;* he is the third man. Although he begins by acting as a mirror for the subject, it is through his refusal to respond at the level consciously or unconsciously demanded by the subject (ultimately the demand for love), that he will eventually (or ideally) pass from the role of "dummy," whose hand the subject seeks to play, to that of the Other with whom the barred subject of his patient is unconsciously communicating.[43]

The dummy fish—impassive, incapable of love—passes from narcissistic mirror to a symbol of perfection—Other, *grande A*—silently spawning the constructions that lead to architecture. As is often the case in the design studio, the designing subject is frustrated by silence, but equally frustrated by a positive response. The fish can be silent because the affirmation of the analyst does no more to stabilize the "being" of the subject than the speech (*parole*) of the subject, who finds that this being—that is, the self—"has never been anything more than his construct in the Imaginary and that this construct disappoints all certainties. For in this labor which he undertakes to reconstruct *for another,* he rediscovers the fundamental alienation that made him construct it *like another,* and which has always destined it to be taken from him *by another.*"[44]

Thus is established a series of relationships not unlike those between an architect and a building. The construction is never wholly authorial for a number of reasons, the most elusive being that the architect cannot stabilize any wholly individual conception of architecture as built form. The "static state or statue"[45]—Lacan's discussion of the "orthopaedic" body image—that each subject fantasizes becoming is perhaps the same wish that produces the monumental architecture of humanism. The speech of the architect—the drawings, models, and buildings—are the *parole vide* of design. Those others who eventually construct an edifice based upon those documents necessarily frustrate the realization of an architecture that never "really" follows the architect's words. All design projects (as projections) are never fully *before* us, just as they never reveal just what we are *after.*

Gehry has described the fish as an affect of such frustrations. After the collaboration with Serra, Gehry said, "the fish evolved further: I kept drawing it and sketching it and it started to become for me like a symbol for a certain kind of perfection that I couldn't achieve with my buildings. Eventually whenever I'd draw something and I couldn't finish the design, I'd draw the fish as a notation…. For me it's a symbol of perfection."[46] According to Gehry's explanation, the fish alleviates the frustration of not finishing. The fish appears when the architecture is missing. In other words, we might think that the fish is a substitute for what buildings lack. Even when Gehry did eventually design a fish at the scale of a building (in the Fish Dance restaurant in Japan), it appeared only as a "monument" that is not habitable, unlike the adjacent coiled snake form (fig. 6.5).[47]

Thus the fish, even when "built," always maintains an ambivalent identity relative to habitable building; like many animals, it survives through its devious mimicry (fig. 6.6). If the fish is perfect, yet cannot be a building, and those buildings that are built are admittedly "dumb," could it not be that the fish operates as a more perfect "dumby" and that buildings are simply not dumb enough? The mistake of most critics who address the psychoanalytic aspects of Gehry's work—Germano Celant is a good example—is to identify the fish as a potential building and, implicitly, as a whole body or a complete, unified humanist self:

> I want to call attention to another feature in Gehry's architecture: its capacity to place on trial the architect's attitude toward himself and toward the object (both client and building). The subject is the identity, the identification, the unitary and totalizing instance that molds all differences into a general statement. By contrast, the object is the dissimilarity, the opposite pole of identification, the particular and resulting instance, the extraneous element that has not yet been assimilated. The object is, therefore, that which activates the reevaluation of differences.[48]

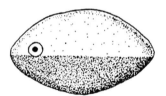

6.5 Frank Gehry, Fish Dance Restaurant, 1986–88.

6.6 Dummies representing male stickleback, from Adolf Portmann, *Das Tier als soziales Wesen,* 1953.

Although Celant concurs with the notion of the fish as a catalyst of differentiation, his notion of the humanist subject—total, assimilating, and willful—contradicts Gehry's imagination of the fish as the ideal other (without apparent desire) of architecture and the architect. In Celant's view, the object—whether architecture or client—is seen as a body to be dissected in order to fulfill the architect's ego, as a response to its own lack. The insistence on the object quality of architecture limits Celant's reading and is a reversion to what Lacan calls the fantasy of *le corps morcelé,* the autoerotic, dismembered body that each subject remembers as existing before the formation of the ego in the mirror stage. But Celant's reading is thoroughly subverted by the Lacanian model of transference, which suggests that Gehry is not regressive or narcissistic in any "normal" sense of ego identification. Further, to say that Gehry is an architect of subjective insights is not simply to say that his work is intuitive, antirational, or personal but to understand him as preoccupied with the concept of the contemporary subject, as Anthony Vidler has noted:

> Rendered introspective by the Romantics, and expressively aerobic by the Modernists, the subject was inherited by Gehry as a strangely ambiguous creature, half traditional, half modern. His response has often been seen as a simple reflection of the subject's postmodern fragmentation, emulating in architecture the morselization and cutting of the body predicated by post-structuralist thought. But another interpretation … would understand Gehry as trying to determine the appropriate limits of his subject with respect to architecture. No longer content to be mirrored in, or confirmed by, its environment, this subject would be self-conscious of the illusion of projection, of the psychological and visual displacements of the mind; it would be a subject that refused to be reformed or rendered healthy.… Architecture, in this sense, would become the stage and the stimulation for this self-enactment … analogous to but not imitative of the subject.[49]

This subjectification of architecture can be taken beyond the analogy offered by Vidler. Both building and architect are situated in an intersubjective relationship. Architecture is not "analogous to the subject" but a virtually present subject (though not a person). Architecture is Other, *grande A,* projecting and structuring a gaze and offering its recognition of the architect and other inhabitants. This is not another version of anthropomorphic architecture; it is mimicry, not an operation of mimesis; it does not attempt to represent the humanist's "whole self." With his fish, Gehry provides the clue toward another, more sophisticated subject-architect who imagines architecture as an uninhabitable, unbuildable body against and toward which all "true" design aspires.

Just about the time I was working on the Indiana apartments an old friend, Elaine May, and I ... discussed the possibility of doing a movie on architects.... She was interested in a particular psychological problem that an architect would have who designed a building that was constructed when he was out of the country. He heard from afar that this was his greatest work, a work of genius.... When he returned to the U.S. and looked at the building he said, 'Oh, my God! They didn't read the plans right ...' And it was just that mistake that made the building so exciting. The movie she wanted would start out on an analyst's couch where this poor guy was trying to deal with that issue in his life. I thought there was nothing an architect could do that would be a mistake like that.... When the Indiana job came along ... we looked at the site and I got a good picture of it and the neighborhood. I came back to the office and we built models of the site from the survey.... A few weeks later, on my way to the airport I drove by the construction.... The [clients] had shown me the wrong site. We went back to the survey and found that the surveyor had put on the wrong north arrow, making the site drawing jive with my vision of the site.... So now the building was under construction and, in a way, Elaine May's scenario had happened.... The space we like best is wrong.

Frank Gehry, from The Architecture of Frank Gehry *(1986)*

More than a decade before the collaboration with Serra, Gehry undertook the project that at once most exemplifies a transferential design process and is enmeshed deeply in the legacy of literalist art. In 1969, Gehry began to work with the painter Ronald Davis on the design of a studio and residence on a hilly site in Malibu, California. Gehry admired Davis's art and attempted to design a building using techniques derived from Davis's work. As a result of that process, the work of both men was altered in significant ways. If the fish is the most polemical statement of Gehry's transdisciplinary recuperation of literalism, the Davis project is his earliest and most systematic effort to devise a transdisciplinary design process.

Following an exhibition of his work at the Tibor de Nagy gallery in the fall of 1966, only his second one-man show, Davis quickly achieved notoriety for a series of polyester resin and fiberglass works that manipulated techniques of perspective and surface reflection (fig. 6.7). Davis was one of several California artists who experimented with unconventional fabrication processes and the production of illusions. Like Larry Bell's Plexiglas cubes or John McCracken's lacquered slabs, Davis's work occupied a space in between Michael Fried's polarities of art and objecthood. In an article on Davis's work published in the April 1967 issue of *Artforum,* just two months before "Art and Objecthood," Fried praised Davis's ability to produce work which, despite being made of plastic and using the seemingly outmoded pictorial device of perspective, was able to "achieve an unequivocal identity as *painting*."[50] Although Davis worked in ways similar to those of literalist sculptors, he had in fact made a wholly original contribution to the medium of painting. Fried thus saw Davis as engaging the same formal problem as Frank Stella and Jules Olitski: he resolved the tension between the literal shape of the work and its painted image. But Davis's techniques were entirely unique. Unlike Olitski, whose brilliance as a colorist allowed him to produce work in which there seemed to be "nothing literal but paint itself,"[51] or Stella, whose paintings were an investigation of the capacity of painting to "defeat" literal shape with depicted shape, Davis used *illusions of objecthood* to overcome the literal shape of his plastic pieces. The perspectival shape of Davis's otherwise flat paintings and the corresponding internal geometry of the image produced the illusion of an object seen in the oblique from above, as though it were sitting on the floor. That three-dimensional illusion contradicts the flatness of the surface, as does the thickness of the plastic construction. As a consequence, "the surface of the painting is experienced in unique isolation from the illusion." Because the shape is so strongly identified with the illusion, Fried writes, "it is virtually impossible to grasp the literal shape" *as* a literal shape. Further, the illusion overwhelms both the material quality of the works and the fact that the color is integral (and in some cases layered in depth), even when one suppresses the illusion and attempts to view the work as a painting: a flat, colored, bounded surface. For Fried, Davis's elaborate (and otherwise suspect) techniques are an elaborate artifice that acknowledges and defeats literalism: "Davis's refusal to settle for anything but ambitious painting … has *compelled* him to use both new materials and two-point perspective."[52]

The complex interplay of illusion, object, surface, and shape in Davis's paintings produces unusual spatial effects. The surface, like that of all painting, is experienced frontally, while the illusive object appears as if it were on the floor, which is somewhat like looking at the plan of a building when it is mounted on the wall. But even the surfaces of Davis's paintings have an unusual spatiality which, Fried argues, is similar to looking in a mirror: "one does not look through them so much as *past* them … [but] not the way one looks past an object so much as how one looks past a reflection."[53] Fried likes Davis's painting, it seems, because it is spatial but not in any literal sense. Like Pollock, who Fried credited with devising a new mode of pictorial "space—if it still makes sense to call it space—in which conditions of seeing prevail rather than one in which objects exist, flat shapes are juxtaposed or physical events transpire," Davis used perspective, if it still makes sense to call it perspective, in a fully modernist manner.[54] That is to say, Davis used perspective not to represent an architectonic space that one can look into, but strictly as a pictorial, formal device.

Gehry was also intrigued by Davis's peculiar use of perspective: "I was fascinated by the fact that he could draw them [perspectival constructions] but he could not make them; he could not turn them into three-dimensional objects."[55] For Fried, of course, it was precisely that inability, or refusal, that made Davis's work *paintings* in a modernist sense. Gehry, on the other hand, saw a possible architecture. Hoping to engage Davis and his work in the design process, Gehry constructed devices to show the artist how to use perspective to represent objects and space (fig. 6.8): "I decided to use the house to teach him how to do it, but I did not succeed.... I took a room and I put vanishing points on the wall with a pen and then I took strings and pinned them down to the site model in the center of the room. When I moved the vanishing points, he made strange drawings in space. It related to his line work in his drawings, and I thought he would get it, but he never got it."[56]

Gehry claims that the experiments were wholly for Davis's benefit: "I did not need to do the wires. I only did them for him to understand what I was doing."[57] Yet Gehry also was learning from the process. His insistence that he "did not need to do the wires" reveals not only how far the painter's imagination was from the architect's, but how far Gehry needed to go to engage Davis on his own terms. By attempting to work in the space between disciplines, Gehry was teaching himself something about Davis and his unique mode of modernist painting.

Gehry's use of perspective to design the Davis Studio is similar to Davis's use of perspective in his paintings; but rather than using illusions to defeat objecthood and literal space, Gehry literalizes the illusion. What Gehry did with the building was exactly what he did with "the wires": he constructed perspectival illusions of space *in actual space.* The room—habitable and conventional architecture—and the site model—a scale replica of a habitable space—served as the stage for a (literal) perspectival illusion: "these beautiful three-dimensional string spaces suspended above the model."[58] In the end, that illusion became the shape of the studio: a distorted cube that is sheathed with a continuous surface of corrugated metal (fig. 6.9). While Davis's paintings use illusion and new materials to produce an innovative pictorial surface, Gehry uses the corrugated metal to heighten one's awareness of the literal shape of the building.

The approach to the building was orchestrated to produce the maximal conflict between the planar geometry of that surface and the perspectival views of the building as an object. If Davis's achievement was to defeat the literalism of his techniques through perspectival illusion, Gehry's achievement was to deploy the same devices as means of engaging architecture, particularly the relationship of the exterior and interior space. When one enters the contained space of the interior, the building can no longer be experienced or conceived as "all surface" and "all outside" (fig. 6.10). For Davis, Gehry's inversion of his techniques was disconcerting and apparently produced something of a crisis. After moving into his new home, Davis did not paint for several months and, according to Charles Kessler, experienced "a period of psychological, physical, and artistic withdrawal."[59] But when he did start working again, his use of perspective was a more conventional pictorial depiction of objects in space and of space in depth. It seems Davis did learn Gehry's lesson after all.

But Gehry also learned Davis's lesson. The building that resulted from the process not only has much in common with the painter's work, but is related to the fish. The fish might be understood as a more perfect version of the Davis Studio, which, for Davis at least, was for a time uninhabitable. Its function as an artist's studio, or as a home for a painter, was not fully realized until some two years after Davis moved into the building. From the painter's perspective, the project was uninhabitable like Gehry's fish. About ten years later, in the collaboration with Serra, Gehry would imagine the fish as an equally dysfunctional architecture—all surface, all outside. Its skin was not perspectival but topological. The space was not architectonic but superficial.

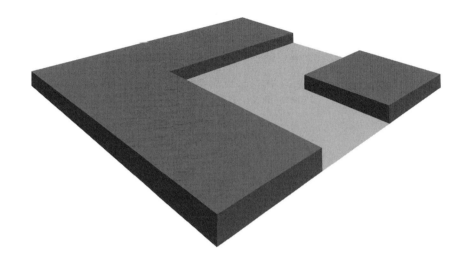

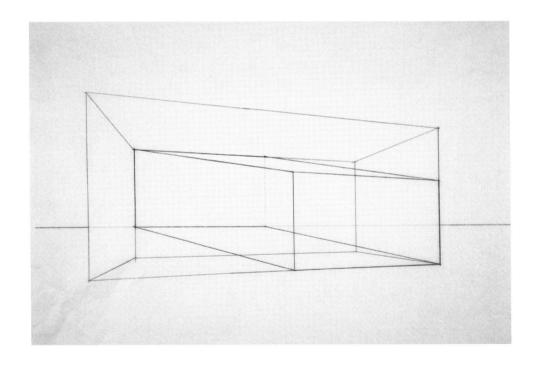

6.7 Diagram of Ronald Davis, *Six-Ninths Red,* 1967. Molded polyester resin, fiberglass, wood, 72 × 131 in. Drawing by Mark Linder.

6.8 Frank Gehry, perspective drawing for Wagner House, 1978.

6.9 Frank Gehry, Ronald Davis Studio, 1969–72. Photo Marvin Rand.

6.10 Frank Gehry, Ronald Davis Studio, 1969–72. Photo Marvin Rand.

Postscript

Alone in an art gallery at Ohio State University in 1969, Barry Le Va produced the artwork he titled *Velocity Piece #1: Impact Run, Energy Drain.* Le Va ran from one end of the large room to the other and slammed into the wall at full speed. He then repeated the act in the opposite direction. This action continued for 103 minutes and was recorded in stereo. For gallery visitors, the encounter with the work consisted only of the damage done to the surfaces of the two gallery walls and two speakers, in the place of the microphones, replaying the audiotape.

Carter Radcliff has recently suggested that Le Va's intention was to show how "cruel" and "oppressive" the "absolutism" of "literalism had become."[1] He argues that Le Va wanted "to demonstrate an impossibility" and to challenge artists to "get out of the box" and "escape imprisonment" by abandoning "the stripped-down, white-walled gallery." But Radcliff's reading of the piece as an *expression* of tragic futility repeats the tendency to cast architecture as the enemy of art. It ratifies Michael Fried's refusal in "Art and Object-hood" of any art that acknowledges its "situation" or its siting "within a room," and epitomizes his accusation that literalist artworks "must be placed not just in [our] space but in [our] way."[2]

What if Le Va's artwork is neither expressive nor an enactment of a desire to escape the gallery, but rather a plea for artists to engage architecture? If that is the case, then accepting the relationship between art and architecture does not mean, as Radcliff implies, that literalism condemns artists to bang their heads against the wall. Rather, Le Va demonstrates the necessity of architecture, and the absurdity and paradox in the promise that it would feel so good if they'd stop.

Notes

INTRODUCTION

1. "Knot" and "navel" are terms borrowed from psychoanalysis. The term "navel" originated in 1900 in Freud's *The Interpretation of Dreams* to designate "a tangle of dream-thoughts which resists unraveling ..., are necessarily interminable and branch out on all sides into the net-like entanglement of our world of thought." Sigmund Freud, *The Interpretation of Dreams,* in *The Standard Edition of the Complete Psychological Works of Sigmund Freud,* ed. James Strachey, 24 vols. (London: Hogarth Press, 1953–74), vol. 5, 530. Jacques Lacan, in 1964, extended the concept to the unconscious and discourse in general. Lacan also consistently described the unconscious as a "knot" that could be understood in terms of topological diagrams, such as what he called the "interior 8." Jacques Lacan, *The Four Fundamental Concepts of Psycho-Analysis,* ed. Jacques-Alain Miller, trans. Alan Sheridan (New York: W. W. Norton, 1977), 23, 131, 155. Samuel Weber, in *The Legend of Freud* (Minneapolis: University of Minnesota Press, 1982), presents an intriguing comparison of Freud's and Lacan's concepts of the navel (75–82).

2. Jacques Lacan, "The Transference and the Drive," in *Four Fundamental Concepts,* 143. First published as *Le séminaire de Jacques Lacan, Livre XI, 'Les quatre concepts fondamentaux de la psychanalyse'* (Paris: Éditions du Seuil, 1973), this seminar was held from January to June 1964.

3. Bhabha explains: "It is not an attempt to strengthen one foundation by drawing from another; it is a reaction to the fact that we are living at the real border of our own disciplines, where some of the fundamental ideas of our discipline are being profoundly shaken. So our interdisciplinary moment is a move of survival—the formulation of knowledges that require our disciplinary scholarship and technique but demand that we abandon disciplinary mastery and surveillance." See W. J. T. Mitchell, "Translator Translated: W. J. T. Mitchell Talks with Homi Bhabha," *Artforum* 33 (March 1995): 118.

4. The most polemical statements on modernism are made in Clement Greenberg's "Modernist Painting," which was first delivered as a radio lecture on the Voice of America in 1960 (and first published in *Arts Yearbook* 4 [1961]); and in Michael Fried's untitled contribution to a 1966 symposium at Brandeis University (published in William Seitz, ed., *Art Criticism in the Sixties* [Boston: October House, 1966], n.p.). For a nuanced and revealing early reassessment of modernist criticism, see Rosalind Krauss, "A View of Modernism," *Artforum* 11 (September 1972): 48–51.

5. Francisco Cerver's *The Architecture of Minimalism* (New York: ARCO, 1997) is a catalog of contemporary architecture that identifies minimalist traits but does not examine their legacy. The most ambitious and productive book to date is Vittorio Savi's and Josep Montaner's *Less Is More: Minimalism in Architecture and the Other Arts* (Barcelona: Col-legi d'Arquitectes de Catalunya, 1993). Savi and Montaner attempt to document a lineage in architecture, sculpture, dance, theater, film, and music, beginning early in the twentieth century with the architecture of Adolf Loos, Hannes Meyer, and Heinrich Tessenow. Montaner's essay in that book, "Taxonomy of Minimalisms," is an ambitious and incisive effort to gather many "strands" of that lineage, but the effort to reconstruct historical relationships is beyond the scope of his writing. Historians of art have almost entirely underestimated (or overlooked) the significance of architecture for the artists of the sixties. Despite the fact that critics and artists in the sixties (notably Lucy Lippard, Robert Mangold, Michael Benedikt, Dan Graham, and Robert Smithson) persisted in making connections to architecture, art historians have not followed those leads. Edward Strickland's *Minimalism: Origins* (Bloomington: Indiana University Press, 1993) gathers evidence of architectural aspects of minimalist art, but its emphasis on origins—specifically the "rudimentary" formal devices introduced in the 1950s by artists such as Barnett Newman and Ellsworth Kelly—implies a linear historical and disciplinary model based in painting. Despite his suggestion that minimalist art "transcends the barriers between media," Strickland's narrative traces a lineage from painting to music to sculpture to literature that leaves disciplinary identities intact. Architecture enters his discussion only allegorically in the figure of the World Trade Center—which he terms the "apotheosis" of minimalist sculpture. This treatment makes architecture twice removed from the "origins" of minimalism, because Strickland defines the works that are usually identified by the term "minimalist movement" (the sculptural and spatial forms of art that emerged in the 1960s) as late "academic" or "mannerist" versions of the "original" minimalism that emerged in painting. James Meyer's recent *Minimalism* (London: Phaidon, 2000) occasionally describes the architectural implications of specific artworks, but completely avoids any elaboration of those associations. For example, Meyer mentions that the early work of Daniel Buren and Michael Asher "disrupted the very architecture of the gallery," but he understands its implications only in terms of critique of the constraints and norms of exhibition. Likewise, Meyer describes Robert Morris's *Box for Standing* in terms of "the architectural form of a doorway," explains that John McCracken's painting contains "forms [that] refer to Neolithic architecture," mentions that Robert Mangold produced a series of paintings titled *Walls* that "suggest windows, doors, or stairwells," and remarks on the importance of scale in the work of Tony Smith and Sol LeWitt, but he does not elaborate the possible significance of these transdisciplinary relationships. Meyer's latest book, *Minimalism: Art and Polemics in the 1960s* (New Haven: Yale University Press, 2001), elaborates on those architectural aspects of minimalist art but still treats them as a marginal issue. Frances Colpitt, in *Minimal Art: The Critical Perspective* (Seattle: University of Washington Press, 1990), goes farthest in identifying texts of the 1960s that make specific references to architecture, but only in a brief section of a larger discussion of perception and space. In a section of her book titled "Architecture and the Environment," Colpitt writes: "By 1966, the larger scale of sculpture was commonly interpreted as architectural, not only in terms of appearance, but because of the interaction between spectator and object, and technical principles. Despite the popularity of the analogy, sculpture was never really confused with architecture" (79).

6. Rosalind Krauss, "Sculpture in the Expanded Field," *October* 8 (Spring 1979): 31, 33.

7. Yve-Alain Bois, "A Picturesque Stroll around *Clara-Clara*," *October* 29 (Summer 1984): 33–62.

8. Christian Bonnefoi, "Louis Kahn and Minimalism," *Oppositions* 24 (Spring 1981): 21.

9. Ibid., 4.

10. Michael Fried, "Art and Objecthood," *Artforum* (June 1967): 12–23; Robert Smithson, "Towards the Development of an Air Terminal Site," *Artforum* (June 1967): 36–40.

11. Donald Judd, "Specific Objects," *Arts Yearbook* 8 (1965): 74.

12. Clement Greenberg, "Towards a Newer Laocoon," *Partisan Review* (July-August 1940): 296.

13. Fried, in Seitz, *Art Criticism in the Sixties,* n.p.

14. Fried, "Art and Objecthood," 23 n. 4.

15. Ibid., 21.

16. Fried, in Seitz, *Art Criticism in the Sixties,* n.p.

17. Greenberg, "Towards a Newer Laocoon," 305.

18. Clement Greenberg, "Abstract and Representational," *Art Digest* (November 1954): 7. As he did in other similar remarks, Greenberg would remove the words "object" and "literally" in the version of this essay published in his book *Art and Culture: Critical Essays* (Boston: Beacon Press, 1961). The revised passage reads: "has now become an entity belonging to the same order of space as our bodies. It is no longer the vehicle of an imagined equivalent of that order."

19. Clement Greenberg, "Picasso at Seventy-Five," *Arts Magazine* (October 1957): 46. In the revised version of this essay published in *Art and Culture,* Greenberg eliminates all implications of physicality: "Modernist pictorial art … calls more attention to the immediate qualities of painting. But like any other kind of picture, the modernist one still assumes that its identity as a picture shuts out awareness of its identity as an object. Otherwise it becomes, at best, sculpture; at worst, a *mere* object" (67).

20. Clement Greenberg, "Sculpture in Our Time," *Arts Magazine* (June 1958): 25.

21. Fried, "Art and Objecthood," 15.

22. Yve-Alain Bois, *Painting as Model* (Cambridge: MIT Press, 1990), xvii.

23. Hartman's essay was first presented at the "Yale Symposium on Literary Criticism" in the spring of 1965 and was published in *Modern Language Notes* 81 (December 1966): 542–556.

24. Judd, "Specific Objects," 74–75.

25. Ibid., 78–80.

26. Robert Smithson, "The Pathetic Fallacy in Esthetics" [1966–67], in *Robert Smithson: The Collected Writings,* ed. Jack Flam, Documents of Twentieth Century Art (Berkeley: University of California Press, 1996), 337.

27. Robert Smithson, "Entropy and the New Monuments," *Artforum* (June 1966): 26–31.

28. Robert Smithson, "Ultramoderne," *Arts Magazine* (September-October 1967): 32.

29. John Hejduk, *Mask of Medusa: Works 1947–1983* (New York: Rizzoli, 1985), 59, 67.

30. Stanley Cavell, "Aesthetic Problems of Modern Philosophy," in Max Black, ed., *Philosophy in America* (Ithaca: Cornell University Press, 1965), 78–81.

31. Walter Benjamin's advocacy of literalism in "The Task of Translator" is offered in the form of an architectural *metaphor:* "a literal rendering of the syntax proves words rather than sentences are the primary element of the translator. For if the sentence is the wall before the language of the original, literalness is the arcade." Walter Benjamin, "The Task of the Translator," in *Illuminations,* ed. Hannah Arendt, trans. Harry Zohn (New York: Schocken Books, 1969), 79.

32. Stanley Cavell, "Ending the Waiting Game: A Reading of Beckett's *Endgame,*" in *Must We Mean What We Say?* (Cambridge: Cambridge University Press, 1969), 119.

1 BLANKLY VISUAL: COLIN ROWE'S PICTORIAL IMPROPRIETY

1. A group including Rowe, John Hejduk, Bernhard Hoesli, and Robert Slutzky taught at the University of Texas from 1954 to 1956 and developed design exercises such as the nine-square problem. For an account of this group and their legacy, see Alexander Caragonne, *The Texas Rangers: Notes from an Architectural Underground* (Cambridge: MIT Press, 1995). From 1963 to 1987, Rowe conducted the Urban Design Studio at Cornell and developed the methods of analysis and design that are now so strongly identified with that school: figure/ground studies, plans generated as negotiations between rotated and overlapping grids, the notion of the "City as Museum" (a collage of legible historical and typological fragments that operates in terms of object/texture dialectics), and a revival of interest in facades, arcades, and porticos as devices of spatial mediation.

2. Colin Rowe, "The Mathematics of the Ideal Villa," *Architectural Review* (March 1947): 101–104; "Mannerism and Modern Architecture," *Architectural Review* 107 (May 1950): 289–299; "Transparency: Literal and Phenomenal," *Perspecta* 8 (1963): 45–54 (by Rowe and Robert Slutzky); "Dominican Monastery of La Tourette, Eveux-sur-Arbresle, Lyons," *Architectural Review* 129 (June 1961): 400–410; and Colin Rowe and Fred Koetter, *Collage City* (Cambridge: MIT Press, 1978). Unless specified otherwise, references to Rowe's essays will be to the first published version, with the corresponding page numbers for the republished versions in Colin Rowe, *The Mathematics of the Ideal Villa and Other Essays* (Cambridge: MIT Press, 1976) given in parentheses.

3. Rowe writes in the acknowledgments of *Collage City* that "the text of this essay was completed in December 1973" and the publication was delayed by "the collection of the illustrations" (186).

4. For divergent claims on Rowe's legacy, see R. E. Somol, "Oublier Rowe," *ANY* 7/8 (1994): 8–15; Peter Eisenman, "Postscript: The Graves of Modernism," *Oppositions* 12 (Spring 1978): 21–22; Thomas Schumacher, "Contextualism: Urban Ideals + Deformations," *Casabella* 35 (1971): 78–86, 359–360; and Stuart Cohen, "Physical Context/Cultural Context: Including It All," *Oppositions* 2 (January 1974): 1–40.

5. Rowe and Koetter, *Collage City,* 58. By far the most dramatic evidence of this change is the two paragraphs Rowe added to his introduction to *Five Architects* at the eleventh hour. (They were inserted into the book as a loose sheet.) His intention was to temper his advocacy for the overt neomodern formalism of the five architects by casting his essay as a pluralist "apologetic" which could be read as also accommodating the emerging contextualist and typological approaches of his colleagues at Cornell. For an account of Rowe's changing views, see Stan Allen, "Addenda and Errata," *ANY* 7/8 (1994): 28–33.

6. Rowe, *Mathematics of the Ideal Villa,* 16.

7. See for example, Henry Millon, "Rudolf Wittkower, *Architectural Principles in the Age of Humanism*: Its Influence on the Development and Interpretation of Modern Architecture," *Journal of the Society of Architectural Historians* 31 (May 1972): 89–90. Also see Caragonne, *Texas Rangers,* 114–124.

8. Colin Rowe, *The Architecture of Good Intentions* (London: Academy Editions, 1994), 50.

9. Meyer Schapiro, "The New Viennese School," *Art Bulletin* 18 (June 1936): 266. In 1965, Vincent Scully made a similar (and characteristically more broad) claim for the ubiquity of pictorialism, writing that "in the America of 1940 architecture was still as fundamentally pictorial as it had been earlier in the American Beaux-Arts." Vincent Scully, "Doldrums in the Suburbs," *Perspecta* 9/10 (1965): 284.

10. Colin Rowe, *As I Was Saying: Reflections and Miscellaneous Essays,* 3 vols., ed. Alexander Caragonne (Cambridge: MIT Press, 1996), 1:73–74, 2:104.

11. For an account of the political implications of Rowe's work, see the first chapter of R. E. Somol, "In Form Falls Fiction" (Ph. D. diss., University of Chicago, 1997). This shift in Rowe's emphasis also corresponds with a broad cultural shift. Mark Jarzombek proposes the term "aesthetic experientialism" for the first stage of pictorial formalism in "De-Scribing the Language of Looking: Wölfflin and the History of Aesthetic Experientialism," *Assemblage* 23 (April 1994): 29–69. Jarzombek distinguishes between "formalism as empathetic experience and formalism as a play of abstract forms" and suggests that a shift occurred from the former to the latter "sometime during the 1940s and 1950s with the popularization in America of abstraction in both painting and architecture." It is clear in Rowe's early essays that he subscribes to some version of empathy theory, and as the shift Jarzombek describes occurred in the broader culture, Rowe's writing becomes increasingly less overt in its formalism, as if trying to avoid guilt by association with the less empathetic and more purely visual formalism. Jarzombek's explanation is an apt description of Rowe's predicament: "Today formalism is generally understood as the manipulation of abstract shapes. In earlier days, it was not about the artist but about the viewer, and not about nonrepresentational forms but about the fundamental *representational* nature of reality, a reality that is not only perceived through the senses but directly linked to our human essence. Formalism was an attempt to reencounter and reawaken the living, human presence in a world stagnating in conceptual immobility" (31).

12. On German aesthetics and architecture, see Harry Francis Mallgrave and Eleftherios Ikonomou, eds. and trans., *Empathy, Form, and Space: Problems in German Aesthetics, 1873–1893* (Santa Monica, Calif.: Getty Center for the History of Art and the Humanities, 1993).

13. See Roger Fry, *Vision and Design* (Cleveland: World Publishing Company, 1920); Clive Bell, *Art* (London: Chatto & Windus, 1914).

14. Alfred Barr, *Picasso: Fifty Years of His Art* (New York: Museum of Modern Art, 1946); Henry-Russell Hitchcock, *Painting toward Architecture* (New York: Duell, Sloan, and Pearce, 1948); Gyorgy Kepes, *Language of Vision* (Chicago: Paul Theobald, 1944); László Moholy-Nagy, *Vision in Motion* (Chicago: Paul Theobald, 1947). A fervent and doctrinaire display of the pictorialist mode is Erle Loran's *Cezanne's Composition* (Berkeley: University of California Press, 1943). While related to the pure design approach of Arthur Wesley Dow's *Composition* (1913) and Denman Ross's *Theory of Pure Design* (1907), the historical lineage of pictorial formalism is quite distinct. See Marie Frank, "The Theory of Pure Design and American Architectural Education in the Early Twentieth Century" (Ph. D. diss., University of Virginia, 1996).

15. Rowe, *As I Was Saying,* 1:43.

16. Henry-Russell Hitchcock, *Modern Architecture: Romanticism and Reintegration* (New York: Payson and Clarke, 1929). One of the introductory essays Rowe wrote for the first volume of *As I Was Saying* is an homage to Hitchcock in which he calls *Modern Architecture* Hitchcock's "best book and the book that brought me to study with him at Yale" (1:16). Hitchcock's 1958 book *Architecture: Nineteenth and Twentieth Centuries* was also significant for Rowe, who wrote a very admiring review as a script for the BBC (Rowe, *As I Was Saying,* 1:177–184).

17. Rowe, *As I Was Saying,* 1:180.

18. Hitchcock, *Modern Architecture,* xxii–xxiii. Armed with that thesis as a critique of modernist architecture's supposed newness, Rowe's early essays offer a series of formal comparisons across centuries: the proportional analysis of Palladio and Le Corbusier in "Mathematics"; the numerous affinities between Zuccheri, Michelangelo, and Le Corbusier in "Mannerism and Modern Architecture"; and the extended analogy between "the Miesian and the Palladian" in "Neo-'Classicism' and Modern Architecture."

19. Rowe, *As I Was Saying,* 1:21.

20. Hitchcock, *Modern Architecture,* 210.

21. Ibid. Rowe's "Character and Composition" can be read as further reflections on the emergence of the New Tradition.

22. Hitchcock, *Modern Architecture,* 158–159.

23. Ibid., 94.

24. Ibid., 220.

25. Rowe, *As I Was Saying,* 1:115–116.

26. Rowe, *Architecture of Good Intentions,* 46–49. A reading list for Rowe's studio in 1969 includes two books by Fiedler, three by Fry, two by Wölfflin, and one each by Hildebrand and Bell. I thank Art McDonald for showing me this document.

27. Clement Greenberg, "Collage," in Clement Greenberg, *Art and Culture: Critical Essays* (Boston: Beacon Press, 1961), 70–83. This essay is a substantial revision (done in 1959) of "The Pasted Paper Revolution," *Art News* (September 1958): 46–49, 60–61.

28. Clement Greenberg, "Avant-Garde and Kitsch," *Partisan Review* (Fall 1939): 34–49.

29. Clement Greenberg, "Modernist Painting," *Arts Yearbook* 4 (1961): 103–108. "Modernist Painting" was first presented as a Forum Lecture on the Voice of America, and was first printed by the U.S. government in 1960. It appeared unrevised in *Arts Yearbook,* and then in a slightly revised form in *Arts and Literature* in 1965, and in various anthologies after that. In Richard Kostelanetz, ed., *Esthetics Contemporary* (Buffalo: Prometheus, 1978), Greenberg wrote a postscript to the essay (205–206).

30. Clement Greenberg, "Towards a Newer Laocoon," *Partisan Review* (July-August 1940): 310.

31. Rosalind Krauss, "Death of a Hermeneutic Phantom: Materialization of the Sign in the Work of Peter Eisenman," *Architecture + Urbanism* (January 1980): 189–219. The next several quotations are taken from page 189. I want to thank Detlef Mertins for leading me to this essay.

32. Krauss is referring to the work of the Russian formalist literary critic Viktor Shklovsky.

33. Krauss, "Death of a Hermeneutic Phantom," 195.

34. Greenberg, "Modernist Painting," 103.

35. Greenberg, "Modernist Painting," 103–104. For an earlier statement on purity and medium, see "Towards a Newer Laocoon": "The arts, then, have been hunted back to their mediums, and there they have been isolated, concentrated and defined.… To restore the identity of an art the opacity of its medium must be emphasized" (305–307).

36. Greenberg, "Modernist Painting," 104. The emphasis on flatness appeared in Greenberg's criticism as early as 1940: in "Towards a Newer Laocoon," he wrote that, with cubism, "the picture plane itself grows shallower and shallower, flattening out and pressing together the fictive planes of depth until they meet as one upon the real and material plane which is the actual surface of the canvas; … a vibrating tension is set up as the objects struggle to maintain their volume against the tendency of the real picture plane to re-assert its material flatness and crush them into silhouettes.… Thus the artist deliberately emphasizes the illusoriness of the illusions which he pretends to create.... But the result is an optical illusion not a realistic one.... As we gaze at a cubist painting of the last phase we witness the birth and death of three-dimensional pictorial space" (308).

37. Clement Greenberg, "After Abstract Expressionism," *Art International* (October 1962): 30.

38. For the definitive account of the significance of the blank picture in formalist discourse, see Thierry de Duve, "The Monochrome and the Blank Canvas," in Serge Guilbaut, ed., *Reconstructing Modernism: Art in New York, Paris, and Montreal, 1945–64* (Cambridge: MIT Press, 1990), 244–310.

39. Krauss, "Death of a Hermeneutic Phantom," 191.

40. Ibid., 195 (emphasis added). Krauss refers only to the "Transparency" essays and quotes from the *revised* version of the first essay which appears in *The Mathematics of the Ideal Villa and Other Essays.*

41. Ibid.

42. Colin Rowe, "Character and Composition; or Some Vicissitudes of Architectural Vocabulary in the Nineteenth Century," *Oppositions* 2 (1974): 43 (61) (emphasis added). This essay was written in 1953–54.

43. In his later writings, Greenberg was consistent in accepting the Kantian separation of the conceptual and the aesthetic. For example, in "Recentness of Sculpture," in Maurice Tuchman, ed., *American Sculpture of the Sixties* (Los Angeles: Los Angeles Museum of Contemporary Art, 1967), Greenberg's critique of literalist and conceptual art was based on that position: "Minimal art remains too much a feat of ideation, and not enough of anything else. Its idea remains an idea, something deduced instead of felt and discovered" (25). Yet at times, particularly in his earlier writings, Greenberg did come close to Rowe's conceptual formalism. A good example is his 1944 essay titled "Abstract Art": "Instead of being aroused, the modern imagination is numbed by visual representation. Unable to represent the exterior world suggestively enough, pictorial art is driven to express as directly as possible what goes on inside the self—or at most the ineluctable *modes* by which that which is outside the self is perceived (Mondrian)." Clement Greenberg, "Abstract Art," *Nation* (April 15, 1944): 450–451.

44. Among Rowe's 1970s revisions to "The Mathematics of the Ideal Villa" is a retrospective application of pictorialism and its impropriety in the place of a form/function opposition (significant additions are capitalized; omissions are in brackets): "this system of horizontal extension WHICH IS *CONCEPTUALLY* logical comes up against the rigid boundary of the [rectangular] block which, ALMOST CERTAINLY, IS FELT TO BE *PERCEPTUALLY* requisite [is fundamental to the programme]" (12).

45. Colin Rowe, "Mannerism and Modern Architecture," *Architectural Review* (May 1950): 295 (40).

46. The first phrase is from "Transparency," 51 (170), and is quoted by Krauss. The second polarity is included in "La Tourette," in *Mathematics of the Ideal Villa*, 200.

47. Greenberg, "Collage," 70.

48. Ibid., 78.

49. By 1971 the cubist controversy had become so involuted and had had such repercussions that critics as seemingly different as Rosalind Krauss and Hilton Kramer could agree in principle. The occasion for the Krauss-Kramer convergence was "The Cubist Epoch," an exhibition curated by the collector and historian Douglas Cooper and staged first at the Los Angeles County Museum of Art and later at New York's Metropolitan Museum of Art. Although Cooper was unable to obtain *Still Life with Chair Caning* for the show, his book-length catalog essay reinforced Barr's realist interpretation (in part, by polemically insisting that the collage's title translates as "Still Life with Caned Chair"). Krauss and Kramer were both provoked by Cooper's position. Krauss ridiculed Cooper for revealing nothing less than gross ignorance, not simply of the names of objects but of any of the recent, innovative interpretations of cubist collage. Kramer accused Cooper of "firmly excluding" any of Picasso's "constructions" from the show, and was quick to imply that it was no coincidence that Picasso had recently decided to donate his first construction sculpture, *Guitar* (1912), to the Museum of Modern Art, the first American museum to exhibit it. Although their general positions are far apart, the alliance of Krauss and Kramer on this matter is no accident; both derive their criticisms from a sympathetic reading of Greenberg, who conceived the first (in Krauss's words) "post-modern interpretation" of (what Kramer termed) "cubist pictorial aesthetics." See Rosalind Krauss, "The Cubist Epoch: The Long Awaited Survey Opens in Los Angeles," *Artforum* 9 (February 1971): 32–38; and Hilton Kramer, "Pablo Picasso's Audacious 'Guitar,'" *New York Times,* March 21, 1971, sec. 2, p. 21; and "Picasso Gives Work to Museum Here," *New York Times,* February 11, 1971, sec. 1, p. 54.

50. Rowe even proposes a *literal* architectural translation of collage based on Barr: "With very slight modifications (for oil cloth caning substitute fake industrial glazing, for painted surface substitute wall, etc.) Alfred Barr's observations could be directly carried over into interpretation of the Ozenfant studio" (*Collage City,* 140, 142).

51. Barr, *Picasso,* 271. Quoted by Rowe in *Collage City,* 139. Greenberg makes precisely the same point, but states it as a negative: "the term 'reality,' always ambiguous when used in connection with art, has never been used more ambiguously than here. A piece of imitation-wood grain wallpaper is not more 'real' under any definition, or closer to nature, than paint on canvas. And even if these materials were more 'real,' the question would still be begged, for 'reality' would still explain next to nothing about the actual *appearance* of the Cubist collage" ("Collage," 70).

52. In the early 1970s, in the course of the quarrel between the Whites and the Grays, Vincent Scully recognized the importance of Villa Schwob in Rowe's thinking, and he criticized the Whites for not seeing the importance of Rowe's reference to that building (or "Le Corbusier's Scala movie theater … which was much the same") in "Mannerism and Modern Architecture." Vincent Scully, *The Shingle Style Today; or, The Historian's Revenge* (New York: Braziller, 1974), 24, 39–40. In the late 1970s, Peter Eisenman identified Rowe's discussion of the blank canvas as the best example of the critical potential of Rowe's pictorialism: "The Rowe critique, in its separation of form and content … was specifically addressed to modern architecture and the Modern Movement and not to the broader philosophical principles of modernism, and as such it was narrowly focused. It dealt only with … a programmatic and perhaps positivistic basis to the relationship between form and content—a kind of mechanistic functionalism. This overtly 'ideological' modernism, which rhetorically anticipated technological and social utopia, co-existed however with another modernism, one that Rowe almost completely ignores. He conveniently fails to note that much of the 'modernist' enterprise had to do with work on the language itself: in architecture this meant a conscious reduction of the discourse, an attempt to assert, for example, the 'blank canvas' of the facade" ("Postscript: The Graves of Modernism," 21–22).

53. Rowe, "Mannerism and Modern Architecture," 294 (38).

54. In 1976 Rowe added references to two critics he considered unusual for their "dispassionate analysis of the Cubist achievement": Christopher Grey [sic], whose *Cubist Aesthetic Theories* appeared in 1953, and Winthrop Judkins, whose "Towards a Reinterpretation of Cubism" appeared in 1948.

55. Rowe and Slutzky, "Transparency: Literal and Phenomenal," 45–46 (161). The 1976 version clarifies the pictorial emphasis (additions and capitalized): "Therefore, at the beginning of any inquiry into transparency, a basic distinction must be established. Transparency might be an inherent quality of substance—as in a wire mesh or glass curtain wall, or it may be an inherent quality of organization—AS BOTH KEPES AND, TO A LESSER

DEGREE, MOHOLY SUGGEST IT TO BE; AND one might, for this reason, distinguish between a REAL OR *literal* and a *phenomenal* OR SEEMING transparency." Subsequent references to this essay are given in the text.

56. Greenberg, "Collage," 70–71. Subsequent references to this essay are given in parentheses in the text.

57. In the final paragraph of "Sculpture in Our Time," Greenberg attributes a similar, but more reductive, fusion to modernist sculpture but suggests a different configuration of the three arts: "A work of sculpture, unlike a building, does not have to carry more than its own weight, nor does it have to be *on* something else, like a picture; it exists for and by itself literally as well as conceptually. And in this self-sufficiency of sculpture, wherein every conceivable as well as perceptible element belongs altogether to the work of art, the positivist aspect of the modernist 'aesthetic' finds itself most fully realized. It is for a like self-sufficiency that both painting and architecture seem to strive." Clement Greenberg, "Sculpture in Our Time," *Arts Magazine* (June 1958): 25.

58. Rowe, "La Tourette," 401 (180).

59. Rowe, "Mannerism and Modern Architecture," 289 (30).

60. Ibid., 289–290 (30–31).

61. Ibid., 290–291 (32).

62. See also his discussion of the frame as both a literal and phenomenal organizing device, in Colin Rowe, "Chicago Frame," *Architectural Review* (November 1956): 285–289.

63. Rowe, "La Tourette," 407 (191).

64. Ibid., 402, 407 (184, 189).

65. In "What Is a Picture," Jacques Lacan makes "a distinction between the picture (or painting) and representation." "The point is not that painting gives an illusory equivalence to an object" but that a picture "pretends to be something other than what it is." This particularly human game of mimicry, or masking, also reflects back on the viewer: "everything is articulated between two terms that act in an antinomic way—on the side of things, there is the gaze, that is to say, things look at me, and yet I see them." The peculiar effect of this "scopic field" is that viewing subjects themselves "turn into a picture." Jacques Lacan, "What Is a Picture," in *The Four Fundamental Concepts of Psycho-Analysis,* ed. Jacques-Alain Miller, trans. Alan Sheridan (New York: W. W. Norton, 1977), 106, 109, 110, 112.

66. Rowe, "La Tourette," 402 (188).

67. See Rowe's "Neo-'Classicism' and Modern Architecture" on the flanking metaphor for theory: "Persuasive, sometimes contradictory, often highly condensed, precisely because it is a climate of opinion, orthodox theory does not submit itself too readily to analysis. It is like a building which resists frontal examination which, in consequence, one is obliged to approach from the flank" (6 [123]).

68. Rowe, "La Tourette," 410 (197). In 1976, he adds images of the earlier Maison Citrohan (1920). The resemblance to works soon to be produced by Donald Judd and Robert Morris, or even to the corridors and rooms of Bruce Nauman, is obvious. Rowe credits Vincent Scully for devising the term "megaron volume." See Vincent Scully, *Modern Architecture* (New York: Braziller, 1961), 42.

69. Anthony Vidler, "Losing Face: Notes on the Modern Museum," *Assemblage* 9 (June 1989): 54. Vidler's provocative interpretation of Rowe's preoccupation with facades, frontality, and faciality was an immense influence on the present work.

70. Rowe, "La Tourette," 407 (192).

71. Ibid., 408, 410 (193, 200).

72. Ibid., 410 (200).

73. Ibid., 410 (197).

74. Rowe, "La Tourette," in *The Mathematics of the Ideal Villa,* 195–200 passim.

75. Ibid., 197, 200.

2 FLATLY CONFUSED: CLEMENT GREENBERG'S FORMALISM ACROSS DISCIPLINES

1. Clement Greenberg, "Modernist Painting," *Arts Yearbook* 4 (1961): 103–108; and "Collage," in Clement Greenberg, *Art and Culture: Critical Essays* (Boston: Beacon Press, 1961), 70–83.

2. The chronology of the two essays is complicated. "Modernist Painting" was first presented as a Forum Lecture on the Voice of America, and was printed first by the U.S. Government in 1960. It appeared unrevised in *Arts Yearbook,* and then in a slightly revised form in *Arts and Literature* in 1965, and in various anthologies after that. Greenberg wrote a postscript to the essay when it appeared in Richard Kostelanetz, ed., *Esthetics Contemporary* (Buffalo: Prometheus, 1978), 205–206. In a way, "Modernist Painting" remained a "new" essay for almost five years as a result of being revised and republished in 1965. The later version received more attention than the earlier version. In fact, many anthologies and bibliographies still mistakenly date the essay to 1965. "Collage" is a substantial revision (done in 1959) of "The Pasted Paper Revolution," *Art News* (September 1958): 46–49, 60–61.

3. The essay titled "The New Sculpture" in *Art and Culture* is a revision of "Sculpture in Our Time," *Arts Magazine* 32 (June 1958): 22–25, which itself is a revision of an earlier essay titled "The New Sculpture," *Partisan Review* 16 (June 1949): 637–642. "Modernist Sculpture, Its Pictorial Past" is a revision of "Cross-Breeding of Modern Sculpture," *Art News* 51 (Summer 1952): 74–77, 123–124.

4. Among the revisions to "Collage" is the addition of "architecture" to the concluding statement that the "monumentality of Cubism" involves "an attitude toward the immediate physical means of pictorial art—thanks to which easel paintings and even 'sketches' acquire the self-evident self-sufficiency of architecture" (83). The final sentence of "The New Sculpture" reads: "It is for a self-sufficiency like sculpture's, and sculpture's alone, that both painting and architecture now strive" (*Art and Culture,* 145). In "Modernist Sculpture, Its Pictorial Past," the essay that develops the most elaborate genealogy of the relationships between the arts, Greenberg argues (also in a revised passage) that "Brancusi, under the influence of Cézannian and Cubist painting as much as anything else, pursued the monolith to an ultimate extreme … that approached the condition of architecture in itself—as pure architecture or as monument" (*Art and Culture,* 162).

5. Clement Greenberg, "David Smith," in Greenberg, *Art and Culture,* 203.

6. As early as 1968, Barbara Reise recognized how in "the 1960s, the tone of Greenberg's criticism changed," becoming "increasingly defensive and academic." Barbara Reise, "Greenberg and the Group: A Retrospective View, Part I," *Studio International* (May 1968): 255. More recently, Peter Osborne has divided Greenberg's writings into three periods: (1) the "two founding essays of 1939–40," (2) the "art criticism of 1941–61 … culminating in the publication of *Art and Culture,*" and (3) the "essentially defensive later writings and interviews from 1962 onwards," which themselves might be "sub-divided thematically into writing of three kinds: i) Attacks on Pop art and Minimalism as 'Novelty Art,' … ii) The modification of the theory of modernism on the basis of Wölfflin's cyclical art history of successive 'painterly' and 'non-painterly' styles … , iii) A meta-critical defense of formalist aesthetics in the form of a vindication of the objectivity of a Kantian concept of 'taste' and the explicit denial of the rational contestability of critical judgments through argument." Peter Osborne, "'Mere Ungovernable Taste': Clement Greenberg Revised," *Architecture-Space-Painting* (London: Academy Editions, 1992), 90.

7. By the late 1960s Greenberg was openly anxious about the survival of his critical model. In an interview in 1968, he admitted, "The question now is one of continuity: will the avant-garde survive in its traditional form? (And there's no paradox in juxtaposing 'avant-garde' and 'tradition.')" Edward Lucie-Smith, "Interview with Clement Greenberg," *Studio International* (January 1968): 5.

8. Early explicit efforts to suggest an alternative approach include Wayne Andersen, "Looking Back from the Sixties," in Maurice Tuchman, ed., *American Sculpture of the Sixties* (Los Angeles: Los Angeles County Museum of Art, 1967), 15–18; Corinne Robins, "Object, Structure, or Sculpture: Where Are We?" *Arts Magazine* 39 (September-October 1966); Max Kozloff, "The Further Adventures of American Sculpture," *Arts Magazine* 39 (February 1965).

9. Clement Greenberg, "Avant-Garde Attitudes: New Art in the Sixties," *Studio International* (April 1970): 142.

10. Ibid.

11. "Post Painterly Abstraction" was the title of an exhibition Greenberg curated at the Los Angeles County Museum of Art in April-June 1964. His catalog essay was reprinted as "Post Painterly Abstraction," *Art International* (Summer 1964): 63–65. In that essay, Greenberg explicitly states his adherence to the dualist principles of the "great Swiss art historian, Heinrich Woelfflin," explaining that the predominant "style" of the fifties, as evident in abstract expressionism, was painterly, in both sculpture and painting. The "style" that succeeded it, that is, the subject of his exhibition, is predominantly linear.

12. Greenberg, "Avant-Garde Attitudes," 143.

13. Greenberg, "Sculpture in Our Time," 25. In the same year, in the essay that would become "Collage," Greenberg was more succinct: "Pictorial illusion begins to give way to what could be more properly called optical illusion" ("Pasted Paper Revolution," 48). In "Modernist Painting," Greenberg would write simply that the illusion of "space in depth" has been abandoned in favor of "a strictly pictorial, strictly optical third dimension" which "can only be seen into; can be traveled through, literally or figuratively, only with the eye" (106).

14. Greenberg, "Sculpture in Our Time," 23, 25. Painting, on the other hand, was required to strenuously avoid any sculptural effects, as Greenberg writes in "Modernist Painting": "three-dimensionality is the province of sculpture. To achieve autonomy, painting has had above all to divest itself of everything it might share with sculpture.... At the same time, however, Modernist painting shows, precisely by its resistance to the sculptural, how firmly attached it remains to tradition, beneath and beyond all appearances to the contrary. For the resistance to the sculptural dates far back before the advent of Modernism" (104).

15. Those shows include "Black White and Grey," Hartford Atheneum (1964); "Seven Sculptors," Philadelphia Institute of Contemporary Art (1965); "The Box Show," Byron Gallery (1965); "Flavin, Judd, Morris, Williams," Green Gallery (1965); "10," Dwan Gallery (1966); "Primary Structures," Jewish Museum (1966); "Sculpture's Ambiguous Image," Walker Art Center (1966); "Eccentric Abstraction," Fischbach Gallery (1966); and Tony Smith's first two solo shows at the Wadsworth Atheneum and the Philadelphia Institute of Contemporary Art, both in late 1966.

16. Clement Greenberg, "Recentness of Sculpture," in Tuchman, *American Sculpture of the Sixties,* 24–26. Greenberg writes: "In the sixties it has been as though art—at least the kind that gets the most attention—set itself as a problem the task of extricating the far out 'in itself' from the merely odd, the incongruous, and the socially shocking.... The Minimalists appear to have realized, finally, that the far-out in itself has to be the far-out as end in itself, and this means the furthest-out and nothing short of that. They appear to have realized that the most original and furthest-out art of the last hundred years ... usually lay on the borderline between art and non-art.... Given that the initial look of non-art was no longer available to painting, since even an unpainted canvas now stated itself as a picture, the borderline between art and non-art had to be sought in the three-dimensional, where sculpture was, and where everything material that was not art also was. Painting had lost the lead because it was so ineluctably art, and it now devolved on sculpture or something like it to head art's advance" (24).

17. Andersen, "Looking Back from the Sixties," 15–18.

18. Clement Greenberg, "America Takes the Lead, 1945–1965," *Art in America* (August-September 1965): 109.

19. But the 1960s were different in one important respect: many artists were also critics, whose theoretical writings emerged simultaneously with their artworks. In fact, Phyllis Tuchman writes that minimalism is significant because critical support preceded actual exhibitions of the work: "Long expository articles appeared quickly in well-circulated art journals (*Art in America, Arts, Artforum, Art Voices,* and *Arts Yearbook*) throughout 1965, even though no major exhibition had yet been held." Phyllis Tuchman, "Minimalism and Critical Response," *Artforum* (May 1977): 27.

20. Wayne Andersen, "The Fifties," *Artforum* (Summer 1967): 60–67. By 1967 *Artforum* had assumed a key role in the turbulent new art movements of the 1960s. Founded in San Francisco in 1962 as a distinctly West Coast magazine, the magazine took up residence in Los Angeles for eighteen months (the November 1965 through May 1967 issues). The Summer 1967 issue coincided with the relocation of *Artforum*'s offices from California to New York, a move that confirmed the end of its role as an "outsider" magazine. Fried joined the magazine as a contributing editor in March 1966.

21. Amy Newman, *Challenging Art: Artforum 1962–74* (New York: Soho Press, 2000), 157.

22. Philip Leider, "American Sculpture at the Los Angeles County Museum of Art," *Artforum* (Summer 1967): 6.

23. Hal Foster has called this situation "the crux of minimalism," and argues that "minimalism threatens modernist practice—more, that it consummates it, completes and breaks with it at once.... In short, minimalism appears as a historical crux in which the formalist autonomy of art is at once achieved and broken up, in which the ideal of pure art becomes the reality of just another specific object among serial others, one thing after another." Hal Foster, "The Crux of Minimalism," in Howard Singerman, ed., *Individuals: A Selected History of Contemporary Art, 1945–1986* (New York: Abbeville Press, 1986), 162, 175.

24. In a discussion of philosophical modernism (in which, curiously, he uses Greenberg's criticism to illustrate his understanding of the logic of modernism), Stephen Melville remarks on another 1967 event to introduce the concept of the "event": a lecture by Jacques Derrida, which would become the essay "Sign, Structure and Play in the Discourse of the Human Sciences." In the essay, Derrida asserts: "Perhaps something has occurred in the history of the concept of structure that could be called an 'event' if this loaded word did not entail a meaning which it is precisely the function of structural—or structuralist—thought to reduce or suspect. But let me use the term 'event' anyway, employing it with caution and as if in quotation marks. In this sense, this event will have the exterior form of a rupture and a redoubling." Stephen Melville, *Philosophy Beside Itself: On Deconstruction and Modernism* (Minneapolis: University of Minnesota Press, 1986), 3.

25. Clement Greenberg, "Where Is the Avant-Garde?" *Vogue,* June 1967, 112–113, 167.

26. In "Modernist Painting" Greenberg is explicitly Kantian, but a decade later, in "Can Taste Be Objective?" he clearly distances himself from Kantian aesthetics and suggests that Hume's empiricism is a more accurate description of the actual development of cultural mores. Clement Greenberg, "Can Taste Be Objective?" *Art News* 72 (February 1973): 22–23, 92.

27. In all his writings after "Towards a Newer Laocoon," Greenberg puts the words "pure" and "purity" in quotation marks. In his 1978 postscript to "Modernist Painting," he explains that he used "quotation marks around *pure* and *purity*" because "'pure' art was a useful illusion, but this doesn't make it any less an illusion. Nor does the possibility of its continuing usefulness make it any less an illusion" (206).

28. Greenberg, *Art and Culture,* vii.

29. Greenberg, "Recentness of Sculpture," 25.

30. Clement Greenberg, "After Abstract Expressionism," *Art International* (October 1962): 30.

31. Greenberg explains that "when it happens that a single art is given the dominant role, it becomes the prototype of all art: the others try to shed their proper characters and imitate its effects. The dominant art in turn tries to absorb the functions of the others. A confusion of the arts results." Greenberg, "Towards a Newer Laocoon," 297.

32. Ibid., 305.

33. In *Art and Culture,* Greenberg added a sentence to the 1957 essay "New York Painting Only Yesterday" (retitled "The Late Thirties in New York") remarking on the political origins of his critical position: "someday it will have to be told how 'anti-Stalinism,' which started out more or less as 'Trotskyism,' turned into art for art's sake, and thereby cleared the way, heroically, for what was to come" (*Art and Culture,* 230). In 1939, Greenberg defended the avant-garde, and even tailored the concept, not because it could serve positive political ends, but because—by definition—it resisted political manipulation and contamination: "the main trouble with avant-garde art and literature, from the point of view of fascists and Stalinists, is not that they are too critical, but that they are too 'innocent,' that it is too difficult to inject effective propaganda into them, that kitsch is more pliable to this end." Clement Greenberg, "Avant-Garde and Kitsch," *Partisan Review* (Fall 1939): 47.

34. For a controversial account of the political situation, see Serge Guilbaut, *How New York Stole the Idea of Modern Art* (Chicago: University of Chicago Press, 1983), 18–47: "When *Partisan Review* resumed publication in December 1937 under a new group of editors, it took a new political line. Working gradually toward disengagement, the magazine abandoned proletarian literature and tried to establish an intellectual community, a community so totally alienated that it could develop into a 'revolutionary force in opposition.' The editors took the position that modern literature must be free of all political interference" (28).

35. Greenberg, "Avant-Garde and Kitsch," 49. In "Towards a Newer Laocoon" Greenberg wrote: "The avant-garde, both child and negation of Romanticism, becomes the embodiment of art's instinct for self-preservation. It is interested in, and feels itself responsible to, only the values of art; and, given society as it is, has an organic sense of what is good and what is bad for art" (301).

36. Greenberg, "Towards a Newer Laocoon," 301.

37. Ibid., 310.

38. Leo Steinberg, "The Eye Is a Part of the Mind," *Partisan Review* (March-April 1953): 200.

39. Clement Greenberg, "Abstract and Representational," *Art Digest* (November 1954): 6–7.

40. Clement Greenberg, "Abstract, Representational, and So Forth," in Greenberg, *Art and Culture,* 136.

41. Clement Greenberg, "Sculpture in Our Time," *Arts Magazine* (June 1958): 23.

42. Ibid., 22.

43. Ibid., 25.

44. Ibid.

45. In 1949, Greenberg claimed that "'International Style' architecture, Cubist and post-Cubist painting and sculpture, 'modern' furniture and decoration and design are the manifestations of a new style.... More directly and less ambiguously than painting and more nakedly than architecture, sculpture realizes the new notion of the work of visual art as an open, more or less transparent object whose effect lies mainly in its total design, its exhibited structure, and which relies relatively little on expressive details. The plastic means are flat planes, lines, and enclosed spaces rather than masses, volumes and modeling. The interest is in lines of force, thrusts, in the 'activation' of empty space." Clement Greenberg, "Our Period Style," *Partisan Review* (November 1949): 1135–1137.

As early as 1948, Greenberg seemed to find hope in modern architecture: "There is a persistent urge, as persistent as it is largely unconscious, to go beyond the cabinet [i.e., easel] picture, which is destined to occupy only a spot on the wall, to a kind of picture that, without actually becoming identified with the wall like a mural, would *spread* over it and acknowledge its physical reality. I do not know whether there is anything in modern architecture itself that explicitly invites this tendency." Clement Greenberg, "The Situation at the Moment," *Partisan Review* (January 1948): 83.

46. Greenberg, "Towards a Newer Laocoon," 307.

47. Clement Greenberg, "Art," review of a joint exhibition of Antoine Pevsner and Naum Gabo, *Nation* (April 17, 1948): 423.

48. Clement Greenberg, "Art," review of an exhibition of Isamu Noguchi and American paintings from the collection of the Museum of Modern Art, *Nation* (March 19, 1949): 341–342.

49. Clement Greenberg, "Art," review of the Whitney Annual and exhibitions of Picasso and Henri Cartier-Bresson, *Nation* (April 5, 1947): 405.

50. Clement Greenberg, "Art," review of the watercolor, drawing, and sculpture sections of the Whitney Annual, *Nation* (February 23, 1946): 242.

51. Clement Greenberg, "David Smith," *Art in America* (Winter 1956): 74.

52. In 1956, Greenberg attacked Herbert Read's "esthetic" of sculpture, particularly its roots in Hegel's evolutionary theory and Riegl's emphasis on haptic perception: "Sculpture does invoke the sense of touch—as well as our sense of space in general—but it does so primarily through the sense of sight and the tactile associations of which that sense is capable." In the end, Greenberg asserts his own genealogy: "The arts have over the last century shown a consistent tendency to withdraw into their respective mediums and 'purify' themselves, by renouncing illusion, among other things. Just as painting ever more insistently declares its flatness, sculpture has declared its roundness and the nature of the materials of which it is made.... But sculpture, having attained a maximum of roundness and compactness with Brancusi and Arp, some forty years ago underwent a mutation without parallel in any other contemporary art and issued from Picasso's hands in a new mode that had its origin in the Cubist collage and bas-relief. This new constructivist and quasi-constructivist sculpture, with its linear and transparent forms and its striving for weightlessness, runs counter to everything in Sir Herbert's canon." Clement Greenberg, "Roundness Isn't All," *New York Times Book Review,* November 25, 1956, 63.

53. Greenberg, "Modernist Sculpture, Its Pictorial Past," 162. While this revised version of "Cross-Breeding of Modern Sculpture" emphasizes the notion of flatness, in the original essay Greenberg wrote: "Brancusi drove this canon [the 'monolithic'] to an ultimate conclusion, and suddenly arrived back at architecture—and painting. Or almost. It was, at any rate, a new kind of painting whose attraction sculpture now felt, a painting infused with sculptural elements out of barbaric and exotic traditions and leading, under the more fundamental influence of Cézanne's painting, toward that sublime and supremely coherent style we call Cubism" ("Cross-Breeding of Modern Sculpture," 77).

54. Greenberg, "Collage," 82–83.

55. Greenberg, "The New Sculpture," 639. Also see Greenberg, "Art" (see note 49), where he writes: "The future seems to belong to sculpture much more than to painting.... The possibilities of post-cubist sculpture have actually become richer than those of post-cubist painting" (405). Perhaps the most important change in Greenberg's writings is that he gradually abandoned theoretical claims or speculative remarks, opting only to offer accounts of art's present in terms of its past. In "Abstract and Representational," Greenberg states: "I will say what I say only about the abstract art I already know, not about abstract art in principle" (6).

56. Greenberg, "The New Sculpture," 640–641. Also see Greenberg's "Art," review of exhibitions of Alberto Giacometti and Kurt Schwitters, *Nation* (February 7, 1948): 165. According to Greenberg, Schwitters's collages show how "contemporary advanced sculpture was able, via the collage, to attach itself to painting and take its point of departure from that medium rather than from anything antecedent in its own medium.... this bridge from painting to sculpture provided by the collage and its derivative bas-relief." In "Sculpture in Our Time," he writes that Picasso "solved—or rather destroyed—the problem [of 'unlocking the flatness of the surface'] by raising the collage's affixed material above the picture surface, thus going over into bas-relief. And soon after he subtracted the picture surface entirely, to let what had been affixed stand free as 'construction.' It is at this point that the new sculpture really began" (23).

57. The following two passages are among those excised from the version of "Cross-Breeding of Modern Sculpture" published in *Art and Culture:* "The last forty years have given birth to a new tradition with an almost entirely new vocabulary of form. But at the same time the old Gothic-Renaissance tradition of sculpture, after a decline of several centuries, has known a rebirth of its own. And curiously enough, both birth and rebirth have been presided over by the art of painting, which has acted as mother to one and physician to the other. The connection of sculpture and painting is closer today than for a long time in the past" (74). "At present, sculpture is on the point of turning the tables on painting with respect to the fertility of ideas and range of possible subject matter. But the new sculptor still remains a little too timid in the face of the other art, too passive, and still too ready to accept any and all of its suggestions. This is excusable when we remember for how long a time and until how recently, painting did lead the way, and how much more interest and excitement could be found in almost any painting than in almost any piece of sculpture contemporaneous with it" (123).

58. See Greenberg, "Art," review of an exhibition of Jean Arp, *Nation* (February 5, 1949): 165. Later in the essay, in an account of the final, regressive, anticubist "return to the statue" in the work of Brancusi and Arp, Greenberg articulates the architectural and urban implications of this evolution: "What was modern in this return to the statue—here Brancusi had already shown the way—was the reduction of the monolith to a simple, quasi-geometrical, ovular form, qualified now and then by protuberances and creases, concavities and convolutions that evoke, if not the forms of the human anatomy, then those of the vegetable kingdom. The works that have resulted from this conception have about them something of garden sculpture: a simplicity and purity that demand to be set in isolation among trees, shrubs and grass. This is a new escape from the city; an escape which seems to me to be the final meaning of the relative academicism of Arp's later work, with its rejection of the object in favor of the statue" (165–166).

59. Greenberg, "America Takes the Lead," 109.

60. Yve-Alain Bois, "Kahnweiler's Lesson," in *Painting as Model* (Cambridge: MIT Press, 1990), 69. Bois's major objective is to elevate the writings of Russian formalist critics and artists such as Malevich, David Burliuk, Yakov Tugendhold, and especially Ivan Aksenov, who as early as 1917 recognized the importance of Picasso's *Guitar*.

61. Greenberg's admiration for Hildebrand is also apparent in "Roundness Isn't All," where he defends Hildebrand against Read's critique: "[Read] calls Adolf von Hildebrand's assertion that the 'sculptor strives to accommodate his three-dimensional form to the visual ease of a two dimensional surface' a heresy. But Hildebrand was at least aware of the crucial problem offered by sculpture's dependence upon the association of virtual tactility and actual visibility, and tried to deal with it" (63).

62. Bois, "Kahnweiler's Lesson," 75. Bois cites Hildebrand's condemnation of the panorama, wax museums, or Canova's tombs, which separate architecture from the life-size sculptural figures. Bois quotes Hildebrand: "What is here constructed is not a picture seen, but a drama acted out…. There is no definite line drawn between the monument and the public." Adolf von Hildebrand, *The Problem of Form in Painting and Sculpture,* trans. Max Meyer and Robert Ogden (New York: G. E. Stechert and Co., 1907), 113. Bois writes: "This passage … explains perfectly the terror of real space that was, for Carl Einstein and Kahnweiler, Western sculpture's indelible defect" ("Kahnweiler's Lesson," 75).

63. Greenberg, "Collage," 79.

64. Greenberg chooses not to "read" the collages. Instead, every "device" is employed to distinguish optically between "literal" and "depicted" flatness. For example, he argues that the "imitation printing" is an "eye-undeceiving *trompe-l'oeil* [that] supplements, rather than replaces, the eye-deceiving kind." Later in the essay, Greenberg elaborates on the distinction between optical and pictorial illusion: "Flatness may now [in the later collages of Picasso and Braque] monopolize everything, but it is a flatness become so ambiguous and expanded as to turn into illusion itself—at least an optical if not, properly speaking, a pictorial illusion" ("Collage," 72–73, 77). In 1962, his disinterest in reading would become explicit: "Whereas space in depth in the abstract or near-abstract art of the 1920's and 1930's had been a matter largely of 'diagram' and association, in the painterly 1940's and 1950's it could not help becoming once again a matter more of *trompe-l'oeil* illusion. Not that space in depth became deeper—not at all—but it did become more tangible, more a thing of immediate perception and less one of 'reading'" (Greenberg, "After Abstract Expressionism," 24).

65. Bois, "Kahnweiler's Lesson," 91.

66. There are numerous examples in Greenberg's writings where he praises, or at least appreciates, artists who cross disciplines, yet in every case he is careful to relegate the work in the "other" discipline to a lesser status. See his 1948 review of an exhibition of Le Corbusier's "good minor painting" and his evaluation of the sculpture of Matisse. Clement Greenberg, "Art," review of exhibitions of Le Corbusier and Robert Motherwell, *Nation* (May 29, 1948): 612; and Clement Greenberg, "'Feeling Is All,'" *Partisan Review* (January-February 1952): 98–99 (revised and published as "Partisan Review, 'Art Chronicle,' 1952," in *Art and Culture*).

67. Clement Greenberg, "Picasso as Revolutionary," *New Leader* (December 10, 1956): 27–28.

68. Clement Greenberg, "Picasso at Seventy-Five," *Arts Magazine* (October 1957): 41.

69. Kahnweiler writes in *The Sculptures of Picasso:* "During the years 1917–1924, while he went on producing pictures wherein he incorporated more and more into painting the device of superimposed planes, Picasso painted a number of works spoken of as 'classical.' Once again, these works are almost painted sculptures.… In contrast, the wire constructions which followed [in 1930] … constitute a kind of *drawing in space,* but, at the same time, a first step towards the conquest, in sculpture, of a field which had never before been claimed by anything but architecture: the *creation of spaces*." David-Henry Kahnweiler, *The Sculpture of Picasso,* trans. A. D. B. Sylvester (London: Rodney Phillips and Co., 1949), n.p. First published as *Les sculptures de Picasso* (Paris: Éditions du Chêne, 1948).

70. Frank Elgar and Robert Maillard, *Picasso,* trans. Francis Scarfe (New York: Praeger, 1956), 148, 150. In their book, Elgar writes the criticism and Maillard the biography, on the top and bottom halves of the pages, respectively.

71. See Kahnweiler's *Les sculptures de Picasso:* "Il imaginait des monuments gigantesques en 1929, qui, maisons d'habitation et sculptures énormes figurant des têtes de femmes à la fois, se seraient dressées devant la Méditerranée. 'Je suis bien obligé de les peindre puisque personne ne m'en commande,' me dit-il" (n.p.). In a footnote, referring to his essay "Das Wesen der Bildhauer" (1919), Kahnweiler directly contradicts the tenets of Greenberg's pictorialism: "I there try to demonstrate, among other things, that in fact relief is always a *branch of painting,* even when executed with sculptural means, for the space it creates is illusory, whereas true sculpture in the round inhabits the same space as we do. Though relief is always a kind of painting, it is obvious, nevertheless, that a picture which creates an illusion of unlimited space is not a relief" (*Sculptures of Picasso,* n.p.).

72. Greenberg, "Our Period Style," 1135–1136.

73. Greenberg, "Abstract and Representational," 7.

74. Greenberg, "'Feeling is All,'" 101. Greenberg would remove the sentences quoted here from the revised version of the essay in *Art and Culture.*

75. Greenberg, "The Situation at the Moment," 84.

76. Greenberg, "Our Period Style," 1949. This essay opens with an epigraph from Pevsner's 1945 book *An Outline of European Architecture* in which he predicts a "recovery of a true style in the visual arts, one in which once again building rules, and painting and sculpture serve." Greenberg proceeds to oppose Pevsner and argue that the new unity of the arts will be achieved by means of "their common tendency to treat all *matter,* as distinguished from *space,* as two-dimensional."

77. Clement Greenberg, "Art," obituary of Piet Mondrian, *Nation* (March 4, 1944): 288.

78. Clement Greenberg, "Cubist, Abstract, Surrealist Art: Guggenheim Collection, Art of this Century Gallery, Permanent," *Nation* (January 30, 1943): 177.

79. Greenberg, "Cross-Breeding of Modern Sculpture," 123. This passage is removed from the revised version of the essay in *Art and Culture.*

80. Greenberg, "Art" (see note 48).

81. Clement Greenberg, "Anthony Caro," *Arts Yearbook* 8 (1965): 106.

82. Leo Steinberg, "Other Criteria," in *Other Criteria* (New York: Oxford University Press, 1972), 88, 90. Chapter 4 of the present work chronicles how the window serves as a key trope in Robert Smithson's artworks and writings.

83. Greenberg, "Abstract and Representational," 7.

84. Clement Greenberg, "Art," review of an exhibition of Victor Brauner, *Nation* (May 17, 1947): 579. Also see a similar passage in Clement Greenberg, "An Essay on Paul Klee," in Merle Armitage, ed., *Five Essays on Klee* (New York: Duell, Sloan, and Pearce, 1950): "Picasso asks you to construct more than to invent, to build large, substantial edifices—not like Klee, to send up demountable tracery and momentary mists. Picasso asks you to be more aware of your surroundings. This does not mean that Picasso is more 'intellectual' or even more deliberate than Klee; in fact, he works faster and less meditatively. The difference is that he sees the picture as a wall, while Klee sees it as a page; and when painting a wall you have to have a more conscious sense of the surroundings and their relation to the picture. Architecture imposes itself then, and with that the monumental and the public" (51–52).

3 INCREDIBLY CONVINCING: MICHAEL FRIED'S DENIAL OF ARCHITECTURE

1. Michael Fried, "Jackson Pollock," *Artforum* (September 1965): 14–17; "Jules Olitski's New Paintings," *Artforum* (November 1965): 36–40; "Shape as Form: Frank Stella's New Paintings," *Artforum* 5 (November 1966): 18–27; "Olitski and Shape," *Artforum* (January 1967): 20–21; "The Achievement of Morris Louis," *Artforum* (February 1967): 34–40; "New Work by Anthony Caro," *Artforum* (February 1967): 46–47; "Ronald Davis: Surface and Illusion," *Artforum* (April 1967): 37–40; "Art and Objecthood," *Artforum* (Summer 1967): 12–23; "Two Sculptures by Anthony Caro," *Artforum* (February 1968): 24–25; "Manet's Sources," *Artforum* (March 1969): 28–82; "Recent Work by Kenneth Noland," *Artforum* (Summer 1969): 36–37; "Thomas Couture and the Theatricalization of Action in 19th-Century French Painting," *Artforum* (June 1970): 36–46; and "Caro's Abstractness," *Artforum* (September 1970): 32–34.

2. Fried, "Art and Objecthood," 15.

3. Ibid., 22.

4. Fried, "Two Sculptures by Anthony Caro," 24.

5. Fried, "Caro's Abstractness," 34.

6. Ibid., 33–34.

7. Clement Greenberg, "Sculpture in Our Time," *Arts Magazine* (June 1958): 23.

8. Greenberg mentioned Stella only twice in his published writings: once in "America Takes the Lead, 1945–1965" (*Art in America* [August-September 1965], 108–109), where he compares Stella with Louis and Noland for their innovative use of stripes around 1959, and again in "Poetry of Vision" (*Artforum* [April 1968]: 21), where he compares the similar "discrepancy between impact and substance" in Stella and Bacon.

9. Michael Fried, *Three American Painters: Kenneth Noland, Jules Olitski, Frank Stella* (Cambridge: Harvard University, Fogg Museum, 1965), 48. Earlier articles, such as "Modernist Painting and the Formalist Criticism," which would be incorporated with some changes into the first section of *Three American Painters,* neither reveal an independent critical position nor suggest a dissatisfaction with Greenberg. Michael Fried, "Modernist Painting and the Formalist Criticism," *American Scholar* (Autumn 1964): 642–648.

10. Michael Fried, in William Seitz, ed., *Art Criticism in the Sixties* (Boston: October House, 1966), n.p.

11. Ibid. On the pervasiveness of historical criticism, see S. C. Foster, *The Critics of Abstract Expressionism* (Ann Arbor: UMI Research Press, 1980): "Quite in opposition to earlier criticism, and perhaps most characteristic of commentary in the 1960s, is the sacrifice of the traditional enterprises of criticism for history. A literature was produced by a new generation of writers, usually trained in art history departments, whose members have been dubbed, historian-critics" (91).

12. Judd in particular was a rival of Fried. He wrote regular reviews for *Arts Magazine* from 1959 to 1965, and was a strong proponent of Stella but in literalist terms that Fried refuted. In *Three American Painters* Fried explains that the notion that "paintings are nothing more than a particular subclass of *things*, invested by tradition with certain conventional characteristics … whose arbitrariness, once recognized, argues for their elimination … is repugnant to me" (43–44). Yet, in a brief catalog essay in 1963, Fried characterized Stella in almost literalist terms. Sounding vaguely like Judd or Morris, Fried explained that in Stella's stripe paintings "the thing-nature of the paintings came to be emphasized, bringing them close to the orbit of Constructivism." See Michael Fried, "Frank Stella," in Ben Heller, ed., *Toward a New Abstraction* (New York: Jewish Museum, 1963), 40. Stella himself, on a radio show with Judd in early 1964, had advocated precisely what Fried found repugnant: "My painting … really is an object. Any painting is an object and anyone who gets involved enough in this finally has to face up to the objectness of whatever it is that he's doing. He is making a thing." Bruce Glaser and Lucy Lippard, "Questions to Stella and Judd," *Art News* (September 1966): 58.

13. As early as 1964 Fried used Stella to exemplify the historical nature of the modernist enterprise and to take issue with Greenberg's emphasis on "purity": "I want to argue that, for example, Reinhardt's paintings are purist in essence whereas Stella's, say, are not. The crux of the distinction I want to make is this: that purism is, in its deepest aspirations, profoundly a-historical. It aims at a kind of metaphysical validity, and proceeds as if on the assumption that by somehow distilling art down to its basic essence one can arrive finally at whatever it is that gives art the power to exist. … In contrast to this, Stella's paintings, like Barnett Newman's, are historically self-aware. They both arise out of and demonstrate a personal interpretation of the particular historical situation in which 'advanced' painting first found itself in the late fifties. … This historically self-aware attitude towards one's work, together with the acceptance of history as that which in the long run determines validity, are the hallmarks of *modernism*." Michael Fried, "New York Letter," *Art International* (April 1964): 59.

14. Fried, in Seitz, *Art Criticism in the Sixties*. While Stella is perhaps the most evident case in painting of what Fried calls "art in question," Fried's confrontation with the literalists presents a more complex instance with more fundamental implications for his project. On the other hand, Fried's critical agreement with Greenberg regarding the failure of literalism might be called a negative case of "art in question." Greenberg and Fried offer different arguments *against* literalism—the exemplar of "bad or meretricious art" *and* "bad or meretricious criticism." Fried sees it as a threat (a supposed alternative), Greenberg as a mere nuisance. Further, their confrontation with literalism was provoked precisely because it did not neglect the modernist paradigm, of which literalism appears either as an alternative or a minor version.

15. In "The Confounding of Confusion" (*Arts Yearbook* 7 [1964]), Fried writes, "superfluous confusion has been manufactured by institutions and persons whose job of work, one would have thought, was rather to make things clear. … Chronic open-mindedness is one of our biggest burdens, and there are few people who are not relieved to come up against a categorical statement with which they can agree or take pride in disagreeing. Either way a decision can be made" (37). Anticipating the coming conflict between their positions, Judd remarks in an article in the same issue of *Arts Yearbook,* "The history of art and art's condition at any time are pretty messy. They should stay that way. One can think about them as much as one likes, but they won't become neater; neatness isn't even a very good reason for thinking about them. A lot of things just can't be con-

nected. The complaints of confusion, lack of common goals, uncertainty and rapid change are naive." Donald Judd, "Local History," *Arts Yearbook* 7 (1964): 26.

16. Fried summarizes his development of an "alternative version of modernism" in "How Modernism Works: A Reply to T. J. Clark," *Critical Inquiry* (September 1982): 217–234.

17. Kynaston McShine, ed., *Primary Structures: Younger British and American Sculptors* (New York: Jewish Museum, 1966), n.p.

18. In "Music Discomposed," Cavell (seemingly responding to Greenberg's notion of an unfolding dialectic of taste) warns that "in waiting for time to tell [what is art and respected as such], we miss what the present tells— that the dangers of fraudulence, and of trust, are essential to the experience of art. If anything in this paper should count as a thesis, that is my thesis." Stanley Cavell, "Music Discomposed," in D. D. Merrill and W. H. Capitan, eds., *Art, Mind and Religion* (Pittsburgh: University of Pittsburgh Press, 1967), 76. Along with Cavell, contemporary philosophers such as Richard Wollheim and Arthur Danto departed from the narrow, logical concerns of the analytic tradition to propose theories of art. All were participating in a complex, if disengaged (from the art world), Wittgensteinian discourse that can be traced in the *Journal of Aesthetics and Art Criticism* and was initiated largely by Morris Weitz's essay "The Role of Theory in Aesthetics," *Journal of Aesthetics and Art Criticism* (September 1956): 27–35.

19. Clement Greenberg, "The Identity of Art," *Country Beautiful* (November 1961). Despite his reference to Kant, and as he would acknowledge in 1973, Greenberg's argument is closer to "Hume, Kant's predecessor." He writes: Kant "could have clinched his case for the time being—and for some time to come too—by remaining content to point to the record, the empirical record with the consensus of taste that it showed.… It's the best taste that … forms the consensus of taste. The best taste develops under the pressure of the best art and is the taste most subject to that pressure. And the best art, in turn, emerges under the pressure of the best taste. The best art and the best taste are indissoluble." Clement Greenberg, "Can Taste Be Objective?" *Art News* (February 1973): 23.

20. Fried, "How Modernism Works," 227.

21. Cavell, "Music Discomposed," 76.

22. Ibid., 93.

23. Stanley Cavell, "Aesthetic Problems of Modern Philosophy," in Max Black, ed., *Philosophy in America* (Ithaca: Cornell University Press, 1965), 86. Cavell's position derives from Wittgenstein's comparison of philosophical method with psychoanalytic therapy. Cavell extends this analogy to art: "for me part of what he means by this comparison is … [t]he more one learns, so to speak, the hang of oneself, and mounts one's problems, the less one is able to *say* what one has learned; not because you have *forgotten* what it was, but because nothing you said would seem like an answer or a solution: there is no longer any question of problem which your words would match. You have reached conviction, but not about a proposition; and consistency, but not in theory. You are different, what you recognize as problems are different, your world is different.… And this is the sense, the only sense in which what a work of art means cannot be *said*. Believing it is seeing it" (ibid.).

24. Fried, "Art and Objecthood," 23 n. 4.

25. Michael Fried, in Hal Foster, ed., *Discussions in Contemporary Culture: Number One* (Seattle: Bay Press, 1987), 56–57.

26. Fried, "How Modernism Works," 217, 222. The essay concludes with a discussion not of painting but of Caro's table sculptures, and Fried's interpretation of those works amounts to another renunciation of architectural issues. That is, Fried proposes that by "tabling" rather than "grounding" the sculptures, Caro made "pieces whose modest dimensions would strike the viewer not as a contingent, quantitative, in that sense merely literal fact about them but rather as a crucial aspect of their identity as abstract works of art—as internal to their 'form,' as part of their very essence as works of sculpture.… Caro's table sculptures thus embody a sense of scale for which there is no obvious precedent in earlier sculpture. And … it is also true that we encounter nothing quite like the abstract smallness of Caro's table sculptures in our ordinary dealings with the world" ("How Modernism Works," 231, 233). Fried first presented these ideas in 1977, in part to refute William Rubin's notion, presented in *Anthony Caro* (New York: Museum of Modern Art, 1975), that Caro's works "occupy a purely literal space." See Michael Fried, "Anthony Caro's Table Sculptures," *Arts Magazine* (March 1977): 97 n. 7.

27. Greenberg, "Modernist Painting," 103–104.

28. Fried, "Shape as Form," 27 n. 11. The accuracy of Fried's intellectual autobiography falters when he claims in "How Modernism Works" that "my argument expressly denies the existence of a distinct *realm* of the pictorial— of a body of suprahistorical, non-context-specific, in that sense 'formalist,' concerns that define the proper aims and limits of the art of painting—maintaining on the contrary that modernist painting, in its constantly renewed effort to discover what it must be, is forever driven 'outside' itself, compelled to place in jeopardy its very identity by engaging what it is not" (226). Leaving aside Fried's description of painting as being "forever 'driven' outside itself" and his denial of a "distinct realm of the pictorial" (two ideas which were definitely *not* present in his writings of the 1960s), Fried follows up these revised ideas with a third that *was* fundamental to his move away from Greenberg and his growing reliance on the writings of the philosopher Stanley Cavell: the claim that modernist painting constantly reformulates "its very identity" through "inquiry into what might be called the politics of conviction" ("How Modernism Works," 227). These retrospective revisions seem to be a response to Stephen Melville who, Fried notes, offers a "highly intelligent, at once sympathetic and deconstructive reading of my account of modernism" in "Notes on the Reemergence of Allegory, the Forgetting of Modernism, the Necessity of Rhetoric, and the Conditions of Publicity in Art in Criticism," *October* 19 (Winter 1981): 55–92. In fact, Melville would later propose that Fried's analysis suggests that painting did not reach outside of itself, but precisely the opposite. Fried "aims not only to relegate a certain (inner) threat to outside the enterprise proper [i.e., to architectural and corporeal space], but even to relegate that place in which the threat can appear to outside the discipline." Thus he "prescribes not only an impulse toward 'pure painting' but also an impulse toward a 'total painting'—some synthesis of all the arts under painting. Such double prescriptions are one of the constants of modernism." Stephen Melville, *Philosophy Beside Itself: On Deconstruction and Modernism* (Minneapolis: University of Minnesota Press, 1986), 10.

29. Of the original footnotes that were not included in *Artforum,* one references Greenberg's 1962 essay "How Art Writing Earns Its Bad Name"; five others simply give sources for images that were referenced in the essay but not included in the catalog; and one quotes Wittgenstein and Cavell. In the entire catalog essay, there are twelve notes (out of a total of thirty seven) that positively reference Greenberg, and only one that is critical. In fact, in the first section of *Three American Painters,* Fried explicitly defends Greenberg against various criticisms, including Hilton Kramer's 1962 review of *Art and Culture,* which argues that Greenberg employs a reductive and ideological (Marxist) historical model. See Hilton Kramer, "A Critic on the Side of History: Notes on

Clement Greenberg," *Arts Magazine* (October 1962): 60–63. Fried responds in the text, not a footnote, that Greenberg has not "forgotten that history, works of art, and essays in art criticism are all made by men who live at a particular moment in history" (*Three American Painters,* 6).

30. Fried, "Jackson Pollock," 14.

31. The quotation is taken from the revised version of Greenberg's "American-Type Painting," published in Greenberg, *Art and Culture.* In the original essay published in *Partisan Review,* Greenberg simply writes: "'Analytical' Cubism is always somewhere in the back of Pollock's mind."

32. Fried, "Jackson Pollock," 17.

33. Ibid., 15. Fried presents a rudimentary version of this interpretation of Pollock in his "New York Letter," *Art International* (April 1964): 57–61.

34. Fried, "Jackson Pollock," 15.

35. Fried, *Three American Painters,* 21. Fried is writing of Barnett Newman as analogous to Pollock; seen note 53.

36. Fried, "Art and Objecthood," 22. Fried would later trace the origins of presentness to the strategy of "absorption" in eighteenth-century French painting. See Fried's *Absorption and Theatricality: Painting and the Beholder in the Age of Diderot* (Berkeley: University of California Press, 1980). Both presentness and absorption entail a preoccupation with the status of the beholder, in relation to what Fried calls "the primordial convention that paintings are made to be beheld" (*Absorption and Theatricality,* 93). In 1978, Fried offered this formulation: "The evolution of painting in France in the nineteenth century up to and including Courbet is largely to be understood in terms of the dialectical unfolding of a problematic of painting and beholder … which received its classic formulation in Diderot's writings on drama and painting of the 1750s and 1760s." See Michael Fried, "The Beholder in Courbet: His Early Self-Portraits and Their Place in His Art," *Glyph* 4 (1978): 116–117. It might even be said that with *Absorption and Theatricality,* by tracing the beginnings of modernism to eighteenth-century academic French sources and displacing the nineteenth-century German theories of aesthetic subjectivism that Greenberg accepted and endorsed, Fried attempts to purge the influence of Wölfflin from contemporary art criticism. Undoubtedly, it is also not by chance that Fried strives to offer a history of modernism that originates simultaneously with the emergence of aesthetics and art criticism as distinct practices.

37. Fried, *Three American Painters,* 19. For an alternative understanding of staining as a photographic process (in terms of "stains of the real"), see Mark Linder, "Wild Kingdom: Frederick Kiesler's Display of the Avant-Garde," in *Autonomy and Ideology: Positioning an Architectural Avant-Garde in America* (New York: Monacelli Press), 124–153.

38. Fried would later make this explicit, writing that "Pollock's 1951 pictures are devoid of a whole range of tactile connotations." He attributes this to "their general openness and extraordinary facture—the paint is, in effect, soaked or stained into the canvas," and to "the fact that a stained edge or line is, in a sense, neither hard nor sharp. (Such an edge, in Greenberg's words, is not a *cutting* edge.)" Michael Fried, introduction to *Morris Louis 1912–1962* (Boston: Museum of Fine Arts, 1967), 13.

39. Fried, *Three American Painters,* 18.

40. An obvious development of the cutout occurs in Stella's "doughnut" paintings of 1963, one of which, *Ileana Sonnabend,* was included in *Three American Painters.* A more literal application of this device, and one that must have seemed depraved to Fried, was employed in Lucio Fontana's numerous sliced canvases of the early sixties with titles such as *Concetto spaziale.*

41. Fried, *Three American Painters,* 17. In support of this notion, in one of the omitted footnotes, Fried quotes Wittgenstein (as cited by Cavell in "The Availability of Wittgenstein's Later Philosophy"): "We don't say that the man who tells us he feels the visual image two inches behind the bridge of his nose is telling a lie or talking nonsense. But we say that we don't understand the meaning of such a phrase." Fried then suggests that his interpretation of Pollock may "count as an explanation" of such a phrase (Fried, *Three American Painters,* 21 n. 52). But perhaps a better reference would be Jacques Lacan, who remarks in "What Is a Picture": "Indeed, there is something whose absence can always be observed in a picture—which is not the case in perception. This is the central field, where the separating power of the eye is exercised to the maximum in vision. In every picture, this central field cannot but be absent, and replaced by a hole—a reflection, in short, of the pupil behind which is situated the gaze." Jacques Lacan, "What Is a Picture," in *The Four Fundamental Concepts of Psycho-Analysis,* ed. Jacques-Alain Miller, trans. Alan Sheridan (New York: W. W. Norton, 1977), 108.

42. Perhaps the most revealing concurrence between Fried and Rowe is their shared deprecation of literalness, which signals a deep alignment in their aesthetics. Thus, there is a correlation between Fried's analysis of shape in Stella—"one's experience of literalness is above all an experience of the literalness of the *individual shapes themselves*"—and Rosalind Krauss's notion of a "hermeneutic phantom" in Rowe's analysis of the villa of Garches. Both Fried and Krauss introduce a formal concept that allows the materiality (e.g., structure, support, literal surface) to disappear or be rendered conceptually irrelevant. See Fried, "Shape as Form," 24, and Rosalind Krauss, "Death of a Hermeneutic Phantom: Materialization of the Sign in the Work of Peter Eisenman," *Architecture and Urbanism* (January 1980): 193–195.

43. Colin Rowe, "Dominican Monastery of La Tourette, Eveux-sur-Arbresle, Lyons," *Architectural Review* 129 (June 1961): 401; and "Mannerism and Modern Architecture," *Architectual Review* 107 (May 1950): 290.

44. Clement Greenberg, "Collage," in Greenberg, *Art and Culture: Critical Essays* (Boston: Beacon Press, 1961), 79.

45. Fried, *Three American Painters,* 18.

46. In *Three American Painters* Fried clarifies what he maintains is a misunderstanding of Greenberg's presentation of the blank canvas as "the expansion of the possibilities of the pictorial." The misunderstanding occurs when it is presumed that "just as modernist painting has enabled one to see a blank canvas, a sequence of random splatters or a length of colored fabric as a picture, Dada and Neo-Dada have equipped one to treat virtually any object as a work of art." For Fried, "it is far from clear exactly what this means," and he is suspicious of the "apparent expansion of the realm of the *artistic* corresponding—ironically, as it were—to the expansion of the realm of the *pictorial* achieved by modernist painting. As we have seen in Stella's case, the expanded realm of the artistic may come into conflict with that of the pictorial; and when this occurs the former must give way" (*Three American Painters,* 47).

47. Ibid., 17.

48. Fried, "Two Sculptures by Anthony Caro," 25.

49. Rowe, "Dominican Monastery of La Tourette," 407.

50. Colin Rowe and Robert Slutzky, "Transparency: Literal and Phenomenal," *Perspecta* (1963): 51.

51. While Rowe remained deeply ambivalent about this dialectic, the work of his students—as exemplified in the work of the New York Five—shares Fried's ambition to *defeat* support and literalness. Rowe's suspicion of such a project emerges explicitly in his introduction to *Five Architects,* where he pokes fun at "the camp of the

'true believer,'" even as he supports the formal investigations by embracing pluralism (which also distinguishes him from Fried). Colin Rowe, introduction to *Five Architects* (New York: Oxford University Press, 1975), 3–8.

52. Michael Fried, "New York Letter," *Art International* (October 1962): 76.

53. Fried, *Three American Painters,* 21–22. Fried admits that "sheerly optical spatiality" "is a hard notion to grasp … we are driven to characterize our visual experience by means of tactile metaphors." Fried allows only that we may use "tactile metaphors" to *describe* art. Drawing upon Merleau-Ponty's *Phenomenology of Perception,* Fried acknowledges that "sight and touch … open onto the same space. If this were not the case … they would lack the fullness of being, the complex, ponderable reality which objects in the world self-evidently possess as we encounter them in experience. What then can it mean to speak of a space addressed to eyesight alone? The answer … is surprisingly simple. Newman's best paintings … comprise an *illusion* of spaciality itself rendered sheerly optical" (*Three American Painters,* 21).

54. Clement Greenberg, "Abstract and Representational," *Art Digest* (November 1954): 7.

55. Clement Greenberg, "The Situation at the Moment," *Partisan Review* (January 1948): 83.

56. Two months after "Jackson Pollock," Fried published "Jules Olitski's New Paintings," in which he affirms that collage is the key to understanding Pollock and that support is the crux of modernist painting by referring to Greenberg's essay "Collage" (which he does not reference in *Three American Painters*) and by restating his claim that modernism should be seen, in Fried's words, "in terms of a growing consciousness of the literal character of the picture-support and a draining of conviction in traditional illusionism" (36).

57. Fried, "Shape as Form," 18. Subsequent references to this essay are given in parentheses in the text.

58. Greenberg's references to shape increase around 1960, for example in "Collage," where he notes "the growing independence of the planar unit in collage as a *shape*" (78), and in "Louis and Noland" where, in explaining Louis's early paintings, he writes that his "revulsion against Cubism was a revulsion against the sculptural. Cubism meant shapes, and shapes meant armatures of light and dark." Clement Greenberg, "Louis and Noland," *Art International* (May 1960): 28. In "Modernist Painting," Greenberg lists "the shape of the support" as one of the three "limitations that constitute the medium of painting," but it is rarely noted that he also forwards the idea that painting and theater "share" shape as basic convention: "For flatness alone was unique and exclusive to pictorial art. The enclosing shape of the picture was a limiting condition, or norm, that was shared with the art of the theater; color was a norm and a means shared not only with the theater, but also with sculpture" (103–104).

59. Fried argues that "Stella's new pictures are a response to the recognition that shape itself may be lost to the art of painting as a resource able to compel conviction," and that the way "to restore shape to health" is by making it "radically illusive" ("Shape as Form," 18, 24). Two months later, in "Olitski and Shape," Fried presents a condensed version of this problem by posing the question of whether the conflict between literal and pictorial shape has reached a "resolution" or an "exhaustion" (20).

60. It is as this point in "Shape as Form" that Fried appends his first long footnote referring to the work of Stanley Cavell.

61. The final paragraph of Donald Judd's "Specific Objects" (*Arts Yearbook* 8 [1965]: 82), discusses Stella's work: "Stella's shaped paintings involve several important characteristics of three-dimensional work. The periphery of a piece and the lines inside correspond. The stripes are nowhere near being discrete parts. The surface is farther from the wall than usual, though it remains parallel to it. Since the surface is exceptionally unified and involves little or no space, the parallel plane is unusually distinct. The order is not rationalistic and underlying but is simply order, like that of a continuity, one thing after another. A painting isn't an image. The shapes, the unity, projection, order and color are specific, aggressive and powerful."

62. For Fried, "post-Cubist" means not just after cubism, but a fundamental shift from an emphasis on flatness to the shape of the support. Thus literalism is a corruption of the modernist project that assimilates "shape" as merely "edge." As he would write in "Jules Olitski's New Paintings": "Deductive structure activates the edge of the support much as Cubism activated its surface" (37). For Greenberg, "post-Cubist" seems to mean those art practices that cubism made possible, such as construction sculpture and abstract expressionism. See, for example, Clement Greenberg, "The European View of American Art," *Nation* (November 25, 1950): "The kind of art that Pollock, de Kooning, and Gorky present does not so much break with the Cubist and post-Cubist past as extend it in an unforeseen way, as does all art that embodies a new 'vision.' Theirs represents, in my opinion, the first genuine and compelled effort to impose Cubist order—the only order possible to ambitious painting in our time—on the experience of the post-Cubist, post 1930 world" (491).

63. "Art and Objecthood" is an event for another reason: it announces and outlines the concerns of a theoretical and historical project that would occupy Fried throughout the next decade, culminating in 1980 with the publication of *Absorption and Theatricality*. In that book's introduction, he makes explicit his intention to close the circle on the arguments and judgments he offered in the 1960s, as the final and most succinct of "six points" that he hopes will "remove grounds for misunderstanding": "The last point I want to make is a somewhat delicate one. In several essays on recent abstract painting and sculpture published in the second half of the 1960s [later in the book, Fried mentions 'Art and Objecthood' and the *Artforum* essays on Caro in 1968 and 1970] I argued that much seemingly difficult and advanced but actually ingratiating and mediocre work of those years sought to establish what I called a *theatrical* relation to the beholder, whereas the very best recent work—the paintings of Louis, Noland, Olitski, and Stella and the sculptures of Smith and Caro—were in essence *anti*-theatrical, which is to say that they treated the beholder as if he were not there" (*Absorption and Theatricality*, 5). Thus, as in the 1960s essays, Fried stakes a claim for modernism at a key moment when it was under intense challenge, in this case, by those promoting the notion of postmodernism.

64. Looking back after three decades, it is often possible to substitute the word "architecture" where Fried uses "theater" or "literal" in "Art and Objecthood." For example: "Literalist sensibility is *architectural* [theatrical] because, to begin with, it is concerned with the actual circumstances in which the beholder encounters literalist work" (15); "*architectural* [literalist] works of art must somehow *confront* the beholder—they must, one might almost say, be placed not just in his space but in his way" (15–16); "the size of much *architectural* [literalist] work … compares fairly closely with that of the human body" (16); "the imperative that modernist painting defeat or suspend its objecthood is at bottom the imperative that it *defeat or suspend architecture [theater]*. And *this* means that there is a war going on between *architecture* [theater] and modernist painting, between the *architectural* [theatrical] and the pictorial" (20); "Literalist sensibility is, therefore, a response to the *same* developments that have largely compelled modernist painting to undo its objecthood—more precisely, the same developments *seen differently,* that is, *architectural* [theatrical] terms, by a sensibility *already architectural* [theatrical], already (to say the worst) corrupted or perverted by *architecture* [theater]" (20); "Art degenerates as it approaches the condition of *architecture* [theater]. *Architecture* [theater] is the common denominator that binds a large and seemingly disparate variety of activities to one another, and which distinguishes those activities from the radically different enterprises of the modernist arts" (21). Subsequent references to Fried, "Art and Objecthood" are given in the text.

65. Fried notes ("Art and Objecthood," p. 16) that "Greenberg was the first to analyze" the role of presence in literalist art by equating what Greenberg in "Shape as Form" called "the look of non-art" with "an effect of *presence.*" Clement Greenberg, "Recentness of Sculpture," in Maurice Tuchman, ed., *American Sculpture of the Sixties* (Los Angeles: Los Angeles County Museum of Art, 1967), 24–26.

66. This point may seem confused to architects, who tend to associate "objects" with autonomous or noncontextual form, that is, painting and sculpture. But, for Fried, objecthood implies ordinariness and thus participation in a context. Such confusions testify to the ways in which definitions of and attitudes toward objects lie at the crux of the interdisciplinary squabbles of the 1960s.

67. Fried simply writes in a footnote: "Stanley Cavell has remarked in seminar that for Kant in the *Critique of Judgment* a work of art is not an object" ("Art and Objecthood," 23 n. 10). In an essay written in 1967, but after "Art and Objecthood" was published, Cavell writes: "the topics of criticism are not objects but works, things which are *already* spoken." Stanley Cavell, "The Avoidance of Love: A Reading of *King Lear,*" in *Must We Mean What We Say?* (New York: Charles Scribner's Sons, 1969), 312. Nevertheless, in none of his writing does Cavell shy away from using the word "object" to denote works of art.

68. Even if the literalists also insisted upon a distinction between art and architecture, they did not deny possible relationships to architecture; rather, they productively exploited the differences between their work and the sites in which it was deployed.

69. Bruce Glaser and Lucy Lippard, "Questions to Stella and Judd," *Art News* (September 1966): 55–61; Donald Judd, "Specific Objects," *Arts Yearbook* (1965): 74–82; Robert Morris, "Notes on Sculpture," *Artforum* (February 1966): 42–43, and "Notes on Sculpture: Part 2," *Artforum* (October 1966): 21; and Samuel Wagstaff, "Talking with Tony Smith," *Artforum* (December 1966): 14–19.

70. Robert Morris, "Notes on Sculpture," 42. In the following sentence Morris mentions Fried's notion that painting is concerned with a "structural" "problematic" that "has been gradually revealed to be located within the literal qualities of the support."

71. Judd, "Specific Objects," 75. In a 1963 review of Noland, Judd wrote: "Painting has to be as powerful as any kind of art; it can't claim a special identity, an existence for its own sake as a medium. If it does it will end up like lithography and etching. Painting now is quite sufficient, although only in terms of plain power. It lacks the specificity and power of actual materials, actual color and actual space. More essentially it seems impossible to further unite the rectangle and the lines, circles or whatever are on it. The image within the rectangle is obviously a relic of pictured objects in their space. This arrangement has been progressively reduced for decades. It has to go entirely. The comparison of painting and three-dimensional work is pretty complicated. There are all sorts of balancing factors. The main qualification to the lesser position of painting is that advances in art are certainly not always formal ones. They always involve innovations, but the actual formal advance, measured by the generalization of historical linearity, may be small. A realistic history would not be a linear one of form, although that enters in. All of this crystallizes or collapses into philosophy." Judd, "Kenneth Noland," 53–54.

72. Judd, "Specific Objects," 76.

73. Ibid., 78.

74. It is curious that while Fried articulates his critique of Greenberg almost entirely in footnotes to his 1960s essays, in "Art and Objecthood" he excuses himself from including footnotes that would identify the sources of his quotations of Judd, Smith, and Morris. Rather than referencing the essays from which the quotations are taken, Fried simply writes: "in laying out what seems to me the position Judd and Morris have in common I have ignored various differences between them, and have used certain remarks in contexts for which they may not have been intended. Moreover, I have not always indicated which of them actually said or wrote a particular phrase; the alternative would have been to litter the text with footnotes" (23 n. 1). On the other hand, Fried goes out of his way to oblige Greenberg in the notes and to explain Cavell's position.

75. Fried first notes Smith's "praise of Le Corbusier as 'more available' than Michelangelo" because the experience of a project such as the High Court Building at Chandigarh, Smith says, is more "direct and primitive." Fried responds that "the availability of modernist art is not of this kind." It is not simply, as Smith says, "something everyone can understand," but rather "one's conviction … is always open to question" ("Art and Objecthood," 19).

76. Brian O'Doherty, *Inside the White Cube: The Ideology of the Gallery Space* (Santa Monica: Lapis Press, 1986). O'Doherty's book is a collection of three essays first published in *Artforum* in March, April, and November 1976.

77. See Judd's various writings on architecture in Marianne Stockebrand, ed., *Donald Judd Architektur* (Münster: Edition Cantz, 1992). Judd claims to have been interested in architecture since he was "thirteen or so" ("Art and Architecture, 1987," *Donald Judd Architektur,* 194), and began to work on architecture as early as 1968 when he purchased and renovated a loft building at 101 Spring Street in New York. But even while he was interested in "a coherent relationship" (ibid., 196) between art and architecture, he insisted on a strict distinction between them: "The configuration and the scale of art cannot be transposed into furniture and architecture. The intent of art is different from that of the latter which must be functional" ("On Furniture," *Donald Judd Architektur,* 133).

78. The "not quite" draws a logical line between the terms "theater" and "architectural," and leaves open "in principle" a possible distinction between them as well as the possibility that architecture too might "defeat objecthood." This possibility, however, seems not only beyond comprehension, but precluded by the logic and language of Fried's polemic.

79. The opposed neo-avant-gardes of architecture and sculpture each became involved in this conflict, but in different ways: architecture evaded domination by embracing pictorial formalism—that is, by proclaiming its autonomy and aesthetic value in pictorial terms—while literalism used architecture to dismantle the supposed autonomy of modernist painting and sculpture.

80. Fried, "Two Sculptures," 24.

81. Fried, "Caro's Abstractness," 32.

82. Ibid., 33–34.

83. Michael Fried, "Anthony Caro and Kenneth Noland: Some Notes on Not Composing," *Lugano Review* (Summer 1965): 198. Donald Judd also argues against composition and uses an architectural example to illustrate his point: "In the new work the shape, image, color and surface are single and not partial or scattered. There aren't any neutral or moderate areas or parts, any connections or transitional areas. The difference between the new work and earlier painting and present sculpture is like that between one of Brunelleschi's windows in the Badia di Fiesole and the facade of the Palazzo Rucellai, which is only an undeveloped rectangle as a whole and is mainly a collection of highly ordered parts" ("Specific Objects," 78, 80).

84. Fried, "Some Notes on Not Composing," 204. Fried explains that deductive structure first appears in Barnett Newman's painting around 1950, and involves establishing the depicted shapes of a painting by deducing them from the canvas shape (or edge). The result, as in Stella's stripe paintings or Noland's chevrons, is "an explicit acknowledgment of the shape of the canvas. They demand to be seen as deriving from the framing-edge—as having been 'deduced from it'—though their exact placement within the colored field has been determined by the painter, with regard to coloristic effect rather than to relations that could be termed geometrical" (Fried, *Three American Painters*, 23).

85. Fried, "Some Notes on Not Composing," 205.

86. Ibid., 204.

87. Ibid., 205. Architecture and space are integral to Fried's intimate, yet nearly incredible, account of his first encounter with Caro's sculpture. In 1998, embellishing remarks he has made before, he recalls "climbing a maze of streets in Hampstead" to arrive at "a gate" and then pass "through it into the courtyard beyond" where he "was alone with [two sculptures] for several minutes before Caro came out of the house." Michael Fried, "An Introduction to My Art Criticism," *Art and Objecthood: Essays and Reviews* (Chicago: University of Chicago Press, 1998), 6–7.

88. Fried, "Art and Objecthood," 16.

89. Cavell, "Music Discomposed," 76.

90. Fried, "Art and Objecthood," 16, 19. As Rosalind Krauss has remarked, there is an affinity between Fried's pictorialism and Lacanian discourse on the "mirror stage" and the "scopic drive." There are in fact remarkable affinities between Fried's vocabulary—statue, stage, identity, anthropomorphism—and Lacan's. Krauss characterizes Fried's notion of "presentness" as "not exactly a situation of nonpresence but one of abstract presence, the viewer floating in front of the work as a pure optical ray. Now it can be argued that this very abstract presence, this disembodied viewer as pure desiring subject, as subject whose disembodiment is, moreover, guaranteed by its sense of total mirroring dependency on what is not itself" (Krauss, in *Discussions in Contemporary Culture*, 61–62).

91. Fried, "Art and Objecthood," 19.

92. Ibid., 15 (Fried's ellipses).

93. Michael Fried, introduction to *Anthony Caro: Sculpture 1960–1963* (London: Whitechapel Art Gallery, 1963), n.p.

94. In 1965, Greenberg credited Fried with introducing the notion of syntax in regard to Caro's work, and added that Caro's "emphasis on syntax is also an emphasis on abstractness, on radical unlikeness to nature. No other sculptor has gone as far from the structural logic of ordinary ponderable things." Clement Greenberg, "Anthony Caro," *Arts Yearbook* (1965): 106.

95. Fried, "Two Sculptures," 24.

96. By way of analogy, Fried explains in "Shape as Form" that a painting "fails" and falls into anthropomorphism if "we see the framing-edge as marking the limits of a spatial *container,* and the canvas itself as something like a background in traditional painting." But, demonstrating the distinction between anthropomorphism and a canvas's being "like a person," he argues that a "narrow vertical format somehow keeps this from happening: not by denying the illusion but, so to speak, by making it self-sufficient, a presence, like that of a human figure, instead of a void waiting to be filled." Thus, in a clear case of the imaginary consuming the real, "the *illusion itself* contains the limits of the support" (Fried, "Shape as Form," 21).

97. Cavell, "The Avoidance of Love," 323–324.

98. Stanley Cavell, "Rejoinders," in Merrill and Capitan, *Art, Mind and Religion,* 119.

99. Cavell, "Music Discomposed," 78.

100. Fried, "Art and Objecthood," 21.

101. Ibid., 22.

4 NON-SITELY WINDOWS: ROBERT SMITHSON'S ARCHITECTURAL CRITICISM

1. Colin Rowe, "Dominican Monastery of La Tourette, Eveux-sur-Arbresle, Lyons," *Architectural Review* (June 1961): 400–410; Clement Greenberg, "After Abstract Expressionism," *Art International* (October 1962): 24–32; Michael Fried, *Three American Painters: Kenneth Noland, Jules Olitski, Frank Stella* (Cambridge: Harvard University, Fogg Museum, 1965); Donald Judd, "Specific Objects," *Arts Yearbook* 8 (1965): 74–82.

2. For a provocative account (drawing on Wittkower) of the relationship between Alberti's trope and modernist painting, see Joseph Mashek, "Alberti's 'Window': Art-Historiographic Notes on an Antimodernist Misprision," *Art Journal* (Spring 1991): 34–41.

3. References to Smithson's writings will cite the first published version. Some of his writings appeared first in one of three posthumous collections: Nancy Holt, ed., *The Collected Writings of Robert Smithson* (New York: New York University Press, 1978); Jack Flam, ed., *Robert Smithson: The Collected Writings,* Documents of Twentieth Century Art (Berkeley: University of California Press, 1996); and Eugenie Tsai, ed., *Robert Smithson Unearthed: Drawings, Collages, Writings* (New York: Columbia University Press, 1991). Subsequent references to these collections will be by editor's name only (Holt, Flam, Tsai). Documents recorded on microfilm from the Archives of American Art will be noted as "AAA" followed by the reel and frame numbers.

4. See Eva Schmidt, ed., "Four Conversations between Dennis Wheeler and Robert Smithson," in Tsai, 107; Robert Smithson, "Pointless Vanishing Points," in Holt, 208; and Robert Smithson, "A Short Description of Two Mirrored Crystal Structures," in Flam, 328.

5. The most frequently cited of these texts include Lawrence Alloway, "Robert Smithson's Development," *Artforum* 11 (November 1972): 52–61; Robert Hobbs, *Robert Smithson: Sculpture* (Ithaca: Cornell University Press, 1981); Craig Owens, "Earthwords," *October* 10 (Fall 1979): 121–130; Gary Shapiro, *Earthwards: Robert Smithson and Art after Babel* (Berkeley: University of California Press, 1995); and Eugenie Tsai, "Robert Smithson's Travelogues and Analogues," in *Robert Smithson: Zeichnungen aus dem Nachlass/Drawings from the Estate* (Munich: Kunstraum München, 1988), 24–40. Another key source are the numerous articles in the special issue of *Arts Magazine* on Smithson's work: *Arts Magazine* 52 (May 1978): 96–144.

6. Among the literalist artists who began to engage architecture is Dan Graham, who claimed he had been photographing "typical suburban houses" since late 1965, although most of the photographs are dated 1968. The article in which they first appeared, "Homes for America," was published in *Arts Magazine* (December-January 1966–67): 21–22. On the chronology of the photographs, see Dan Graham, *Rock My Religion,* ed. Brian Wallis (Cambridge: MIT Press, 1993), 21. Graham also wrote a review of three quasi-architectural group shows ("Scale Models and Drawings" at Dwan, "Macrostructures" at Richard Feigen, and "Architecture Sculpture, Sculpture Architecture" at Visual Arts) titled "Models and Monuments: The Plague of Architecture," *Arts* (March 1967): 32–34. Sol LeWitt, who worked for a time for I. M. Pei, published a short article titled "'Ziggurats': Liberating Set-backs to Architectural Fashion," *Arts Magazine* (November 1966): 24–25.

7. In Smithson's words: "I invented this job for myself as artist-consultant." See Paul Cummings, "Interview for the Archives of American Art," in Holt, 152. Smithson almost always noted his experience as an "artist-consultant" in the bios, however brief, that he submitted to publications and galleries, beginning as early as May 1967 on a form for the Whitney Museum documenting their purchase of *Alogon #1*. Under the heading "Occupations other than artist" (one of the few categories he filled out), he wrote: "Bookstore clerk—8th Street Bookshop, P.A.L. Teacher, 'artist consultant' to Tippetts-Abbett-McCarthy-Stratton (engineers and architects)." AAA 3832/982. Also see AAA 3833/238, 449.

8. The symposium was sponsored by the Yale Art Association, and was the School of Art and Architecture's offering for Alumni Week activities. Smithson's panel included Brian O'Doherty, John Hightower, and Paul Weiss. See AAA 3832/869–870, 892, 894–896.

9. The initial contract ran from July 1 to December 31, 1966, and was apparently renewed for a second six-month term, after which Prokosch tactfully informed Smithson that the architects' contract with the Airport Board no longer included funds for his position. See two letters from Prokosch: AAA 3832/902 (7.20.66), and 3832/999 (8.29.67).

10. Smithson claimed, "I would say I began to function as a conscious artist around 1964–5. I think I started doing works then that were mature. I would say that prior to the 1964–5 period I was in a kind of groping, investigating period." Cummings, "Interview for the Archives," 146.

11. Robert Smithson, "Entropy and the New Monuments," *Artforum* (June 1966): 26–31; and "The Monuments of Passaic," *Artforum* (December 1967): 48–51. "Entropy and the New Monuments" is ostensibly a review of the "Primary Structures" show at the Jewish Museum, but Smithson had written it at least one month before the show's opening in late April 1966.

12. This would be the theme of Smithson's contribution to the 1966 Yale symposium. See Cummings, "Interview for the Archives": "I guess a lot of my thinking about crystalline structures came through there because I was discussing the whole city in terms of crystalline network" (152).

13. Robert Smithson, "The Crystal Land," *Harper's Bazaar* (May 1966), 72–73. The article is a result of a trip "to go rock hunting in New Jersey." That excursion is the prototype of the "site-selection" trips he would take with friends as part of the production of his non-sites. The first site-selection trip was in December 1966 to the Paterson quarry with Nancy Holt and Robert Morris, during which Holt took the well-known photos of Smithson and Morris scaling a chainlink fence to enter the quarry. The second trip was in April 1967 to the Pine Barrens and Atlantic City with Holt, Morris, Virginia Dwan, and Carl Andre. The third, unaccompanied trip was in October 1967 to Passaic. See Lawrence Alloway, "Sites/Nonsites," in Hobbs, *Robert Smithson: Sculpture,* 41.

14. Cummings, "Interview for the Archives," 147.

15. Schmidt, "Four Conversations," 96. This logic is first presented in "Towards the Development of an Air Terminal Site," *Artforum* (June 1967): 36–40, Smithson's first published account of his work on the Dallas–Fort Worth project. In that essay, Smithson moves from the observation that "the maps that surveyors develop from coordinating land and air masses resemble crystalline grid networks" through a discussion of Alexander Graham Bell's "prefabricated, standardized and crystalline" kites and outdoor observation station (which Smithson called "linguistic objects") to the speculation that "we will someday see … aircraft that will be more crystalline in shape" ("Towards the Development," 37, 40).

16. Cummings, "Interview for the Archives," 149.

17. Smithson, "Donald Judd," in *7 Sculptors* (Philadelphia: Institute of Contemporary Arts, 1965), n.p.

18. Robert Smithson, "Artist's Statement," in Wayne Andersen and Brian O'Doherty, eds., *Art '65: Lesser and Unknown Painters, Young American Sculpture—East to West* (New York: American Express Company, 1965), 131. Smithson's work was included in the painting section ("Lesser and Unknown Painters"), curated by O'Doherty.

19. Smithson, "Entropy and the New Monuments," 26.

20. Ibid., 27. Two years later, the architect Alex Tzonis would publish an article titled "Lobbies: Ambiguous Voids in the Urban Fabric," *Arts Magazine* 41 (May 1967): 20–21.

21. Those essays are "Entropy and the New Monuments"; "The Domain of the Great Bear" (with Mel Bochner), *Art Voices* (Fall 1966): 44–51; "Quasi-Infinities and the Waning of Space," *Arts Magazine* (November 1966): 28–31; "Towards the Development of an Air Terminal Site," *Artforum* (June 1967): 36–40; "Ultramoderne," *Arts Magazine* (September-October 1967): 31–33; and "The Monuments of Passaic." Two other important articles from this period deal with museums: Robert Smithson, "Some Void Thoughts on Museums," *Arts Magazine* (November 1967): 41; and "What Is a Museum? A Dialogue between Allan Kaprow and Robert Smithson," *Arts Yearbook* 10 (1967): 94–107.

22. "What Really Spoils Michelangelo's Sculpture" (1966–67) is an extended response to Clement Greenberg's contention in *Art and Culture* (1961) that "what really spoils Michelangelo's sculpture is not so much its naturalism as, on the contrary, its unnaturalistic exaggerations and distortions, which place themselves more in the context of pictorial illusion than in that of sculptural self-evidence." Smithson uses that quotation as one of his two epigraphs, and writes in the first paragraph: "His [Michelangelo's] 'figures' are geometric edifices, more like buildings than human beings." The essays ends: "In Michelangelo's cosmological system of *figures* the direction is *downward* toward infinity. This is not true of his Dome in the Medici Chapel which is *not architecture or sculpture,* but rather one of his most non-anthropocentric progressions into an infinite abstract sphere." Robert Smithson, "What Really Spoils Michelangelo's Sculpture," in Tsai, 71, 73.

23. Robert Smithson, "Interpolation of the Enantiomorphic Chambers," in *Art in Process: The Visual Development of a Structure* (New York: Finch College Museum of Art, 1966).

24. Robert Smithson, "A Provisional Theory of Non-sites," in Flam, 364.

25. Schmidt, "Four Conversations," 107.

26. Smithson explains this process in numerous interviews. See, for example, P. A. Norvell, "Robert Smithson: Fragments of an Interview," in Lucy Lippard, ed., *Six Years: The Dematerialization of the Art Object* (New York: Praeger, 1969), 87–90: "The site selection is by chance. There is no willful choice. A site at degree zero, where the material strikes the mind, where absences become apparent, appeals to me, where the disintegrating space and time seems very apparent. Sort of an end of selfhood … the ego vanishes for a while." For more extensive descriptions and commentary on the non-sites, see Anthony Robbin, "Smithson's Non-site Sights," *Art News* (February 1969): 51–53; Hobbs, *Robert Smithson: Sculpture*, 104–127; and Alloway, "Sites/Nonsites," 41–46.

27. Smithson, "A Provisional Theory of Non-sites," 364.

28. Ibid.

29. The most didactic of the non-sites in regard to the conventions of painting is the *Mono Lake Non-site,* which has the form of a rectangular loop, mimicking the ecologically unique shoreline of the volcanic lake and resembling an empty picture frame. For Greenberg on the inside and outside of painting, see Clement Greenberg, "Our Period Style," *Partisan Review* (November 1949): "inside and outside are interwoven. The artist no longer seals his figure or construction off from the rest of space behind an impenetrable surface, but instead permits space to enter into its core and the core to reach out into and organize the ambience" (1136).

30. While Smithson's remarks refer specifically to fringes and interiors, it should be noted that the general center/edge dialectic is also at work in Fried's notion of deductive structure. See Michael Fried, *Three American Painters,* 41–42; and "Shape as Form: Frank Stella's New Paintings," *Artforum* (November 1966): 18, 24.

31. Norvell, "Fragments of an Interview," 88. In the Cummings interview, Smithson offers this explanation of his move from making sculptural objects to constructing non-sites: "The very construction of the gallery with its neutral white walls became questionable. So I became interested in bringing attention to the abstractness of the gallery as a room, and yet at the same time taking into account less neutral sites, you know, sites that would in a sense be neutralized by the gallery" ("Interview for the Archives," 155–156). Usually Smithson's explanations were more sophisticated, even enigmatic. For example, in his 1968 essay "A Sedimentation of the Mind," he writes that the non-site "actually exists as a fragment of a greater fragmentation. It is a three-dimensional *perspective* that has broken away from the whole, while containing the lack of its own containment." Robert Smithson, "A Sedimentation of the Mind: Earth Projects," *Artforum* (September 1968): 50.

32. See Michael Heizer, Dennis Oppenheim, and Robert Smithson, "Discussions with Heizer, Oppenheim, Smithson," *Avalanche* 1 (Fall 1970): 63. The Cummings interview ends with a similar but less specific speculation: "it got me to think about large land areas and the dialogue between the terminal and the fringe of the terminal—once again, between the center and the edge of things. This has been a sort of ongoing preoccupation with me, part of the dialectic between the inner and the outer" ("Interview for the Archives," 156). For more on this "preoccupation," see William Lipke, "Fragments of a Conversation," in Holt, 168.

33. The quotation continues: "In fact, the entire air terminal may be considered conceptually as an *artificial universe,* and as everyone knows everything in the known universe isn't entirely visible. There is no reason why one shouldn't look at art through a telescope." Robert Smithson, "Aerial Art," *Studio International* (April 1969): 180.

34. Smithson, "A Short Description of Two Mirrored Crystal Structures," 328.

35. Smithson, "A Provisional Theory of Non-sites," 364.

36. Eva Schmidt mentions that Smithson derived the fiction-myth dichotomy from a theory first proposed in 1965 by Frank Kermode ("Four Conversations," 125). See Frank Kermode, *The Sense of an Ending: Studies in the Theory of Fiction* (New York: Oxford University Press, 1967). Smithson may have been attracted to this book because it was first presented as a lecture series titled "The Long Perspective" at Bryn Mawr College in October and November 1965. Kermode distinguished between myths—"which presuppose total and adequate explanations of things as they are and were"—and fictions—which "can degenerate into myths whenever they are not consciously held to be fictive.… Fictions are for finding things out, and they change as the needs of sense-making change. Myths are the agents of stability, fictions the agents of change. Myths call for absolute, fictions for conditional assent" (*The Sense of an Ending,* 39). The forms of fiction that most inspired Smithson were popular science fiction and the writings of Jorge Luis Borges. For more on Smithson's notion of fiction, see Robert Smithson, "A Museum of Language in the Vicinity of Art," *Art International* (March 1968): "When the word 'fiction' is used, most of us think of literature, and practically never of fictions in a general sense. The rational notion of 'realism,' it seems, has prevented esthetics from coming to terms with the place of fiction in all the arts. Realism does not draw from the direct evidence of the mind, but rather refers back to 'naturalistic expressiveness' or 'slices of life.' This happens when art competes with life, and esthetics is replaced by rational imperatives. The fictional betrays its privileged position when it abdicates to mindless 'realism.' The status of fiction has vanished into the myth of fact. It is thought that facts have a greater reality than fiction—that 'science fiction' through the myth of progress becomes 'science fact.' Fiction is not believed to be part of the world. Rationalism confines fiction to literary categories in order to protect its own interests or systems of knowledge" (24).

37. See Robert Smithson, "The Iconography of Desolation" (c. 1962), in Tsai, 61–68; "The Shape and the Future of Memory" (1966), in Holt, 211; and "The Crystal Land," 72–73.

38. Some parts of "Quasi-Infinities and the Waning of Space" are fragments that had been discarded from other writings or that appear in various parts of Smithson's notebooks; in fact, much of the writing in "Quasi-Infinities" is culled from "The Pathetic Fallacy in Esthetics" in Flam, 337–338. Also, one page in a notebook (probably from 1966) has the title "The Magazine as Quasi-Object," and includes this statement: "If we consider magazines in terms of space and form we discover rectangular sheets composed of strata" (AAA 3834/84).

39. Smithson wrote in "A Sedimentation of the Mind": "A great artist can make art by simply casting a glance. A set of glances could be as solid as any thing or place, but the society continues to cheat the artist out of his 'art of looking,' by only valuing 'art objects.'" (50).

40. The opening sentence reads: "Around four blocks of print I shall postulate four ultramundane margins that shall contain indeterminate information as well as reproduced reproductions." In the galleys the first sentence reads: "Around a series of inaccessible abstractions, I shall construct an inaccessible system that has no inside or outside, but only the dimension of reproduced reproductions" (AAA 3834/1060).

41. Leo Steinberg, "Reflections on the State of Criticism," *Artforum* (March 1972): 41. This essay is based on a lecture at given at the Museum of Modern Art in March 1968. It was republished, with additions to the beginning of the essay, as "Other Criteria," in *Other Criteria: Confrontations with Twentieth Century Art* (New York: Oxford University Press, 1972), 55–91.

42. Steinberg, "Reflections on the State of Criticism," 49.

43. In his published writings, Smithson first mentions "printed-matter" in "Entropy and the New Monuments": "Like the movies and the movie houses, 'printed matter' plays an entropic role. Maps, charts, advertisements, art books, science books, money, architectural plans, math books, graphs, diagrams, newspapers, comic books, booklets and pamphlet from industrial companies are all treated the same. Judd has a labyrinthine collection of 'printed matter,' some of which he 'looks' at rather than reads. By this means he might take a math equation, and by sight, translate it into a mental progression of structured intervals. In this context, it is best to think of 'printed-matter' the way Borges thinks of it, as 'The universe (which others call the library),' or like McLuhan's 'Gutenberg Galaxy,' in other words as an unending 'library of Babel'" (29).

44. Douglas Crimp has written that Rauschenberg's "combines" employ "a radically different pictorial logic." See Douglas Crimp "On the Museum's Ruins," in Hal Foster, ed., *The Anti-Aesthetic* (Port Townsend, Wash.: Bay Press, 1983), 47.

45. Smithson, "Towards the Development of an Air Terminal Site," 40. An early example of such a "building" is "The Domain of the Great Bear," which Smithson described in Cummings, "Interview for the Archives": "in 1966 I did an article with Mel Bochner on the Hayden Planetarium which, once again, was sort of an investigation of a specific place; but not on the level of science, but in terms of discussing the actual construction of the building; once again, an almost anthropological study of the planetarium from the point of view of an artist" (156).

46. Smithson, "Towards the Development," 40.

47. Ibid., 37.

48. Ibid., 40.

49. Wittgenstein's *Philosophical Investigations* begins (section 2–21) with the famous parable portraying "a tribe" whose "*whole* language" includes only "the words 'block', 'pillar', 'slab', 'beam'…." A few paragraphs later, to support his notion that such a primitive language is possibly a *whole* language, Wittgenstein introduces the claim: "For a *large* class of cases—though not for all—in which we employ the word 'meaning' it can be defined thus: the meaning of a word is its use in the language." Ludwig Wittgenstein, *Philosophical Investigations,* trans. G. E. M. Anscombe, 2d ed. (Oxford: Blackwell, 1958).

50. Perhaps the best examples occur in "A Sedimentation of the Mind," where, for example, Smithson writes: "Look at any *word* long enough and you will see it open up into a series of faults" (49).

51. Stanley Cavell, "Existentialism and Analytic Philosophy," *Daedalus* (Summer 1964): 953.

52. Virginia Dwar, quoted in Robert Hobbs, "Smithson's Unresolvable Dialectics," in *Robert Smithson: Sculpture,* 20.

53. Smithson, "Towards the Development," 40.

54. Ibid., 40.

55. Robert Smithson, "Untitled (Air Terminal—Windows)" (1967), in Flam, 355–356 (my emphasis).

56. Ibid.

57. Smithson owned a volume of reproductions of the *Carceri* etchings.

58. Schmidt, "Four Conversations," 104.

59. Smithson, "Pointless Vanishing Points," 209. Or even more obliquely: "an illusion without an illusion."

60. Schmidt, "Four Conversations," 104.

61. Smithson's "A Short Description of Two Mirrored Crystal Structures" reads in part: "Both structures have symmetric frameworks, these frameworks are on top of the faceted mirrored surfaces, rather than hidden behind the surfaces. The frameworks have broken through the surfaces, so to speak, and have become 'paintings.' … Each framework supports the reflections of a concatenated interior. The interior structure of the room surrounding the work is instantaneously undermined. The surfaces seem thrown back into the wall. 'Space' is permuted into a multiplicity of directions. One becomes conscious of space attenuated in the form of elusive flat planes. The space is both crystalline and collapsible. In the rose [colored] piece the floor hovers over the ceiling. Vanishing points are deliberately inverted in order to increase one's awareness of total artifice" (328).

62. Also see AAA 3834/96 (probably 1966): at the end of a short paragraph titled "The Morphology of Mirrors," Smithson scratched out: "The mental architecture of the South American Jorge Luis Borges gives us many clues about the looking-glass world."

63. Smithson, "The Cryosphere," in *Primary Structures* (New York: Jewish Museum, 1966), n.p.

64. Smithson's notebooks are filled with remarks on mirrors. See his letter (October 12, 1967) to James Fitzsimons (AAA 3832/1002–1004); "An Infinity of Mirrors" (AAA 3834/92); and "A Morphology of Mirrors" (AAA 3834/96) in a 1966 notebook. The latter reads in part: "This will be an attempt to consider mirrors apart from their function. The content that each one of us sees every morning in the mirror will not be our prime concern. Instead, we shall consider the mirror as a formal or structural medium. Spatially speaking the mirror surface is precise but ungraspable, extensive but impenetrable."

65. Smithson, "Pointless Vanishing Points." Smithson writes that spatial artifice had been "smothered" and "muddle[d]" in the painting of the last four centuries. "And in our own times, perspective is swamped by 'stains' and puddles of paint." Almost certainly Smithson was referring not only to abstract expressionism, but to the more recent work such as that of Jules Olitski, as well as that by Friedl Dzubas, Morris Louis, or Kenneth Noland: that is, the artists most strongly supported by Greenberg or Fried.

66. In "Towards the Development of an Air Terminal Site," Smithson extends these logics to what he calls "aero-surveying" of a "high altitude satellite. The farther out an object goes in space, the less it represents the old rational idea of visible speed. The stream-lines of *space* are replaced by the crystalline structure of *time*." He also relates it to all sorts of grids, including "our city system of avenues and streets. In short, all air and land is locked into a vast lattice" (Smithson, "Towards the Development," 37).

67. Smithson, "Pointless Vanishing Points."

68. Ibid.

69. In *Robert Smithson: Sculpture,* Robert Hobbs describes *Leaning Strata* as one of several projects in which Smithson "conflates two systems for representing space-perspective and cartography" (103). Mihai Craciun, in a student project at the Harvard Graduate School of Design, has suggested that a similar reading of Marcel Breuer's trapezoidal windows at the Whitney Museum (completed 1966) is possible.

70. Smithson was an attentive reader of Greenberg and Fried, although most of his more elaborate remarks and critiques of their position were not published in his lifetime. An obvious exception is his letter to the editor written in response to "Art and Objecthood" and published in the October 1967 *Artforum,* in which Smithson satirized "Fried, the orthodox modernist, the keeper of the gospel of Clement Greenberg" who "is trying hard not to fall from the 'grip' of grace." Directly contradicting Greenberg's loathing for mannerism, Smithson credits Fried with having "set the critical stage for *manneristic modernism.*" Smithson thereby turns the tables on his adversaries and recuperates formalism in his otherwise heretical criticism. (See Greenberg, "After Abstract Expressionism": "Badness becomes endemic to a manner only when it hardens into mannerism" [25].)

71. Smithson, "The Iconography of Desolation," 64.

72. Smithson also mentions Greenberg in "Donald Judd" (1965); "Abstract Mannerism" (1967); "Ultramoderne" (1967); letter to the editor (1967); "Outline for a Yale Symposium: Against Absolute Categories" (1968) in Holt, 218; and "Frederick Law Olmsted and the Dialectical Landscape" (1972), *Artforum* 11 (February 1973): 62–68.

73. Smithson, "Pathetic Fallacy," 337–338. Also see "Conversation with Robert Smithson on April 22nd, 1972," ed. Bruce Kurtz, in *The Fox II* (1975): "You're supposed to not even think of the wall that the painting is hanging on. You're supposed to just respond metaphysically to the painting in terms of color, line, structure, you know, and talk about the framing support, but forget about where you're standing, where you are and the ambience of the entire space" (72). Smithson summarized "Greenberg's space speculations" in similar terms in "Quasi-Infinities" (parts of which appear to be revised extracts from "Pathetic Fallacy"), and in one of the most prominent marginal notes (at the top of the second page) he insists that painting, in Greenberg's sense, "is not abstract, but representational. Space is represented. Critics who interpret art in terms of space see the history of art as a reduction of three dimensional illusionistic space to 'the same order of space as our bodies.' (Clement Greenberg—*Abstract, Representational, and so forth.*) Here Greenberg equates 'space' with 'our bodies' and interprets this reduction as abstract. This anthropomorphizing of space is aesthetically a 'pathetic fallacy' and is in no way abstract."

74. This remark is edited out of published versions in Tsai and Flam. See AAA 3833/1127. Also see AAA 3833/1105: "In terms of Michael Fried, even though he's an adversary of mine, I respect the syntax of his delivery."

75. Smithson, "A Sedimentation of the Mind," 109.

76. Smithson refers to an article on Caro "with photographs of his sculpture in settings and landscapes that suggest English gardening. One work, *Prima Luce 1966*, painted yellow, matches the yellow daffodils peeking out behind it, and it sits on a well cut lawn ... Somehow, Caro's work picks up its surroundings, and gives one a sense of a contrived, but tamed, 'wildness' that echoes the traditions of English gardening.... The traces of weak naturalism cling to the background of Caro's *Prima Luce*." He then satirizes "Clement Greenberg's notion of 'the landscape'" and "Anglicizing tastes." Smithson, "Sedimentation of the Mind," 46.

77. These three sentences occupy an interesting "site" in Smithson's writings. The essay, "The Artist as Site-Seer; or, A Dintorphic Essay" (in Tsai, 74–80), is one of Smithson's most mannered: there is an endnote for each sentence. Tsai notes that the final five footnotes (notes 71–75, including those for these three sentences) "have either been lost or never completed." However, the Archives of American Art microfilm (AAA 3834/160–162) includes what are certainly those notes as well as fifteen additional segments of the essay. See Mark Linder, "Non-sitely Windows: Robert Smithson's Architectural Criticism," *Assemblage* 39 (August 2000): 30 n. 17.

78. Apparently aware of Smithson's query in "The Monuments of Passaic"—"Has Passaic replaced Rome as the eternal city?"—Smithson's friend Howard Junker sent him a copy of an excerpt from Robert Venturi and Denise Scott Brown's *Learning from Las Vegas,* published in *Architectural Forum* in March 1968, three months after "Passaic." See AAA 3832/832–841. Also see AAA 3836/306–309, which consists of marked up galleys for an article (source unknown) titled "Bedding Down in Bali, Brasilia, or Bimini" which includes excerpts, some of which discuss airports, from George Nelson, "Architecture for the New Itinerants," *Saturday Review* (April 22, 1967): 30–31.

79. The artifacts that Smithson identifies as "The Monuments of Passaic"—concrete abutments, bridges, waste pipes, parking lots, and so on—would normally be categorized as infrastructure. This term is particularly interesting terminology considering that, soon after the article appeared, Smithson would write a letter to Martin Friedman, the director of the Walker Art Center, describing his own artwork as "infraphysical" (which he opposed to his use of the word "metaphysical" in an earlier conversation, with its implications of the idealism of conceptual art, which he did not support). Smithson explained: "By infra I mean an order that is not visible to the natural eye, but rather an order that remains hidden until it is made physical by the artist." See undated draft of letter (probably early 1968) AAA 3834/49. Smithson would receive a letter in reply dated March 5, 1968 (AAA 3832/1053). Smithson's use of certain prefixes is consistent enough to suggest clear meanings in his criticism. "Ultra" suggests his notion of mannerism and the literary or metaphorical dimension of materials. "Quasi" implies various hybrid conditions or confusions with affinities to Rauschenberg's "combines." "Infra" relates to what Smithson called "contraction"; that is, raw physicality and literalness. In "A Museum of Language" Smithson coined the term "infra-criticism" to characterize the writing of several artists in his circle. Smithson's essay discusses the writings of Dan Flavin, Carl Andre, Robert Morris, Donald Judd, Sol LeWitt, Ad Reinhardt, Peter Hutchinson, and Dan Graham, as well as Andy Warhol's interviews.

80. Norvell, "Fragments of an Interview," 89. In this interview, Smithson calls both the non-site and photography "contractions," and implies that ordinary language should be understood conversely as an expansion.

81. See July 20, 1966, letter from Prokosch. AAA 3832/902.

82. Cummings, "Interview for the Archives," 152. In "Towards the Development of an Air Terminal Site," one paragraph explains Smithson's fascination with the early parts of the building process, and two photographs of different dams at different stages of construction illustrate how buildings move from a "discrete stage" as a "work of art" (during construction) to a functioning "utility."

83. "Architecture is built by computers. People have all these statistics going on in their heads, so that they'll do something based on that level, completely detached from any kind of physicality of the site." Kurtz, "Conversation with Robert Smithson," 73.

84. Cummings, "Interview for the Archives," 152. At a symposium for an exhibition titled "Earth," at White Museum, Cornell University (February 6, 1969), Smithson's opening statement was: "I first got involved in the earth project situation when I was contracted to do some work for an architectural company as an artist consultant, and they asked me to give them suggestions on what to do with sculpture and things like that. I felt it was wrong to consider sculpture as an object that you would tack onto a building after the building is done, so I worked with these architects from the ground up. As a result I found myself surrounded by all this material that I didn't know anything about—like aerial photographs, maps, large-scale systems" (Holt, 160).

85. As a result, the architects decided to terminate Smithson's contract several months before they learned that the Airport Board would terminate theirs. Also see Prokosch's letter dated December 21, 1967, granting permission (but also disclaiming financial or other responsibility) to Smithson to publish an article and stage an "Airport Sculpture" exhibition to tour Europe. ΛAA 3832/1017.

86. See Paul Toner and Robert Smithson, "Interview with Robert Smithson," in Flam, 234; and Schmidt, "Four Conversations," 107.

87. Smithson, "Aerial Art," 180.

88. Ibid., 181.

89. Smithson, "A Sedimentation of the Mind," 50.

90. Eugenie Tsai, "Robert Smithson's Travelogues and Analogues," 24, 26.

91. This notion of bricks is elaborated in "Ultramoderne." The work of Carl Andre also comes to mind.

92. For a similar interpretation, see Shapiro, *Earthwards,* 157.

93. In December 1966, Mel Bochner staged an exhibit titled "Working Drawings and Other Visible Things on Paper Not Necessarily Meant to Be Viewed as Art" at the Visual Arts Gallery of the School of Visual Arts, New York University. Smithson, as well as Flavin, Judd, LeWitt, "and poet Dan Graham," were invited to participate. See letter from Visual Arts Gallery dated October 10, 1966: "The objective of the exhibition is to present such divergent visual phenomena as working drawings by artists, industrial drawings, engineering plans, musical scores such as those by John Cage, mathematical diagrams, computer data sheets and programs, and certain graphic poetry. The premise is to present work which is not based on preconceived aesthetic assumptions common to most visual art.... Most of the material will be in black and white, blueprint or zerox [sic]." AAA 3832/922.

94. Robert Smithson, "Press Release: Language to Be Looked At and/or Things to Be Read," in Holt, 104. For the early draft, see AAA 3834/170.

95. AAA 3834/182.

96. Smithson, "A Museum of Language," 21.

97. Ibid. Four years later, Smithson would offer a more conventional but parallel critique of actual museums: "Museums, like asylums or jails, have wards and cells—in other words, neutral rooms called 'galleries.' A work of art when placed in a gallery loses its charge, and becomes a portable object or surface disengaged from the outside world. A vacant white room with lights is still a submission to the neutral." Robert Smithson, "Cultural Confinement," *Artforum* (October 1972): 32.

98. Robert Smithson, "The Magazine" (1966), AAA 3834/85. Also see Robert Smithson, "LOOK" (1970) in Flam, 370; "Hidden Trails in Art" (1969) in Tsai, 83–84. On the relationship between Dan Graham and Smithson on magazines as sites, see Eugenie Tsai, "Interview with Dan Graham," in *Robert Smithson: Zeichnungen aus dem Nachlass/Drawings from the Estate*, 8–22; and Dan Graham, "The Book as Object," *Arts Magazine* (Summer 1967): 23.

99. Robert Smithson, "Untitled (Site Data)" (1968), in Flam, 362–363. In another piece of writing, titled "Sites and Settings," Smithson opposes those two terms: settings are the stage for "happenings," while sites are "empty or abstract settings," such as "landscapes without the look of history," "buildings' (suburban factories, rectilinear interiors and exteriors) hard, impenetrable surfaces," or "museums without painting and sculpture, lots without cars, shopping centers without commodities, office buildings without business activities." Robert Smithson, "Sites and Settings" (1968), in Flam, 362.

100. Smithson, "Untitled (Site Data)," 363.

101. The asterisk in the quotation refers to the single footnote in the essay, which reads: "Impressionism is a popular theory derived from 'symbolist theory.' It has nothing to do with individual artists. I use the word 'impressionism' according to its recent linguistic mutation. The original meaning of the word is less important than its recent usage. We are not concerned with what 'impressionism' was but rather with what it is today. But it should be remembered that symbolist theory is prior to impressionist theory." For other remarks on impressionism see Flam 355–356, 360.

102. Smithson, "Ultramoderne," 31–33.

103. Steinberg, "Reflections on the State of Criticism," 41.

104. Smithson, "Ultramoderne," 49–50.

5 OBLIQUELY DENSE: JOHN HEJDUK'S WALL HOUSE

1. John Hejduk, *Mask of Medusa* (New York: Rizzoli, 1985), 36. A precise date for the Wall House is difficult to establish. The earliest sketches, which resemble the basic diagram—a single wall with circulation and habitable space on either side—were most likely produced in 1968, while the final drawings and models were completed between 1970 and 1972, the year the project was exhibited at the Foundation Le Corbusier in Paris.

2. Richard Pommer, "Architecture: Structures of the Imagination," *Art in America* (March-April 1978): 76.

3. Kenneth Frampton, "Notes from Underground," *Artforum* 10 (April 1972): 40–41.

4. Ibid., 46.

5. Ibid., 45–46.

6. Hejduk, *Mask of Medusa,* 36. Hejduk explained the motivation of the Texas Houses as a desire to work through "the conflict between two worlds: the modernist world, so called, and the classicizing world; America and Europe.… The overtones and overtures of the Texas houses was getting Italy out of the system … getting rid of the classicizing aspect, by *working it out*" (*Mask of Medusa,* 35, 36).

7. Frampton, "Notes from Underground," 41.

8. Hejduk, *Mask of Medusa*, 35.

9. Ibid., 36.

10. Ibid., 62.

11. Ibid., 67.

12. Stan Allen, "Nothing but Architecture," in K. Michael Hays, ed., *Hejduk's Chronotope* (New York: Princeton Architectural Press, 1996), 90.

13. John Hejduk, "Out of Time and into Space," *Architecture and Urbanism* (May 1975): 3–4, 24. The essay was first published in French as "Hors de temps dans l'espace," *Architecture Aujourd'hui* (September/November 1965): xxi–xxiii. In *Mask of Medusa* Hejduk mentions a series of lectures he presented at Cornell and Chicago Circle in the early and mid-sixties in which he elaborated further on these ideas.

14. Hejduk, "Out of Time and into Space," 24.

15. Ibid., 4.

16. The text was first published in John Hejduk, *Three Projects* (New York: Cooper Union, 1969), a folio of loose plates (also known as the Diamond Catalog) that is slightly different from the text for the exhibition panels, the only version where this quotation appears.

17. Hejduk, *Three Projects,* n.p.

18. Ibid.

19. Hejduk, "Out of Time and into Space," 4.

20. Hejduk, *Three Projects,* n.p.

21. Hejduk, "Out of Time and into Space," 4.

22. Hejduk, *Mask of Medusa,* 128. Hejduk also claimed to have no interest in contemporary painting. When asked if the work of Morris Louis was similar to Mondrian's, Hejduk replied: "You see, I find it hard to discuss this. My interest in painting, for what ever reason stops with Mondrian" (ibid).

23. Frampton, "Notes from Underground," 43.

24. In retrospect, Hejduk preferred to explain this intensification as a search for "the elusive still life in architecture," a search that culminates in the Wall House where "the vertical wall plane becomes the table of the architectural still life" or, more concisely, a "centralized relief on a tableau." John Hejduk, "Architecture and Education," lecture at the Academy of Architecture, Amsterdam, October 5, 1995. Quoted in Joan Ockman, "Review [of Hejduk exhibition at the Canadian Centre for Architecture]," *Casabella* (October 1997): 13.

25. Hejduk, *Three Projects,* n.p.

26. Hejduk, *Mask of Medusa,* 50, 62.

27. Clement Greenberg, "After Abstract Expressionism," *Art International* (October 1962): 30.

28. In a 1984 catalog for an exhibition of Slutzky's painting, both he and Hejduk write explicitly of the reciprocity of plans and paintings. Hejduk claims that the "horizontal plane is the architect's 'plan'" while "the vertical plane is the painter's datum" upon which she or he builds a "city of the mind." In an essay written with Joan Ockman, Slutzky terms the canvas an "earth-ground, suggesting a horizontal plane/plain of landscape" that when "flipped up into the frontalized picture plane, los[es] its verdancy and gain[s] instead earthy opacity and compaction." John Hejduk, "Painting as City of the Mind," and Robert Slutzky with Joan Ockman, "Color/Structure/Painting," both in *Robert Slutzky: 15 Paintings, 1980–1984* (San Francisco, 1984), n.p.

29. Colin Rowe and Robert Slutzky, "Transparency: Literal and Phenomenal," *Perspecta* (1963): 51, 49.

30. Colin Rowe, "Dominican Monastery of La Tourette, Eveux-sur-Arbresle, Lyons," *Architectural Review* 129 (June 1961): 407.

31. Hejduk, *Mask of Medusa,* 36

32. Rowe, "Dominican Monastery of La Tourette," 402.

33. Several of the early Wall House sketches include renderings of tea cups and wine glasses.

34. See note 24.

35. Hejduk, *Mask of Medusa,* 33.

36. The sketch (with its text) is contained in a folio of "Miscellaneous Diamond Sketches" at the Canadian Centre for Architecture. Hejduk writes here that "an idea of our time is the reinforcing of the periphery of a field—it has been demonstrated both in painting and in architecture; it has not been demonstrated in city planning. NYC is a unique specific example where because of the natural elements of topography and water the … peripheric reinforcement and horizontal extension of the elements seems natural. At present N.Y. has taken on the old form of centralized areas of compact activity—the periphery is dead—the waters on the periphery are not operating to their capacity. If the periphery is activated in its entirety there will be true tension and implication."

37. Jay Fellows, *The Failing Distance: The Autobiographical Impulse in John Ruskin* (Baltimore: Johns Hopkins University Press, 1975), 133.

38. Ibid., ix.

39. Ibid., 135.

40. See *The Works of John Ruskin,* ed. E. Cook and A. Wedderburn (London: G. Allen, 1903–12), vol. 3, 321.

41. See ibid., vol. 15, 241–243.

6 DUMBY BUILDING: FRANK GEHRY'S ARCHITECTURAL IDENTITY

1. The project was sponsored by the Architectural League of New York, which invited pairs of architects and artists to collaborate on projects of their own choice.

2. Gehry said: "Architecture is so cluttered with problems of function, things that the painter confronting the white canvas doesn't have to deal with, that architects hide behind alot of those things and develop rationales based upon functional issues.… But how do we go further? For me there was the one-room building. It was as close as I could get to that pure problem in which the functional issues are so simple that you are faced with only the formal gesture." Frank Gehry, "Beyond Function," *Design Quarterly* 138 (1987): 3. Elsewhere Gehry has said: "How do you get close to [the painter's] experience in architecture? It's very simple: you have to deal with yourself." Adele Freedman, "The Next Wave," *Progressive Architecture* (November 1986): 99. Between those two identifying statements—the first epitomizing the basic conventions of architecture, and the second implying that the discipline of architecture is no less subjective than that of any other art—lies a complex architectural engagement with literalism.

3. Peter Arnell and Frank Gehry, "No, I'm an Architect," in *Frank Gehry: Buildings and Projects* (New York: Rizzoli, 1985), xvii.

4. Jacques Lacan, *The Four Fundamental Concepts of Psycho-Analysis,* trans. Alan Sheridan (New York: W. W. Norton, 1978), 124.

5. Arnell and Gehry, "No, I'm an Architect," xvii.

6. Joseph Giovannini, "Edges, Easy and Experimental," *The Architecture of Frank Gehry* (New York: Rizzoli, 1986), 77.

7. Robert Smithson, "Quasi-Infinities and the Waning of Space," *Arts Magazine* 41 (November 1966): 33. Donald Judd, "Specific Objects," *Arts Yearbook* 8 (1965): 78.

8. Michael Fried, "Art and Objecthood," *Artforum* (Summer 1967): 19.

9. See chapter 3 for a more complete discussion of Fried's "analogous and abstract anthropomorphism" and its relationship to the philosophical writings of Stanley Cavell.

10. Michael Fried, "Jules Olitski's New Paintings," *Artforum* (November 1965): 40.

11. Michael Fried, "New York Letter," *Art International* 7 (May 1963): 69.

12. Fried, "Olitski's New Paintings," 40.

13. Michael Fried, "Shape as Form: Frank Stella's New Paintings," *Artforum* 5 (November 1966): 21

14. Fried, "Art and Objecthood," 19.

15. In 1954 Greenberg wrote: "The picture has now become an object of literally the same spatial order as our bodies and no longer the vehicle of an imagined equivalent of that order. It has lost its 'inside' and become all 'outside,' all plane surface [and] the abstract … picture … returns [the spectator] to that space in all its brute literalness." Clement Greenberg, "Abstract and Representational," *Art Digest* 29 (November 1954): 7. In 1966 Fried wrote: "It is as though, finally, the opticality toward which advanced sculpture aspires brings one up short, not against its literalness exactly, but against the *fact* that when we perceive a solid object eyesight makes contact with no more than its surface (and then only part of that). That is to say, advanced sculpture, such as Caro's, makes this fact a disturbing one, and in effect thrusts it into our awareness. It makes us *note* it, whereas painting, one wants to say, in comparison with sculpture, is all *surface*" ("Shape as Form," 25–26). The following year, Fried described Jules Olitski's sculpture *Bunga* as "more like … a painting than like … an object: like painting, and unlike both ordinary objects and other sculpture, *Bunga* is *all* surface" ("Art and Objecthood," 21).

16. In more recent formalist discourse in architecture, a similar polarity is exemplified in the battles between "blobs"—the production of digitally designed objects comprised of complex topologies—and "boxes"—highly crafted "minimal" forms.

17. J. C. Cooper, *An Illustrated Encyclopedia of Traditional Symbols* (London: Thames and Hudson, 1978), 68. The fish has myriad and contradictory symbolic connotations, considered from both a historical and a contemporary perspective. Another encyclopedia identifies the fish with "abundance, baptism, generative power, knowledge, proflicacy [sic], wisdom, woman.… Also foolishness, greediness, oafishness, sexual indifference, stupidity." Gertrude Jobe, *Dictionary of Mythology Folklore and Symbols* (New York: Scarecrow Press, 1962), 574. In the visual arts, and particularly Asian arts, numerous studies of fish iconography exist. Dawn Rooney's "The Fish Motif in Sukhothai Ceramics," *Oriental Art* 35 (Spring 1981): 135–143, treats the carp specifically and almost seems to be a description of Gehry's self-image: "The carp symbolized perseverance. It is believed to be able to overcome obstacles because it has strength and endurance enabling it to swim against the current. A carp leaping out of the waves signif[ies] freedom." Other iconographic interpretations of the fish align with Gehry's personal explanations of his interest in the fish symbol, and many of those explanations circulate through and around his own ambivalent Jewish identity. Gehry claims that as a child he was given the derogatory nickname "Fish" by his non-Jewish schoolmates. The early Christian association of the fish with the name of Christ (ICHTHUS = Iesous CHristos THeou HUios Soter [Jesus Christ, Son of God, Saviour]) resonates with Gehry's fixation on the significance of that nickname as well as of his distinctly Jewish family name—Goldberg—which he changed in his twenties.

18. Sarah Kofman has explained Freud's attempt to rewrite the concepts of creativity and genius in ways that resonate with the function of Gehry's fish: "The cult of the artist is ambiguous in that it consists of the worship of the hero and father alike; the cult of the hero is always a form of self worship, since the hero is the first ego ideal. This attitude is religious but also narcissistic in character, and repeats that of the child toward the father, and of the parents toward the child, to whom they attribute all the 'gifts' and good fortune that they granted to themselves during the narcissistic period in infancy." According to Kofman, "Freud opposes the ideological conception of art as an imitation of reality and a reflection of the author, a conception which presupposes truth to mean correspondence to reality and the identity of oneself to oneself. The work of art, on the contrary, makes it possible for the nonunified and absent self to be structured, to constitute its identity. The work of art is not external to the 'psychic reality' that it 'represents' and so cannot imitate it. The fantasy that it 'expresses' is a construction after the fact." Sarah Kofman, *The Childhood of Art: An Interpretation of Freud's Aesthetics,* trans. Winifred Woodhull (New York: Columbia University Press, 1975), 18, 100.

19. In fact, Gehry's fish operates something like a totem. As early as 1912, when the first portions of *Totem and Taboo* were published, Freud applied psychoanalytic principles to the study of social forms: art, morals, and religion. "What is a totem? It is as a rule an animal (whether edible and harmless or dangerous and feared) … which stands in a peculiar relation to the whole clan [architects]. In the first place, the totem is the common ancestor of the clan; at the same time it is their guardian spirit and helper, which sends them oracles." Sigmund Freud, *Totem and Taboo,* trans. James Strachey (New York: W. W. Norton, 1950), 5. Also, Gehry's use of the fish aligns with the strong connections Freud makes between primitive notions of the totem and modern obsessional neuroses. For example, the taboos that are applied to the totem—the prohibition against touching and the sexual mores that derive from it, in short the Oedipal complex—have psychoanalytical counterparts. The fish seems to function in a similar way relative to the "fathers" of American modernism. Finally, the deep ambivalence toward the totem is also apparent in Gehry's attitude toward the fish.

20. Freud, "Constructions in Analysis," in *The Standard Edition of the Complete Psychological Works of Sigmund Freud,* ed. James Strachey, 24 vols. (London: Hogarth Press, 1953–74), vol. 23, 261.

21. Ibid., 259.

22. For a detailed reading of the strengths and weaknesses of the archaeological metaphor, see Donald Kuspit, "A Mighty Metaphor: The Analogy of Archaeology and Psychoanalysis," in Lynn Gamwell and Richard Wells, eds., *Sigmund Freud and Art: His Personal Collection of Antiquities* (New York: Harry N. Abrams, 1989), 133–152.

23. Freud, "Constructions in Analysis," 260. This argument is supplemented by his more famous invocation of the archaeological metaphor: "By a flight of the imagination, suppose that Rome is not a human habitation but a psychical entity.… [But] our phantasy … leads to things that are unimaginable and even absurd. If we want to represent historical sequence in spatial terms we can only do it by juxtaposition in space: the same space cannot have two different contents.… The fact remains that only in the mind is such a preservation of all the earlier stages alongside of the final form possible, and that we are not in a position to represent this phenomenon in pictorial terms." Sigmund Freud, *Civilization and Its Discontents,* trans. James Strachey (New York: W. W. Norton, 1961), 17–18.

24. Freud, "Constructions in Analysis," 260.

25. Ibid., 267–268.

26. Kofman, *The Childhood of Art,* 71.

27. Freud, "Constructions in Analysis," 265.

28. Quoted in Barbaralee Diamonstein, *American Architecture Now* (New York: Rizzoli, 1980), 44.

29. Diana Ketcham, "Frank Gehry in Vogue," *New Criterion* (March 1988): 56.

30. Jacques Lacan, *The Seminar of Jacques Lacan, Book I: Freud's Papers on Technique 1953–1954,* ed. Jacques-Alain Miller, trans. John Forrester (New York: W. W. Norton, 1991), 13.

31. Ibid., 157, 14.

32. Frank Gehry, "Excerpts from the Rietveld Lecture," *Kunst & Museum Journal* 2, no. 6 (1991): 48. Another version of this story is: "The fish thing started because of Postmodernism. I got upset with people regurgitating the architecture of the past, which has its origins in anthropomorphism, so I said, 'well, why not go before man … to fish.' That's the way my head works. So I started drawing fish." Quoted in Charles Gandee, "Catch of the Day," *Architectural Record* (January 1988): 81.

33. Or, as Freud writes in *Totem and Taboo,* one cannot dismiss any obsession as merely a personal matter: "It is not accurate to say that obsessional neurotics, weighed down under the burden of an excessive morality, are defending themselves only against *psychical* reality and are punishing themselves for impulses that are merely *felt. Historical* reality has a share in the matter as well" (199).

34. Arnell and Gehry, "No, I'm an Architect," xvii.

35. Freud, "Constructions in Analysis," 269. Also see "Moses and Monotheism," *Standard Edition,* vol. 23, passim.

36. Lacan, *The Seminar, Book I,* 79.

37. Jacques Lacan, "The Mirror Stage as Formative of the Function of the I as Revealed in Psychoanalytic Experience," *Écrits: A Selection,* trans. Alan Sheridan (New York: W. W. Norton, 1977), 4.

38. The mirror stage is not an isolated event or situation that results in a particular configuration of the subject: it is both a loss (of a primordial, polymorphous, autoerotic wholeness) and an "achieved anxiety" (a precocious anticipation of an impossible maturity or return to wholeness). The mirror stage, Lacan writes, is recurrently "experienced as a temporal dialectic that decisively projects the formation of the individual into history. The *mirror stage* is a drama whose internal thrust is precipitated from insufficiency to anticipation" ("The Mirror Stage," 4).

39. Lacan responds negatively to the question of "whether or not the transference is … a product, not to say an artefact, of analytic practice…. Even if we must regard the transference as a product of the analytic situation, we may say that this situation cannot create the phenomenon in its entirety, and that, in order to produce it, there must be, outside the analytic situation, possibilities already present to which it will give their perhaps unique composition" (*Four Fundamental Concepts,* 124–125).

40. Loos wrote, "If we find a mound in the forest, six foot long and three foot wide, formed into a pyramid shape by a shovel, we become serious and something within us says, 'Someone lies buried here.' This is architecture." Adolf Loos, "Architecture" (1910), in *Architecture and Design: 1890–1939* (New York: Whitney Library of Design, 1975), 45. On the billboards, Venturi et al. wrote, "The big sign leaps to connect the driver to the store, and down the road the cake mixes and detergents are advertised by their national manufacturers on enormous billboards inflected toward the highway. The graphic sign in space has become the architecture." Robert Venturi, Denise Scott Brown, and Steven Izenour, *Learning from Las Vegas,* 2nd ed. (Cambridge: MIT Press, 1977), 13.

41. Lacan, *Four Fundamental Concepts,* 143.

42. Jacques Lacan, *Écrits I* (Paris: Éditions du Seuil, 1966), 118.

43. Anthony Wilden, "Lacan and the Discourse of the Other," in Jacques Lacan, *The Language of the Self,* trans. Anthony Wilden (New York: Delta, 1968), 167–168.

44. Jacques Lacan, "The Function and Field of Speech and Language," in Lacan, *Écrits: A Selection*, 42.

45. Ibid., 43, 50.

46. Arnell and Gehry, "No, I'm an Architect," xvii.

47. The project was an accident, according to Gehry, who claims that the fish was built only as a result of a mistranslation by the Japanese client who produced working drawings from a sketch and without Gehry's assistance.

48. Germano Celant, "Reflections on Frank Gehry," in *Frank Gehry: Buildings and Projects,* 8.

49. Anthony Vidler, "Frank Gehry's Architectural Movement," *Casabella* (March 1989): 60.

50. Michael Fried, "Ronald Davis: Surface and Illusion," *Artforum* 5 (April 1967): 37–40.

51. Fried, "Jules Olitski's New Paintings," 40.

52. Fried, "Ronald Davis," 37. For an alternative, protoliteralist reading of the appearance of perspective in sixties art, see Rosalind Krauss, "Illusion and Allusion in Donald Judd," *Artforum* 4 (May 1966): 24–26; and "Robert Motherwell's New Paintings," *Artforum* 7 (May 1970): 26–28.

53. Fried, "Ronald Davis," 39.

54. Michael Fried, *Three American Painters: Kenneth Noland, Jules Olitski, Frank Stella* (Cambridge: Harvard University, Fogg Museum, 1965), 14.

55. Frank Gehry, "Conversations with Frank O. Gehry," *El Croquis* 74/75 (1995): 19.

56. Ibid., 20.

57. Ibid., 22.

58. Ibid., 20.

59. Charles Kessler, *Ronald Davis: Paintings 1962–1976* (Oakland: Oakland Museum, 1976), 11.

POSTSCRIPT

1. Carter Radcliff, *Out of the Box: The Reinvention of Art, 1965–1975* (New York: Allworth Press, 2000), viii–xii.

2. Michael Fried, "Art and Objecthood," *Artforum* (Summer 1976): 15–16, 19.

Figure Credits

0.1 Courtesy Paula Cooper Gallery, New York. Photo Tom Powel. © 2003 Estate of Tony Smith / Artists Rights Society (ARS), New York.

0.2 © Jasper Johns / Licensed by VAGA, New York, NY. Courtesy ULAE.

0.3 Courtesy the Allen Memorial Art Museum, Oberlin College, Ohio; Eva Hesse Archives. Reproduced with the permission of the Estate of Eva Hesse. Galerie Hauser & Wirth, Zurich.

0.4 © Robert Ryman.

0.5 Courtesy Richard Tuttle.

1.2, 1.4 Reproduced courtesy of The Architectural Review. First published May 1950.

1.6 Reproduced courtesy of Birkhäuser Verlag.

1.7 Digital Image © The Museum of Modern Art, New York / Licensed by SCALA / Art Resource, New York. © 2003 Estate of Pablo Picasso / Artists Rights Society (ARS), New York.

1.8, 1.24 Courtesy of Réunion des Musées Nationaux / Art Resource, New York. © 2003 Estate of Pablo Picasso / Artists Rights Society (ARS), New York.

1.9, 1.14 Reproduced courtesy of The Architectural Review. First published June 1961.

1.10, 1.21, 1.22 © 2003 Artists Rights Society (ARS), New York / ADAGP, Paris / FLC.

1.11 © 2003 Estate of Pablo Picasso / Artists Rights Society (ARS), New York. © The Solomon R. Guggenheim Foundation, New York.

1.12 Courtesy SCALA / Art Resource, New York. © 2003 Estate of Pablo Picasso / Artists Rights Society (ARS), New York.

1.13 © 2003 Estate of Pablo Picasso / Artists Rights Society (ARS), New York.

1.15 © 2003 Artists Rights Society (ARS), New York / ADAGP, Paris / FLC. Photograph Mark Linder.

1.16 © 2003 Richard Serra / Artists Rights Society (ARS), New York.

1.17, 1.19 © 2003 Artists Rights Society (ARS), New York / ADAGP, Paris / FLC. Photograph Yukio Futagawa.

1.18 Art © Donald Judd Foundation / Licensed by VAGA, New York, NY.

1.20 Courtesy Tate Gallery, London / Art Resource, New York. © 2003 Estate of Pablo Picasso / Artists Rights Society (ARS), New York.

1.23 © 2003 Estate of Tony Smith / Artists Rights Society (ARS), New York.

1.25 Courtesy James Cohan Gallery, New York. Art © Estate of Robert Smithson / Licensed by VAGA, New York, NY.

2.1 Courtesy Wadsworth Atheneum Archives. Art © 2003 Robert Morris / Artists Rights Society (ARS), New York.

2.2 Courtesy of Virginia Dwan. Photo John D. Schiff. Art © Donald Judd Foundation / Licensed by VAGA, New York, NY.

2.3 Courtesy the Jewish Museum, New York / Art Resource, New York. Art © Donald Judd Foundation / Licensed by VAGA, New York, NY. Art © 2003 Robert Morris / Artists Rights Society (ARS), New York.

2.6 Courtesy Edward Ruscha and the Hirschhorn Museum. Gift of Joseph H. Hirshhorn, 1972. Photo Lee Stalsworth.

2.7 Courtesy Tate Gallery, London / Art Resource, New York.

2.8 Courtesy the Isamu Noguchi Foundation. Photo © Estate of Rudy. Burckhardt / Licensed by VAGA, New York, NY.

2.9 Art © Estate of David Smith / Licensed by VAGA, New York, NY.

2.10 © 2003 Artists Rights Society (ARS), New York / ADAGP, Paris. Courtesy Sheldon Memorial Art Gallery, University of Nebraska-Lincoln, Gift of Mrs. Olga N. Sheldon in Memory of Adams Bromley Sheldon.

2.11 Courtesy of Réunion des Musées Nationaux / Art Resource, New York. © 2003 Estate of Pablo Picasso / Artists Rights Society (ARS), New York.

2.12, 2.13 © 2003 Estate of Pablo Picasso / Artists Rights Society (ARS), New York.

2.14, 2.15 © Austrian Frederick and Lillian Kiesler Private Foundation. © The Solomon R. Guggenheim Foundation, New York. Photo Berenice Abbott.

2.16 Art © Donald Judd Foundation / Licensed by VAGA, New York, NY. Photo © Estate of Rudy Burckhardt / Licensed by VAGA, New York, NY.

2.17 © 2003 Robert Morris / Artists Rights Society (ARS), New York.

2.18 Courtesy Anthony Caro.

2.19 © 2003 Agnes Martin. Digital Image © The Museum of Modern Art, New York / Licensed by SCALA / Art Resource, New York.

2.20 Photo courtesy David Zwirner Gallery.

2.21 Courtesy of Virginia Dwan.

2.22 Photo © Museum of Contemporary Art, Chicago.

2.23 Courtesy PaceWildenstein. Photo Ellen Page Wilson. © 2003 Robert Mangold / Artists Rights Society (ARS), New York.

2.24 © 2003 Robert Mangold / Artists Rights Society (ARS), New York. Photo © Estate of Rudy Burckhardt / Licensed by VAGA, New York, NY.

2.25, 2.26 Courtesy Mel Bochner.

3.1, 3.11 Courtesy Anthony Caro.

3.2 © Kenneth Noland / Licensed by VAGA, New York, NY.

3.3 © Jules Olitski / Licensed by VAGA, New York, NY. Purchased with the aid of funds from the National Endowment for the Arts; 1977.617. Photo © 2003 Museum of Fine Arts, Boston.

3.4 © 2003 Frank Stella / Artists Rights Society (ARS), New York. Photo © Estate of Rudy Burckhardt / Licensed by VAGA, New York, NY.

3.5 Courtesy Staatsgalerie Stuttgart. © 2003 The Pollock-Krasner Foundation / Artists Rights Society (ARS), New York.

3.6 Photo © Board of Trustees, National Gallery of Art, Washington. Gift of the Collectors Committee. © 2003 The Pollock-Krasner Foundation / Artists Rights Society (ARS), New York.

3.7 Courtesy Smithsonian American Art Museum, Washington, D.C. / Art Resource, New York.

3.8, 3.10 © 2003 Frank Stella / Artists Rights Society (ARS), New York.

3.9 Courtesy Tate Gallery, London / Art Resource, New York.

3.12 © 2003 Robert Morris / Artists Rights Society (ARS), New York.

4.1, 4.2, 4.3, 4.4, 4.5, 4.7, 4.8, 4.9, 4.10, 4.11, 4.12, 4.13, 4.15, 4.16, 4.17, 4.18 Courtesy James Cohan Gallery, New York. Art © Estate of Robert Smithson / Licensed by VAGA, New York, NY.

4.6, 4.14 Art © Estate of Robert Smithson / Licensed by VAGA, New York, NY.

5.1, 5.2, 5.3, 5.6, 5.7, 5.8, 5.9, 5.11, 5.12, 5.13, 5.14, 5.16, 5.17, 5.18, 5.19, 5.20, 5.21 John Hejduk Archive, Collection Centre Canadien d'Architecture / Canadian Center for Architecture, Montréal.

5.4, 5.5 © 1971, The Irwin S. Chanin School of Architecture of The Cooper Union.

5.10 Courtesy Robert Slutzky.

6.1, 6.2, 6.3, 6.5, 6.8 Courtesy Gehry Partners.

6.4 © Jules Olitski / Licensed by VAGA, New York, NY.

6.9, 6.10 © 2003 Marvin Rand Associates.

Index